INCOME TRANSFERS IN TEN WELFARE STATES

CASH & CARE

Editors: Sally Baldwin, Jonathan Bradshaw and Robert Walker

Cash benefits and care services together make a fundamental contribution to human welfare. After income derived from work, they are arguably the most important determinants of living standards. Indeed, many householders are almost entirely dependent on benefits and services which are socially provided. Moreover, welfare benefits and services consume the lion's share of public expenditure. The operation, impact and interaction of benefits and services is thus an important focus of research in social policy.

Policy related work in this field tends to be disseminated to small specialist audiences in the form of mimeographed research reports or working papers and perhaps later published, more briefly in journal articles. In consequence public debate about vital social issues is sadly ill-informed. This series is designed to fill this gap by making the details of important empirically-based research more widely available.

THE AUTHOR

Dr Deborah Mitchell is a research fellow in the Research School of Social Sciences at the Australian National University.

This book is dedicated to Judy Welsh.

Income Transfers in Ten Welfare States

DEBORAH MITCHELL

Public Policy Program
Australian National University

Avebury

Aldershot · Brookfield USA · Hong Kong · Singapore · Sydney

Published by
Avebury
Academic Publishing Group
Gower House
Croft Road
Aldershot
Hants GU11 3HR
England

Gower Publishing Company
Old Post Road
Brookfield
Vermont 05036
USA

A CIP catalogue record for this book
is available from the British Library.

ISBN 1 85628 225 2

Printed and Bound in Great Britain by
Athenaeum Press Ltd., Newcastle upon Tyne.

Contents

Acknowledgements

My first thanks go to the staff of the Luxembourg Income Study Project. In particular, Tim Smeeding (Syracuse University) and Lee Rainwater (Harvard University) who conducted the Luxembourg Income Study Workshop in August, 1988. The Workshop introduced me to the exciting possibilities of the LIS data, as well as the theoretical and methodological minefields which surround comparative analyses of economic well-being. Subsequently John Coder, the then LIS Technical Director, provided advice on the LIS data sets and guided me through the remote accessing of the LIS data base.

My understanding and interpretation of the LIS data was enhanced greatly by discussion - and argument - with Francis Castles and Steve Dowrick of the Australian National University. Jonathan Bradshaw (University of York) and Tony Atkinson (London School of Economics) made useful suggestions on the final form of the text.

In a previous life, this book was a doctoral dissertation in the Public Policy Program at the Australian National University. I wish to thank all the staff of the Program for their past and present support.

The financial support which made this work possible came from several sources. The Australian Department of Finance provided me with a scholarship and leave to commence the study - many thanks to Malcolm Holmes who supported this project from the outset. A post-graduate award from the Australian National University allowed the original dissertation to be completed; and the British Council provided me with a stipend and travelling costs to the UK where the manuscript was completed.

Introduction

Income transfer programs are a fundamental component of the welfare state in most, if not all, advanced western societies. We know this from the proportion of government budgets devoted to such programs; from their primary role in the establishment and subsequent development of the welfare state; and from the universal impact which social security and taxation have on the economic well-being of families and individuals.

Income transfer programs in OECD countries have highly diverse attributes. A cursory glance at the comparative social policy literature tells us that among OECD countries transfer programs vary enormously in respect of their goals, the level of government expenditure devoted to such programs, the proportion of the population in receipt of transfers, how the programs are financed, and the types of transfer instruments used in each country. Indeed it is the detailed description of these variations which constitutes a large proportion of the comparative literature. What the literature lacks, however, is a clear assessment of how, and whether, these variations result in tangible differences in the impact of these programs on, for example, poverty and inequality. This gap in the literature is directly attributable to a lack of comparable data on incomes across a range of countries.

Since 1986, researchers at the Luxembourg Income Study Project (LIS) have been compiling a new data set based on microdata collected in a number of OECD countries in the form of income, expenditure (consumption) or tax file surveys. At present, there are sixteen countries participating in the LIS project and two waves of data, collected *circa* 1980 and 1985, are available. Until the advent of LIS, the comparability of the individual microdata sets

1

from different countries was extremely low and could not be used with any confidence to make cross-national comparisons of the incidence and impact of income transfers. The outstanding feature of the LIS data is that a number of income and demographic variables have been drawn from these surveys to form a common framework. The LIS database consists of approximately 60 income and demographic variables (listed in Appendix A) which have been coded according to a common set of criteria.

Each of these variables is identified with the same variable name across the data sets and across the two waves of data. For example, income variable V1 *'Gross wage and salary income'* can be specified for each country and in each wave of the data without the user being familiar with the finer details of the original data sets. Commenting on this feature of the LIS data and its implications for comparative study, Heidenheimer et al (1990:10) note:

> Elementary though it seems, one key problem in comparative policy studies is the difficulty of finding truly comparable measurements of the same things in different countries. For example, every major nation produces statistics on the distribution of income. However, income is measured differently in different countries; definitions of household versus individual income are often not the same; methods for estimating the underreporting of income in government statistical surveys vary greatly, and so on. Only in the last few years ... has it been possible to go back to each nation's income surveys, create a common accounting framework, and recalculate the millions of individual household income reports on that common basis. Only then can we begin to address sensibly questions about the distribution of well-being ... and public policy in different nations.

Thus the LIS data presents an invaluable opportunity for comparing income transfers in a number of welfare states. A challenge for comparative analysts now is how to exploit the LIS data to shed new light on the relationship between the operation of income transfer systems in different welfare states and the **outcomes** of these transfer programs. This book represents a first response to this challenge.

In addition, the LIS Project raises new questions for those attempting comparative studies in this field. Is it possible to make meaningful comparisons of transfer programs with such widely varying attributes? Which goals of transfer programs are important? Which criteria should be used to make comparisons? Which methodologies should be used? It is these issues which form the basis of Part I of this study. Ten countries have been selected from the LIS data for analysis in this study: Australia, Canada, France, (West) Germany, the Netherlands, Norway, Sweden, Switzerland, United Kingdom and United States. Appendix A provides a list of all the participating countries, details of the surveys from which the LIS data have been drawn and the sample sizes.[1]

Using the LIS data, Part I focuses on the outcomes of transfer programs in relation to two core goals: the alleviation of poverty and the reduction of income inequality. Chapter 1 discusses the centrality of these two goals to the welfare state and develops a model which illustrates how efficiency and effectiveness criteria may be used to elucidate the extent to which different welfare states achieve these goals.

Whereas most studies of income transfer programs concentrate exclusively on direct transfers through the social security system, this study takes a comprehensive view of transfer policies by using the microdata to examine the incidence and impact of both social security transfers and income taxes.

It does so for two reasons. First, tax 'expenditures' (in the form of deductions, rebates and exemptions) may be used in place of, or in addition to, social security transfers to increase the disposable income of families or households. Second, in many of the countries to be studied, social security policy and policy instruments are specifically designed to interact with taxation policy to produce certain desired outcomes. For example, progressive income taxes may 'clawback' universal transfers from high income families or households. To neglect the effects of taxation may result in the under-estimation of income transfer expenditures designed to effect redistributive aims and present an incomplete view of those transfer systems which crucially depend on the interaction of social security and taxation policy instruments.

To expose the interaction of these alternative instruments, the study uses a three stage analysis of the formation of family disposable income commencing with the initial distribution of income through the market, the distribution post- social security transfers and finally, the distribution post-tax.

Using the observations from each stage of the redistribution process, the study draws conclusions about the effectiveness of alternative policy instruments in relation to income redistribution and poverty alleviation. Alternative policy instruments in this context refers not only to the choice of different social security instruments (*eg*: universal versus income-tested transfers) but also the choice between direct and indirect transfers (*eg*: child benefits versus tax deductions for children.)

A key innovation of this study is its attempt to quantify the efficiency with which the poverty reduction and income redistribution outcomes are achieved, for example, the extent to which transfers close the poverty gap, the proportion of transfers which accrue to lower income earners, the amount of redistribution achieved for each social security dollar. This issue has become critical in recent years as governments of many of the OECD countries react to new perceptions of economic scarcity and seek ways to manage the growth of income transfer programs that do not 'incur disastrous political costs' (Heidenheimer et al, 1990:255).

There are limitations on the LIS data which are discussed in detail in Chapter 2. The four which most concern this study are: the type of unit for which the original data was reported; the treatment of zero and negative disposable incomes; the under-reporting of income in the original surveys; and the stage of the macro-economic business cycle when the data was collected in each country. Although not entirely perfect, the degree of comparability between the data sets has been argued to be extremely high (Smeeding et al,1985a) and certainly represents the best available data for cross-national comparison of income transfers.

In Chapters 3 to 8 of Part I, the goals of poverty alleviation and reduction of income inequality are considered separately and the discussion is further sub-divided into efficiency and effectiveness issues.

Chapter 3 discusses the poverty measurement literature, outlines the methodology to be used to specify a poverty line for each country in the study and describes the assumptions made to accommodate the LIS data. Chapter 4 analyses how effective the LIS countries are in alleviating poverty while Chapter 5 examines how efficiently the transfer systems of the LIS countries direct expenditure to the poor.

Chapter 6 reviews the alternative methods employed in the income inequality field, outlines the methodology adopted by the study and describes the assumptions made to accommodate the data. Chapter 7 examines the extent to which income inequality is reduced by transfers in these countries and Chapter 8 looks at the efficiency with which the reduction is produced.

Chapter 9 reviews the empirical results of the above chapters and discusses the relationship between poverty alleviation and inequality reduction. It also examines whether there is a policy trade-off between the efficiency and effectiveness goals of transfer systems.

Part II of the study turns to the larger issues of comparing welfare states. Chapter 10 examines the place of studies based on microdata in the overall comparative welfare state literature and use the results of Part I to comment on this literature. These comments concern both specific problems and debates in the literature as well as more general observations about the contribution which microdata based studies may make in this field.

The specific issues include: whether the conventional division of countries into welfare *leaders* and *laggards*, based on the level of government expenditures, corresponds with the outcomes of transfer processes. In other words, do higher expenditures on social security, for example, necessarily equate with better outcomes? If not, can the microdata identify and explain the intervening processes which might prevent the 'straight line' translation of expenditures to outcomes? These questions are tackled in Chapter 11.

Chapter 12 examines several well-known typologies of the welfare state which use characteristics of the social security system (*eg:* universal versus selective assistance, replacement rates, methods of financing) to identify distinctive models of welfare provision. The study compares the assignment of the LIS countries within each typology to examine the extent to which the selection of different attributes of social security systems may lead to different groupings of countries.

Using one of these typologies, the chapter examines whether the 'types' of welfare states identified are consistently associated with particular outcomes. This leads to a more general discussion about the relationship of findings based on microdata to this area of the comparative literature. The discussion is advanced on several fronts: can the use of microdata inform welfare state typologies? For example, if the validity of these typologies rests on the characteristics of the social security system are there critical characteristics which have been overlooked? One area which the results of Part I points to is taxation. Here, the implications of taking a more comprehensive view of income transfers by presenting a balance between the characteristics of direct transfers (social security payments) and indirect transfers (taxes) is discussed and used to construct an alternative typology of welfare state types.

It is important to stress here that the analysis presented in this study draws on the first wave of the LIS data (*circa* 1980). At the time of writing, the coverage of countries in the second wave of data (*circa* 1985) was considerably smaller and therefore less attractive given the aims of the study. There is no doubt that the income transfer policies of the early eighties will have undergone considerable transformation in the intervening period and the outcomes observed may well be different today.

Despite the age of the data, the analysis presented here maintains its relevance for two reasons. First, a major aim of the study is the investigation, and application, of methodologies suited to cross-national comparisons using microdata. From this perspective, the importance of the analysis lies in the sensitivity of the poverty and inequality measures to alternative forms of transfer policies and instruments rather than providing a 'league table' of how each country is currently performing. A second aim is to develop a model of transfer processes which traces the relationship between government expenditure, transfer instruments and outcomes in a consistent fashion. This model is found to 'work well' for the early 1980s, in that it successfully illuminates the links between expenditure, instruments and outcomes. There is no reason to doubt that it will also work well on subsequent data sets.

A glossary of terms

The study draws on the theoretical and methodological work of several disciplines, each of which use a number of core terms and concepts in slightly different ways. The purpose of this section is to make clear to readers how this study defines and uses these terms.

Direct transfers refers to payments made through social security and closely allied programs. For example, it includes veterans' pensions but not education or health benefits. The measurement of direct transfers across the countries in the study are defined by the variable 'SOCTRANS' on the LIS database, the detailed composition of this variable is set out in Appendix A. In certain contexts, I will abbreviate 'direct transfers' to 'transfers' and this will be clear from the context.

Indirect transfers refers to income taxes and allied deductions. For example, it includes mandatory social insurance contributions for wage earners and the self-employed. The measurement of indirect transfers is given by the variables 'PAYROLL' plus 'V11', as described in Appendix A. Indirect transfers will be abbreviated to 'taxes' and this usage will also be clear from the context.

Income transfer system refers to the set of policies and policy instruments used to make direct and indirect transfers. In the course of the study I may refer to it as 'the transfer system' or the 'tax-transfer system'. The combined effect of transfers and taxes is referred to as 'net transfers' for the sake of brevity.

Market income refers to income from private sources: wages, property, self-employment, private pensions and superannuation. That is, it is pre-transfer, pre-tax income. It is the variable labelled as 'MI' on the LIS database, see Appendix A.

Gross income refers to all income from private and public sources. That is, it is post-transfer, pre-tax income. It is labelled as 'GI' on the LIS database and is equivalent to market income plus social security transfers plus private transfers such as alimony. It may be referred to as pre-tax income.

Disposable income refers to income net of taxes and social insurance contributions. That is, it is post-transfer, post-tax income. It is labelled as 'DPI' on the LIS database and is equivalent to gross income less the taxes described above. It may be referred to as post-tax income.

Notes

[1] For a detailed discussion of the LIS Project, readers are referred to Smeeding et al,1990.

PART I
AN EMPIRICAL
INVESTIGATION OF
INCOME TRANSFER
SYSTEMS

1 Focusing on outcomes

As noted in the Introduction, the emphasis of this study is on the **outcomes** of income transfer programs in the LIS countries. This chapter sets out the implications of adopting an outcomes perspective; what this means in the context of income transfers; which outcomes will be considered; and how these can be measured.

One way of viewing outcomes is presented in Figure 1.1 which has been adapted from a model of the 'production of welfare' developed by Hill and Bramley (1986:181). An advantage of using this model is that it shows the relationship of welfare policies to policy instruments, the environment in which they operate and the linkages between program inputs and program outcomes. Applying this to social security transfers, for example, **inputs** would include the actual payments; **production** would refer to the policy instruments used to distribute these payments; **outputs** would include the size and incidence of the payments; while **outcomes** might be measured in terms of the final distributions of income or welfare. In the course of this study I will touch on each of these four stages individually, as well as linking inputs to outcomes; production to outcomes; and outputs to outcomes.

As a first step in this analysis we need to consider which outcomes should be measured. There are, of course, many ways of describing, defining and measuring the outcomes of income transfer policies. In large part, the range of possible outcomes is a direct reflection of the diversity of the goals of these policies. This raises two problems first, defining the central goals common to each of the ten countries and second, establishing a set of criteria to assess the achievement of these goals.

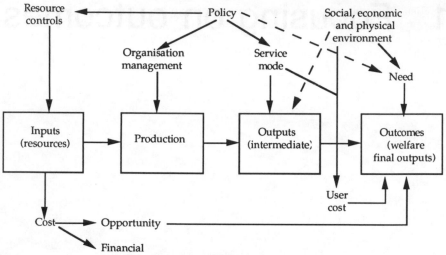

Figure 1.1. A model of the production of welfare

1.1. The goals of income transfer policies

The variation in the goals of income transfer programs is illustrated by the following sample of statements of goals from respectively, Sweden, Germany and the United States:

> The aim of this section... is to evaluate the success of the Swedish Welfare State by its own standards ... improved social security among the total population; greater equality between social classes and between single persons and families, as well as between retired persons and the labour force; and an elimination of poverty.[1]

> Following the policy statements of various federal governments and the platforms of the major political parties, the German income maintenance schemes have three basic aims: to prevent poverty, to provide social security in the sense of helping people to preserve their social status in the case of lost earnings, and to reduce inequalities in living conditions.[2]

> The clearest statement of goals, which did not appear until the early 1970s, outlined eight:
>
> 1.   Provision of a nominally adequate income level to those who cannot work and, in tandem with social insurance and employment programs, to those who can work.
> 2   Targeting benefits on those most in need.
> 3.   Coordination and integration of programs to achieve administrative efficiency.
> 4.   Similar treatment of similar individuals (horizontal equity) ...
> 5.   Vertically equitable treatment ...
> 6.   Encouragement of self-sufficiency by providing work incentives.
> 7.   Reduction or elimination of incentives for family breakup.
> 8.   Attention to making the system understandable, coherent, and subject to fiscal control.[3]

It is possible to detect some common themes in these goals as well as substantial variations - for example, different emphases on the balance of social and private responsibilities. To start with a basic theme, Ringen (1987:7) argues that redistribution policies in general have equality as their immediate goal, that the aim is to make the distribution of welfare more egalitarian or 'fairer' than it would have been in the absence of such policies.

> That equality is a goal in the welfare state we know from what politicians say, from what we can read in policy documents, and from the existence of policies that cannot be understood independently of some redistributive intention.

Where welfare states diverge, according to Ringen (1987:8), is in the strength of their commitment to equality:

> The goal of equality can be given a weak or strong interpretation. In its weak interpretation, it implies a guaranteed *minimum standard* for all members of society ... In its strong formulation, the redistributive goal refers not only to the minimum standard but to the entire *structure of inequality*...

It is on the basis of this division of the goal of equality that the study examines the outcomes of income transfer policies. In the first instance, all the countries in this study have income transfer policies which are aimed at ensuring that a minimum standard of income is enjoyed by all. In this context it is reasonable to assume, as a first approximation, that this indicates a desire to ensure that poverty is avoided or alleviated. As Ringen (1987:141) argues:

> To ask about poverty in the welfare state is to question the elementary effectiveness of social policy... While there is disagreement about the responsibility of government with regard to overall inequality, its responsibility in relation to poverty has been accepted for generations and is not seriously contested today.

In addition to this goal there are some countries, as the examples from Sweden and Germany illustrate, whose policies are aimed at decreasing the level of inequality in society. In this context, progress toward this goal would be reflected in the level of income redistribution achieved by transfer policies. Thus the two goals of income transfer policies which form the focus of this study are: the alleviation or reduction of poverty and the reduction of income inequality.

In comparing each country's progress towards both these goals, we could simply construct measures to indicate the level of poverty and income inequality and conclude which countries do best or worst in each regard. However a more challenging task, and one which may be of interest to both the wider welfare state literature and to social policy analysis, is to consider the various stages in the production of these outcomes and the relationship between each stage and the outcomes. In particular, the contribution of various policy instruments to these outcomes is of interest to writers in both these areas. It enables us, for example, to make more informed judgements about whether universal or selective programs are better at achieving one or both of these goals or how taxation contributes to these goals.

In addition to the assessment of the effectiveness of these policy instruments, the study also examines their efficiency in producing the observed outcomes. I indicated in the Introduction that efficiency issues are gaining momentum in the discussion of welfare states, even in those countries where such concerns are of secondary importance in transfer policy (Heidenheimer et al, 1990:255). There are other countries where efficiency questions have always dominated transfer policy and this is demonstrated by the goals of transfer policy in the United States cited earlier. No less than five of the eight goals directly address the efficiency issue in its various guises: targeting, administrative efficiency, disincentive effects, fiscal control. Many of these goals are shared by other countries in this study such as Australia, Canada and the United Kingdom.

As with the effectiveness issue, efficiency questions are of interest to writers in both the general welfare state literature and social policy literature. For example, Ringen (1987:13) raises this issue in debating the pros and cons of different welfare state 'types':

> The large and/or universal welfare state may be seen as wasteful and as giving benefits to people who do not need them, at the cost of unnecessarily high taxes, and the small welfare state as more effective because selective and targeted policies give more bang for the buck.

Policy analysts may also be interested in this issue when making comparisons of different transfer policies (for example, whether some policies are more efficient in reducing poverty or inequality and in what respect). Where transfer instruments result in fairly similar outcomes we may wish to know which instrument produces this outcome most efficiently. On the other hand, where different outcomes result we may wish to know the costs or benefits involved in adopting the instrument which produces a superior outcome. A third reason is that all transfer systems, no matter which policy instruments they use, aim to minimise the costs of transferring income. This may be a primary or secondary goal of transfers although, as noted above, it is increasingly becoming a primary goal even in those countries where formerly such concerns were not explicit.

Defining efficiency and effectiveness

The terms efficiency and effectiveness in this study are defined by the relationship between the various stages of production identified in the Hill and Bramley model. Hill and Bramley (1986:182) offer the following definitions of efficiency, effectiveness and cost-effectiveness in the general context of welfare programs:

> *Efficiency* is the relationship between outputs and inputs ... greater efficiency is achieved by increasing the output from given inputs or by reducing the inputs required to produce a given output.
> *Effectiveness* is the extent to which a service increases welfare ...
> *Cost-effectiveness* is the relationship between the cost of inputs and the increase in welfare achieved ... greater cost-effectiveness is achieved by reducing inputs for a given level of welfare increase or by increasing welfare for a given level of inputs.

12

Hill and Bramley's definitions are adopted in this study, with the cost-effectiveness measures being grouped with the efficiency measures for ease of exposition. In the following sections I set out how efficiency and effectiveness are to be measured in relation to each of the two goals and identify the salient characteristics of each part of the transfer process which influence the outcomes.

1.2. The effectiveness criteria

The effectiveness of transfer policies in alleviating poverty may be measured by the extent to which they reduce the number of families in poverty and the extent to which they decrease the poverty gap. These are measured in aggregate, and for particular family types. Figure 1.2 adapts the Hill and Bramley model in relation to the poverty alleviation goal.

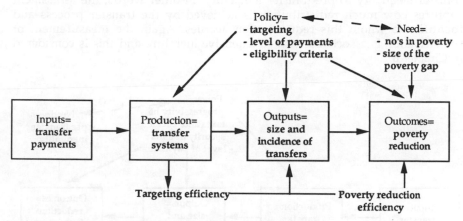

Figure 1.2. The production of welfare: a view of poverty alleviation

The inputs are defined as income transfer payments and income taxes. Production here refers to the transfer instrument (and its characteristics) which distributes the payments to, or deducts taxes from, the recipients. The outputs are the size and incidence of transfers and are determined by government policy on the level of payments, eligibility criteria (*ie* who should receive income support) and the operation of means-tests (*ie* how much income support). The assessment of outcomes is dependent on the relationship of the size and incidence of the payments to a defined poverty line. The specification of a poverty line allows us to assess welfare outcomes in terms of both a head-count (*ie* the number of individuals or families who are lifted out of poverty) and the size of the poverty gap before and after transfers.[4]

A critical issue in the assessment of outcomes in terms of poverty alleviation is the specification of the poverty line. There is a considerable literature on how poverty lines can be specified and this is discussed in detail in Chapter 3.

The effectiveness of transfer policies in reducing income inequality may be measured by the amount of redistribution achieved by transfers *ie* a decrease (or increase) in income inequality which depends, in part, upon the progressivity of the transfers.[5] The effectiveness of transfer policies in reducing income inequality may be measured by the extent to which indices of inequality such as the Gini coefficient fall during the income transfer process and therefore reflect the amount of redistribution achieved.

Figure 1.3 illustrates how the model is adapted in relation to the goal of reducing income inequality. The inputs are the average level of transfers received, or taxes paid, by the individual, family or household. Production again refers to the transfer instruments. The outputs are the size and incidence of transfers across the income distribution and are determined by the progressivity of taxes and social security payments. The assessment of welfare outcomes in this instance relies on measuring the level of beneficiaries' incomes relative to the incomes of non-beneficiaries, or post-transfer inequality to pre-transfer inequality. In other words, the assessment captures how much redistribution is achieved by the transfer process and identifies to whom this redistribution accrues. Again the measurement of redistribution is associated with an extensive literature and this is considered in Chapter 6.

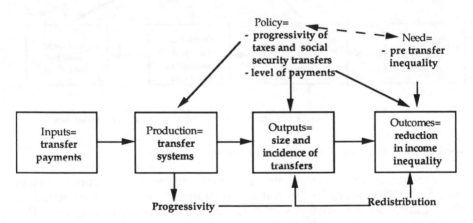

Figure 1.3. The production of welfare: the reduction of income inequality

1.3. The efficiency criteria

The efficiency of transfer policies in alleviating poverty can be measured by the extent to which the inputs (transfers) accrue to the pre-transfer poor (target efficiency) and the amount by which each unit of input reduces the poverty gap (poverty reduction efficiency).

Referring to Figure 1.2, we see that the link between inputs and outputs is the transfer instrument, so that the characteristics of this instrument (for example, whether it is a universal or selective transfer) will determine target efficiency. In turn, the level of output - the size and incidence of the transfers

- in relation to the existing level of need, will determine the amount of poverty reduction achieved per unit of transfer. The final outcome is measured by the difference between the pre- and post- transfer levels of inequality.

The efficiency of transfer policies in reducing income inequality may be measured by how progressive the transfer instruments are in distributing the transfer payments or taxes and by the amount of redistribution achieved for each unit of transfer payment or tax receipt.

Referring to Figure 1.3, we see that it is the progressivity of the transfer instrument which determines how efficiently the inputs are distributed; so that an instrument with low progressivity will require a higher level of inputs to achieve the same output as a more progressive instrument.

1.4. Discerning the effects of the transfer instruments

The LIS data identifies the components of household income and transfers in a fairly detailed fashion. For each family or household 'case' on the file it is possible to identify its sources of income from either the private sector (*eg*: wages, property, self-employment) or the public sector (*eg*: unemployment benefits, aged pensions, housing benefits, family allowances); as well as deductions in the form of income taxes, property taxes and social insurance contributions.

In order to measure and analyse the transfer process a theoretical division of the formation of income into three stages - market income (MI), gross income (GI) and disposable income (DPI) - is used in the study. In moving from market income to gross income it is the direct transfers (social security payments) which form the first set of inputs to the transfer system. This produces an output in the form of gross income. The movement from gross to disposable income is via indirect transfers (taxes) which form the second set of inputs to the transfer system, with disposable income the resultant output. It is through this division of the transfer process that the separate, as well as net, effects of each instrument can be identified and measured. Figure 1.4 illustrates this separation and relates each stage to the Hill and Bramley model.

In following the stages of redistribution illustrated in Figure 1.4, the analysis presented in Part I reports the efficiency and effectiveness measures at each stage of income formation. The interpretation and discussion, however, varies in the degree of space devoted to the changes between each stage. The primary concern will be with the change between the pre- and post-transfer measures, with the intermediate stages being analysed in greater or lesser detail as warranted. For example, in analysing the changes to the poverty head-count the analysis may be more concerned with social security transfers than with taxation. On the other hand, changes in income inequality may require equally detailed analysis of both types of transfers.

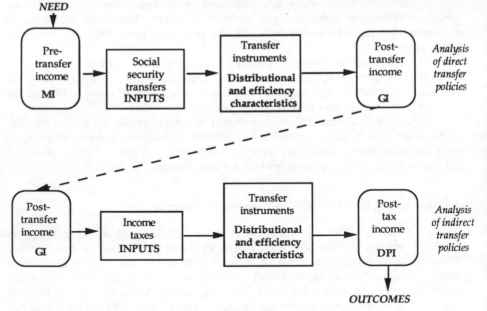

Figure 1.4. The 'three stage' approach to analysing income transfers

1.5. Summary

In this chapter I have identified poverty alleviation and the reduction of income inequality as two goals central to income transfers. In examining the progress of the various welfare states towards these goals, the study uses several measures of efficiency and effectiveness to compare the various policy instruments employed in each country to achieve these goals. Thus, the focus is not just on the outcomes of transfer processes, but also on how the various instruments of policy contribute to these outcomes.

Notes

[1] Flora (1986a:41).

[2] Flora (1986b:53).

[3] Haveman (1987:91).

[4] The poverty gap refers to the difference between household or family income and the poverty line. This difference may be expressed in actual monetary terms *eg* $X required to bring the family up to the poverty line income; or expressed as a percentage of the poverty line rather than in monetary units. The latter approach is frequently adopted in cross-national comparisons to standardise comparisons.

[5] The precise definition and measurement of progressivity is set out in Chapter 5. Briefly, progressivity refers to the extent to which higher income

earners pay taxes at a higher rate than low income earners; conversely, the extent to which lower income earners receive more generous social security payments than higher income earners.

2 Using the LIS data

While Chapters 3 and 6 discuss measurement issues specific to the poverty and income inequality methodologies, there are several important methodological and operational problems common to both which are discussed in this chapter. These problems arise from: the unit of analysis; the use of equivalence scales; the choice between recipient characteristics and family types to analyse the incidence of transfers; and the treatment of zero and negative incomes. In each instance, there is no consensus in the literature as to a 'best approach' to solving these problems and it should be emphasised that different choices in each of these areas will lead to quite different results being obtained. Moreover, the form of the LIS data may constrain choices in some areas. The purpose of this chapter is to set out the choices made in each instance so that the reader is quite clear about the assumptions underpinning the empirical results reported in later chapters.

2.1. The unit of analysis

The LIS data sets are derived from three main sources: surveys of tax files, specifically designed income or consumption surveys or general population surveys. The surveys cover three main types of units, the tax (administrative) unit; the household unit; and the family unit. For a number of countries in the study it is possible to analyse the data from more than one perspective, in others there may be no choice at all. In the LIS database units have been coded in such a way as to allow researchers to identify what type of unit the survey data originally covered. For a majority of countries researchers can select units for analysis on either a family or household basis. Appendix A sets out the availability of data for each type of unit. On balance, the 'family' based definition can be applied more uniformly across the data sets than the 'household.' For this reason the family is chosen as the unit of analysis for the study. The selection is reinforced by the fact that in most of the countries, social security and taxation policy is directed toward the family rather than the household unit.[1]

The comparability of the unit of observation in the LIS data has been discussed by Smeeding et al (1990:6-8), Hagenaars (1989) and Coder (1990).[2] The comparability of the unit poses two problems here. First, calculating the total amount of income, transfers and taxes which accrues to the unit and second, in estimating the number of people among whom the unit's income is shared.[3]

The problem may be demonstrated by the example of a family comprising a married couple together with a student aged 18 years residing at home. In the Swedish data set, this 'family' would be considered as two tax units, *ie* a married couple and a single taxpayer. In Canada, if the student received some economic support from her/his parents, all three would form a single 'economic family'; if not, then two 'economic families' would be reported. In the UK, the student would form part of a single family household regardless of whether the student was financially dependent or independent.

To illustrate the difference which the unit makes to the analysis consider the situations shown in Table 2.1. The table shows a family of identical composition with identical income in Sweden and in the UK. In Sweden, this family would comprise two tax units with income of $9,000 (married couple) and $5,000 (single person); in the UK, the joint family income is $14,000. Using the poverty lines shown in the table, both tax units in Sweden would be considered as poor, adding three persons (or two families) to the poverty head count, while in the UK the joint income puts the unit above the relevant poverty line with no addition to the poverty head count.

Table 2.1.
An illustration of the unit of analysis problem

	Sweden	UK
	$	$
Married couple income:	9000	14000 }
Student income	5000	combined)
Poverty line income :	MC = 10,000	MC + 1 = 13,000
	S = 6,000	
Total poverty gap:	2000	0
Poverty head count:	3 persons or	
	2 families	0

While the incidence of units such as the one described above are generally a small part of the survey populations, they do affect the results of a number of the measures and these will be noted where relevant.[4]

An additional consideration in the choice of unit of analysis is the weight given to each unit in the various surveys. Essentially, each survey attempts to weight each observation according to the make up of the unit in the total population. Thus if a family comprising a married couple with two children

20

represents 10% of a country's family units, then the weight given to each unit in the survey will ensure these units will be counted as 10% of the sample. This weight is reported in the LIS database as the variable HWEIGHT. A second weighting variable is constructed to reflect the weighted number of persons by unit type reported as PWEIGHT=HWEIGHT X NUMBER OF PERSONS. For most of the empirical results reported here, the sample was weighted by HWEIGHT. For the inequality measures results are reported for PWEIGHT weighted samples.

The analysis of family types

The results of the analysis are reported and interpreted on a 'family type' basis. Although there is sufficient detail in the LIS data to allow analysis from the perspective of beneficiary type - for example, those in receipt of age pensions - this level of analysis is difficult in comparative studies. The reasons for this are: beneficiaries may have several sources of transfer income and could therefore be identified with several groups and/or some beneficiary categories may not match, may overlap, or may not exist in some countries. Therefore, the approach adopted is to analyse the incidence of transfers for the family types described in Table 2.2. The table also shows the abbreviated references for each type which are used in reporting the results in the following chapters.

Table 2.2.
Description of family types used in the study

Family type	Description of family	Table reference
Aged single	Single person of official retirement age	Aged (S)
Aged couple	Couple, head has reached official retirement age	Aged (C)
Single person, no children	Single person household, no children, head less than official retirement age	Single (NC)
Couple, no children	Couple, no children, head less than retirement age	Couple (NC)
Lone parent	Single person less than official retirement age, with one or more children under 18 years	Lone parent
Couple with children	Couple, head less than official retirement age, with one or more children under 18 years	Couple (Ch)
Other	All other units	Other

The category of 'other' family types includes units such as shared households with two or more unrelated adults. In Norway, Sweden and Switzerland there are no units coded as 'other'; in the example just cited these persons would be coded as single person units in a multi-family household. In some countries, depending on resource-sharing or declared relationships, such a group would be coded as other in a single-family household.

Table 2.3 sets out the incidence of each family type in the LIS countries as represented on the LIS files.

Table 2.3.
Percentage of family types in population, circa 1980

	Aged (S)	Aged (C)	Single (NC)	Couple (NC)	Lone Parent	Couple (CH)	Other	Total
Australia	7.7	8.1	20.6	20.2	5.3	34.4	3.7	100
Canada	7.8	8.0	20.2	20.1	5.6	34.0	4.2	100
France	12.2	11.3	10.9	21.4	2.9	36.7	4.5	100
Germany	15.6	11.3	18.3	19.0	2.9	29.6	3.3	100
Netherlands	9.9	9.7	12.4	25.0	3.4	36.0	3.7	100
Norway	16.8	10.5	18.0	10.8	8.4	35.5	*	100
Sweden	16.3	9.4	34.2	15.4	4.4	20.2	*	100
Switzerland	14.2	8.1	35.5	15.2	4.0	23.0	*	100
UK	12.5	11.2	11.7	20.6	4.3	34.3	5.5	100
USA	9.3	8.7	21.1	18.8	8.3	29.5	4.4	100

2.2. Equivalence scales

Equivalence scales are used to adjust family incomes to reflect the needs of families of different sizes and composition. Table 2.4 illustrates how equivalence adjustments are made. In this example, a family income of $5,000 is deflated by 0.7 for each additional adult and by 0.5 for each child, this produces an adult equivalent unit (AEU) income for each family. Alternatively, the incomes could be expressed in terms of the amount of income required by different families to reach the same level of well-being for a fixed standard. In the example, a couple without children would require $8,500 to have an equivalent income to a single person with $5,000 and a couple with two children would require $11,000.

Table 2.4.
The calculation of equivalent incomes

Family type	Equivalence	Family income	AEU income	Single equivalence
Single person	1.0	5000	5000	5000
Couple	1.7	5000	2940	8500
Couple + 2 ch	2.2	5000	2270	11000

There is a considerable range of methods which can be used to derive equivalence scales and a large number of scales are used in OECD countries (Whiteford,1985). The issue of equivalence adjustment has been widely discussed in the literature and there is no general agreement on a best approach or approaches (Whiteford,1985; Buhmann et al,1988). Additionally, as the work of both Whiteford and Buhmann demonstrates, the equivalence factors used in OECD countries vary considerably with no obvious central tendencies. Therefore, in a comparative context, there is no scale which has any clear advantage over others. The choice is essentially arbitrary, as Atkinson (1989b:2) makes clear in this discussion on the measurement of inequality in a comparative context:

> It is a field in which there are large differences in social judgments, which translate themselves into differences in the tools which are applied, such as the measure of inequality or the choice of equivalence scale.

The extensive study of equivalence scales carried out on the LIS data by Buhmann et al (1988) shows that poverty estimates, and particularly head-counts, are sensitive to the choice of scale. One way around this problem has been discussed by Atkinson (1989b:3), who suggests that comparative researchers use a range of analytical tools - for example, more than one equivalence scale or poverty line - to produce a range of estimates which give partial rather than absolute answers to questions about levels of poverty or inequality. Atkinson's arguments draw on the earlier work of Sen (1979:286) who noted that:

> ... one may be forced to use more than one criterion because of non-uniformity of accepted standards, and look at the *partial* ordering generated by the criteria taken together ..

In this analysis two equivalence scales are used to generate a partial ordering of the countries, results are reported for both, and where significant differences emerge this is noted. The first scale used in the analysis (designated as EQ1) is a conventional scale adopted by the OECD (1982:36) in its list of social indicators. The second (designated EQ2) is based on statistical work carried out by Whiteford (1985) which calculated the geometric mean of 59 scales based on consumption surveys, adopted in government transfer programs or official poverty lines. The two scales are shown in Table 2.5.

Table 2.5.
OECD and Whiteford geometric mean equivalence scales

Equivalence scale	1st adult	2nd & subseq. adults	Each child
OECD (EQ1)	1	0.70	0.50
Whiteford (EQ2)	1	0.56	0.32

2.3. Income measurement issues

Chapter 1 detailed the basis on which income will be measured in the study *ie* in terms of market, gross and disposable incomes. These measures reflect the sum of all incomes of the family unit at each stage of income formation. In the analysis in the following chapters family income is expressed in equivalent terms, unless otherwise indicated.

An issue of general concern in income surveys is the apparent under-reporting of income by survey respondents. Cross-checks between national income data and income reported in surveys of this kind, reveal that frequently, the expected level of income does not match that which is actually reported. This is less true of data based on tax file surveys than on income or consumption surveys. Some preliminary work on this problem has been done by several LIS researchers, who find that in three of the countries so far analysed that reported income is about 90% of expected income (Smeeding et al, 1990:16). It is difficult to make any correction for this under-reporting, except to note that it exists for a number of the LIS files.

Treatment of zero and negative incomes

Table 2.6 shows the percentage of families with zero and negative incomes for each data set using various definitions of income. The percentage of zero and negative incomes reported for these countries at the disposable income stage, is generally small for each country with the exception of the Netherlands which has a level of both zero and negative incomes far in excess of the other LIS countries. There would appear to be two sources of explanation for this. First, a large percentage of the zero incomes are concentrated in the non-aged single (no children) group. This suggests that some of this group may be students or young unemployed who are residing with parents without an independent income. Second, as will be discussed in the following section, the data for the Netherlands was collected in 1983 and thus it is the country furthest on in the downturn in the business cycle that occurred in the early and mid- 1980s.

Table 2.6.
Zero and negative incomes reported for families

Country	Families with negative incomes (%)			Families with zero incomes (%)		
	MI	GI	DPI	MI	GI	DPI
Australia	-	-	-	10.2	0.5	0.5
Canada	0.2	0.1	0.1	7.4	0.5	0.5
France	0.3	0.1	0.2	14.9	0.2	0.1
Germany	-	-	0.1	23.4	0.2	0.2
Netherlands	-	-	1.4	21.2	3.4	2.1
Norway	0.1	0.1	0.1	11.9	0.2	0.2
Sweden	1.0	-	0.1	6.5	0.3	0.3
Switzerland	-	-	0.1	3.4	1.0	0.9
UK	-	-	0.1	8.3	-	-
US	0.3	0.2	0.2	7.4	0.8	0.8

The treatment of zero and negative incomes varied with the operational constraint of each measure. The management of these observations is set out in Table 2.7. Overall, the approach was to include as many observations as possible in the analysis. Thus zero and negative incomes were included, at face value, in all measures except those which could not be computed on a negative basis, in which case they were recoded to zero.[5]

Table 2.7.
Operational treatment of zero and negative incomes

Measure	Zero incomes	Negative incomes
Median income	included	included
Poverty measures	included	recoded as zero
Inequality measures	included	recoded as zero

2.4. Different years of observations

The period which the first wave of LIS data spans runs from 1979-80 to 1983. Two countries, Switzerland (1982) and the Netherlands (1983) are at the later end of this wave and therefore the data are more likely to be influenced by the downturn in the business cycle experienced in the OECD area in the early

1980s. For example, unemployment doubled in the Netherlands between 1980 and 1983 from 7% to 14% (OECD,1989). The effect of the downturn is also likely to increase the number of small business failures and bankruptcies. Negative incomes may arise through tax liabilities on previous earnings when current income is low.

Blank (1989) finds that poverty and income inequality move anti-cyclically. This implies that if the data for the Netherlands (and to a lesser extent Switzerland) had been collected in 1980, we might expect to have observed a lower level of poverty and inequality in these countries. The fact that data was collected at different stages of the business cycle for different countries implies that cross-national comparisons of levels of poverty and inequality may be biased. On the other hand, proportional reduction in these measures may give a less biased comparison of the effectiveness of transfer systems.

Notes

[1] Researchers using the LIS database also appear to favour the family unit, reporting results for either families, or individuals in family units. See for example, Buhmann et al (1988), O'Higgins et al (1985), Smeeding et al (1990:57-76).

[2] A general discussion of the unit of analysis problem can be found in Danziger and Taussig (1979).

[3] As the discussion in the following section makes clear, this estimate is critical for the application of equivalence scales. The study leaves aside the related issue raised by the work of Pahl (1980;1984) and Edwards (1981) which challenges the assumption that income is in fact shared equally among the members of a family/household.

[4] Smeeding et al (1985a:10) estimate, for example, that the overall poverty rate for Sweden would fall from 5.0% to 4.2% if students are excluded from the poor population. This may also affect the results for the Netherlands.

[5] As suggested by Smeeding et al (1985b:4).

3 Poverty measurement issues

The investigation of poverty in a comparative context adds a new dimension to the debate on the definition and measurement of poverty. Cross-national comparisons of poverty raise questions about which sorts of measures are appropriate and how these should be applied across national and cultural boundaries.

Previously, the analysis of poverty was largely confined to national settings where any single approach to defining and setting a poverty line could not be demonstrated to be superior to others. Alternative approaches are suited to some tasks and not others. In a comparative context, however, are some approaches more appropriate than others? In the following section I examine this question in terms of the basic debates on approach and methodology, noting the importance of the type of comparative data which is available and how this might influence the approach to be adopted.

On the basis of this discussion, Section 3.2 describes the approach adopted by the study; and Section 3.3 outlines how the poverty line for each country was established using the LIS data.

The chapter also considers a number of the perennial questions associated with empirical work on poverty: how sensitive are poverty estimates to where the poverty line is drawn? What are the effects of using different equivalence scales? In presenting a picture of poverty in a cross-national context, are head-counts or poverty gaps the better measure? How confident can we be in the empirical results and how should the results be presented and interpreted?

3.1. Defining and measuring poverty in a comparative context

Broadly speaking there are two conceptual approaches to the definition of poverty. The **absolute** approach aims to set a poverty standard based on the minimum requirements of an individual or family, irrespective of the standard of living enjoyed by a society as a whole. Conversely, **relative** approaches aim to set a standard which is commensurate with societal living standards or expectations.

The debate between Amartya Sen and Peter Townsend in the UK in the early eighties on the relative merits of each of these approaches demonstrated that neither approach is intrinsically superior in theory, but in practice, each has advantages in differing circumstances.[1] As Atkinson (1989b:13) concludes:

> The problems which arise in the determination of the poverty line have been extensively discussed in the literature and it is now generally recognized that there is scope for a wide variety of opinion.

Here I give a brief account of five approaches to defining and measuring poverty which exemplify the absolute and relative approaches as well as several intermediate approaches. In addition to the choice of definitional perspective, Atkinson (1989b:13-17) has also pointed out that the indicator of poverty may take a variety of forms. He distinguishes three types of indicators - the consumption of specific commodities, total expenditure and total income. In the discussion below I note which indicators are used by the various approaches as this is a critical issue in the approach chosen for this study.

Five approaches to poverty measurement

The following discussion of approaches to measuring poverty is selective, aiming to describe some of the main methodologies used by government agencies to determine poverty lines and to illustrate the contexts in which the different indicators distinguished by Atkinson are used. The approaches are referred to as:

    (1) budgetary or basket-of-goods;
    (2) consumer expenditure patterns;
    (3) budget standards;
    (4) attitudinal surveys;
    (5) relative standards.

Budgetary approach

The first studies to determine poverty lines were conducted in the UK and US around the end of the nineteenth century and were based on a fairly simplistic basket-of-goods approach. The best examples of this approach are the various studies conducted by Rowntree (1902;1941;1951) who established his poverty line by drawing up a list of necessities under the headings of food, clothing, fuel and household sundries to form a basket-of-goods and then estimating the cost of purchasing these items.

In Rowntree's studies, the food allowance was based on the cost of standard diets required by low income families specified by nutritional experts. Estimates for clothing, fuel, rent and miscellaneous household goods were based on actual expenditures by low income earners.

While the determination of the poverty line under this approach was based on the expenditure required to consume certain levels of commodities, the actual indicator of poverty used was income.

A related approach which is used in the context of developing countries, sets specific consumption targets for what are termed 'basic needs' (Chichilnisky,1982). In this instance, the consumption of target levels of specified commodities is the indicator of poverty, rather than income or expenditure equivalents.

Consumer expenditure theory

A number of methods for determining poverty lines have been developed by economists within the broad area of consumer behaviour. Principally these are based on proportional expenditure, Engel curve and utility theory approaches. Here only the first two of these approaches will be considered since the methodology derived from utility theory has not been used by government agencies for the purposes of calculating poverty lines. A number of methods for estimating poverty lines derives from the work of Ernst Engel who, in a study of the economic development of a province in Germany in 1857, observed that:

> ... the proportion of outgo (total expenditure) used for food, other things being equal, is the best measure of the material standard of living of a population.[2]

It is now a well established economic law that expenditure on food as a proportion of total expenditure decreases as income increases.[3] Expenditure on other goods and services such as fuel, clothing and housing has also been found to decrease as household income increases. Thus there appears to be a systematic relationship between a household's expenditures on what can be termed 'necessities' and its standard of living, as determined by income.

This relationship is illustrated in Figure 3.1. Conversely, expenditure on other items termed 'luxuries' shows an opposite relationship in Figure 3.2. Expenditure on necessities, singly or in combination, has consequently been used in a variety of ways as a measure of living standards and for the derivation of equivalence scales.

There are several well known poverty lines based on the proportional approach. In the US, the Orshansky poverty line assumes that a family which spends more than 30 per cent of its income on food is in poverty.[4] Alternative studies in the US which use expenditure on food as a proportion of total expenditure (as opposed to income) found that low income families on average spent 25 to 35 per cent of their total expenditure on food (Nicholson,1976:1-12).

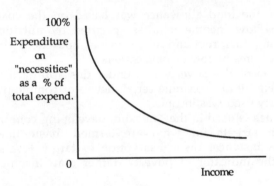

Figure 3.1. Engel curve for 'necessities'

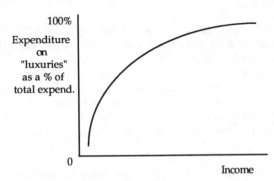

Figure 3.2. Engel curve for 'luxuries'

In Canada, the proportional approach has been applied by the government bureau, Statistics Canada, to derive its poverty line. Statistics Canada chose food, clothing and shelter as necessities and, using expenditure data for Canadian households, calculated the amount spent on these goods as a proportion of income. This proportion was around 42 per cent in 1969. An arbitrary figure of 20 per cent was then added to give a 'reference level' of expenditure. Households which spent more than this proportion of income on necessities were deemed to be in poverty.[5]

The proportional expenditure approach uses expenditure data to set poverty standards; however the poverty indicator can be either income or expenditure.

Budget standards

The development of budget standards, particularly in the US, can be viewed as a combination of the basket-of-goods and consumer expenditure approaches described above. The US Bureau of Labour Statistics (USBLS) opted for an approach to setting reference incomes which involves the selective estimation of consumption budgets based on a combination of survey data analysis together with normative minimum standards for commodities such as food and housing.[6]

The USBLS has devised techniques for estimating a 'minimum required expenditure' for various commodities known as S-curve analysis. This technique is based on the observation that consumption patterns for necessary commodities typically follows a progression whereby as income increases, expenditure is directed firstly, towards increased quantities of the commodity, then increased variety, and finally improved quality. On this basis, it was anticipated that the analysis of expenditure data would show a relationship between amounts bought with changes in income. It was expected that if expenditures in relation to income followed the trend described above, and if, initially, quantity not quality increased, then a quantity- income curve would result that was roughly S-shaped.

Using expenditure as a proxy for quantity, the budget level for a particular commodity was determined by the point where the increase in expenditure showed a tendency to decline relative to income. This point (x') is shown in Figure 3.3. The reference income is set by combining the minimum expenditure levels for food and housing with the S-curve estimates for other commodity groups. The USBLS argued that a standard based on this approach represents the cost of maintaining a family or individual at a 'modest but adequate' level. Budget standards are set by expenditure based data, although the poverty indicator itself is income.

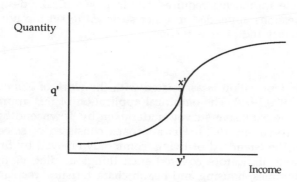

Figure 3.3. Quantity-income elasticity function, the 'S-curve'

Attitudinal surveys: the social consensus approach

This approach represents a radical departure from those described above. It relies on direct questioning of the population about their views on welfare levels. This usually takes one of two forms. In the first, the respondent is asked to estimate the minimum income needed to maintain a 'reference' family (eg: a couple with two children). This produces a poverty line via the averaging of all responses (Rainwater,1974).

Alternatively, the respondent is asked for details of their household composition, current income and the minimum income they would require for necessary costs. The respondents' minimum income estimates are then plotted against their actual income to produce a poverty line as follows: if the amount individuals consider to be their minimum income is an increasing function of income, with an elasticity between 0 and 1, a minimum income function can be derived. The intersection of the actual and minimum income function curves is the poverty line. This point is shown in Figure 3.4, where y^* represents the poverty level income. This approach was introduced by Goedhart et al (1977) and has been developed and applied in the Netherlands to produce the 'Leyden' poverty line.

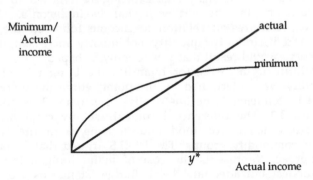

Figure 3.4. The determination of the 'Leyden' poverty line

Using either of these approaches requires data from specifically designed surveys (or specific questions appended to other surveys) to set the poverty line. Thereafter, the poverty indicator is income.

Relative deprivation

The concept of relative deprivation is associated with the work of Runciman (1966) and Townsend (1970,1979). The empirical application of this approach is best exemplified by the extensive survey undertaken by Townsend in the UK in the late 1970s (Townsend,1979). His approach consisted of selecting around 60 indicators of the 'standard of living' commonly enjoyed by British society at the time. These indicators covered such things as diet, clothing, household consumer durables, housing and health characteristics, recreation.

Townsend then conducted a survey to uncover the characteristics of those who lacked, or did not participate in, the amenities or activities represented by each of these indicators. By correlating this lack or non-participation with income and demographic characteristics, Townsend was able to construct a deprivation threshold or poverty line and to identify significant groups within this threshold.

Like the attitudinal approach, Townsend's approach requires a specifically designed survey to set the deprivation index. Although Townsend converted his index to an income level, his approach essentially relies on the consumption of specific commodities as the indicator of poverty.

Relative income approaches

The best known example of the relative income approach was developed by Victor Fuchs in the US in 1965. Fuchs' approach is based on a concept of

economic distance. He argued that a definition of poverty was required which sets a standard that changes with the growth of real income:

> Absolute standards of poverty constantly change. It is more reasonable, therefore, to think of poverty in terms of relative incomes... In any given society at any given point in time the "poor" are those in the bottom tail of the income distribution. While there will always be a bottom tail, how far those in it are from those in the middle is ... of critical importance.[7]

Fuchs proposed a standard of 50% of median income. At the time he recognised that there was no special claim to be made for choosing 50%, however in time this interval has become a widely adopted standard. Researchers using the LIS database have favoured this approach in their analyses and the following section examines the advantages and disadvantages of this approach.

The median income approach is set and measured using income data which may be collected in a number of ways - usually through surveys of tax files or by large-scale social surveys.

3.2. Observing poverty: appropriate measures for the comparative context

In this study the potential range of approaches to measuring poverty is limited by: the conceptual appropriateness of different measures in the comparative context; the availability of suitable comparative data to set a poverty line; and related to this, the availability and comparability of the indicative data. In this section I discuss these issues, using the approaches outlined above to illustrate the arguments. While the discussion focuses on the theoretical advantages and disadvantages of the different approaches, the data required to support each approach is also important. Table 3.1 summarises the relationship between the concepts and the type of data used to set and/or measure the incidence of poverty.

Table 3.1.
The relationship between poverty concepts and indicators

Indicator	Conceptual approach	
	ABSOLUTE	RELATIVE
SPECIFIC COMMODITIES	Chichilnisky	Townsend
INCOME	Rowntree	Fuchs
EXPENDITURE	Orshansky	USBLS Budget standards

The advantages and disadvantages of each approach vary with the purpose for which the measure is to be used. For example, if we wanted to know whether a particular transfer payment provided an 'adequate' standard of living for recipients it might be appropriate to examine the expenditure patterns of recipients and compare these with a poverty line which has been set using dietary, housing and clothing requirements. In answering this question such an absolute approach might be more appropriate than, perhaps, a relative income approach, which would tell us how far below the average or median income the recipients are, but not whether this seriously impairs their ability to consume certain necessary commodities. There are of course the usual objections regarding the subjectivity of such an absolute approach, for example, variations in consumption due to age, sex, cultural background. However, the interval chosen to set a relative standard is equally arbitrary.

Shifting the focus of the question, and asking whether a transfer payment is set at a level which might be regarded as 'fair', would require a shift in approach. In this instance, the judgement of fairness may be best conducted on a basis which relates the income of recipients to the average or median incomes of the society as a whole. Absolute approaches may be inappropriate in this context because they do not capture the change in inter-group differences, particularly over time. The objections which might be raised against the relative measure in this case include the definition of income, for example, measuring income but not assets.

The debate on absolute versus relative measures in the UK and US in the 1970s paid considerable attention to the question of the subjectivity of each approach. In this, and indeed many other respects, there is room for doubt about the validity of criticisms made by adherents of each particular approach of the other approaches. Quite often the charges being levelled at other approaches are equally applicable to the approach being advocated. For example, a frequently cited criticism of absolute approaches to defining poverty is that it involves an unacceptably high level of subjective judgement with respect to defining what constitutes a minimum standard. This is a valid criticism but it is one which is equally applicable to relative approaches. For example, the Townsend and median income approaches also suffer from considerable subjectivity: Townsend because his indicators of style of living were based on his judgements; the median income approach because of its arbitrary specification of the interval of comparison. Essentially, there seems little point in making abstract criticisms of each approach, all measures are problematic and the problems specific to each approach are probably best dealt with in the context of application.

Many of the problems associated with the application of an absolute approach in national contexts become even more apparent cross-nationally. For example, consumption patterns will vary substantially between different groups of commodities - fuel consumption will vary with climate; similarly clothing budgets and customary diets will differ; housing costs will vary with patterns of public and private provision, and so on. It would be difficult to construct a budget standard or basket-of-goods which could be confidently applied cross-nationally. This is also true of a relative approach such as Townsend's. In addition, the data required to generate such standards does not exist on a comparable basis.

For these reasons approaches which rely on the consumption of specific goods and expenditure based measures are difficult to use with any confidence in a comparative context.

The social consensus approach in the comparative context could be adopted if the appropriate survey data were available for each country. However we would not be contrasting the countries on the basis of a single standard, but on a series of standards which might prove difficult to compare to each other. For example, they would reflect national differences in standards of living, customary consumption patterns and so on.

The relative income approach to setting a poverty line has a number of advantages and disadvantages in the comparative context. In terms of advantages, consider the example of adopting Fuch's approach to setting the poverty line (*eg*: 50% of median income). Using this approach we would be able to compare, in a consistent fashion, the relative economic distances between higher and lower income earners across countries. A second advantage is that, unlike expenditure data, income data pose fewer problems in terms of building comparable variables for analysis. Third, an approach such as Fuchs' allows the specification and measurement of poverty to proceed from the same type of data.

There are a number of problems with the relative income approach, some of which are shared with other approaches and others which are specific to income approaches. In the first instance, the period of observation of the income is limited, usually to an annual or even weekly basis. It is possible that units defined as poor one week or year may not be defined so in the following survey - the duration of 'poverty' may vary considerably for some families or households and is frequently related to the stage of the 'life-cycle' which the unit being observed has reached. This is a problem common to all approaches, even those which do not use income to set the poverty line, but as the indicator of poverty.

Second, income as an indicator has specific weaknesses in distinguishing the poor in that, assets or capital in the form of home ownership or savings, are not included in the measure. Some families which we might not regard as poor - relative to community standards - because of their asset holdings, may be defined as such on an income basis.

A third problem specific to the income approach in a comparative setting is that those defined as poor in relatively wealthy countries, may be well above the poverty line in others. This issue is particularly important when comparing developed and developing economies. However, in the group of OECD countries under consideration here, this poses less concern. The problem is one of degree in these countries and requires consideration about the relative standard that is chosen: for example, whether one uses median income rather than average income as a standard.

To conclude, the relative income approach generally appears to have the strongest claims in the comparative context. Its immediate attractions are strongly linked to data constraints, but it should also be recognised that there are sound theoretical reasons for using relative income approaches rather than consumption or expenditure approaches to make meaningful comparisons. In terms of the specific focus of this study, the ability of the income transfer systems to decrease the economic distance between higher and lower income earners is a central element of the effectiveness of these systems. For these reasons the Fuchs' approach is adopted for the analysis. In the following sections I set out how the Fuchs' approach is applied; discuss a number of related empirical issues which concern how the poverty measures are to be presented (head-counts versus poverty gaps); and how the countries are to be compared (ranking and partial ordering versus absolute measures).

3.3. Setting a relative poverty line

The basis of the poverty line measures used in the analysis is 50% of adjusted median family income. This poverty line is calculated using the following steps. First, family disposable income (DPI) is divided by the equivalence scale (OECD or Whiteford scale) to give adjusted family income. The observations are then sorted in ascending order and the median adjusted income observed. A poverty line for all AEU is set at 50% of this median. This is, in effect, the poverty line for a single person since the equivalence scale equals 1 for a single person. Finally, poverty lines for other family sizes are calculated by multiplying the AEU line by the appropriate equivalence factor. Table 3.2 illustrates how the adjusted median income poverty line is calculated for several family types, using the OECD equivalence scale.

Table 3.2.
Calculation of the adjusted median income poverty line

Family type	AEU Poverty line	OECD scale	Family type poverty line
Single person	1000	1.0	1000
Lone parent + 1 child	1000	1.5	1500
Couple	1000	1.7	1700
Couple + 2 children	1000	2.7	2700

3.4. Head-counts and poverty gaps

Poverty estimates are frequently presented in the form of a **head-count** measure, that is, the proportion of the population below a given poverty line. The count itself may be based on persons, families or households. While the head-count is a useful presentational measure, by virtue of its simplicity, it does have a number of drawbacks which have been widely discussed in the poverty measurement literature.[8] Of these, there are three which most concern this study: first, the head-count is sensitive to where the poverty line is drawn; second, head-counts may be misleading in comparing the degree of poverty cross-nationally; and third, head-counts are insensitive to transfers from the poor to the non-poor.

To illustrate these problems consider the examples shown in Tables 3.3 and 3.4. Table 3.3 shows the poverty head-counts for two countries based on two poverty line incomes. When the poverty line is drawn at $100 per week, both countries have identical head-counts of 20%, however, when the poverty line is decreased by 10% there is a significant drop in the level of poverty in Country A with very little change in Country B. This illustrates that head-counts may vary quite dramatically with a small variation in the poverty line. It also shows that if we were to compare these two countries solely on the basis of *Poverty line 1*, the head-count would suggest that the two countries have similar levels of poverty; however we know from *Poverty line 2* that the degree of poverty is substantially different. The most common reason for such changes is the 'clustering' of income units around the poverty line.

Table 3.3.
The sensitivity of poverty estimates

	Poverty line 1	Poverty line 2	Poverty head-count (%)	
	$	$	PL1	PL2
Country A	100	90	20	5
Country B	100	90	20	18
	Poverty line 1	Poverty line 2	Average poverty gap ($)	
	$	$	PL1	PL2
Country A	100	90	5	2
Country B	100	90	9	8

This problem is handled in two ways in the empirical analysis. First, to avoid clustering effects, three poverty intervals are used: in addition to setting the poverty line at 50% of median income, one line was set slightly lower (at 40% of median income) and another slightly higher (60% of median income). Poverty measures are reported at each of these levels.

Second, the concept of the **poverty gap** is used in the study. The poverty gap is the difference between the income of the unit in question and the income that would be required to bring that unit up to its defined poverty line. Returning to the example in Table 3.3, we see that in Country A the poor are clustered just below PL1 and on average, have incomes which are $5 below the poverty line. In Country B the poor are, on average, $9 below the poverty line. This accounts for the dramatic shift in the head-count for Country A when the poverty line is set at a slightly lower level, while the head-count for Country B falls to a much lesser extent. In Chapter 4 the analysis of poverty is presented using both the head-count and poverty gap measures.

Table 3.4 illustrates the transfer sensitivity problem identified earlier. We see that a transfer occurs between Person A, who is below the poverty line pre-transfer and Person B, who is above the poverty line pre-transfer. If the head-count measure is used there appears to be no change in poverty levels; however using the poverty gap measure we see that poverty has increased.

Table 3.4.
Transfer sensitivity

	Poverty line ($)	Pre-transfer income ($)	Post-transfer income ($)	Head-count		Poverty gap($)	
				Pre-	Post-	Pre-	Post-
Person A	100	90	70	1	1	-10	-30
Person B	100	100	120	0	0	0	+20

This property of the poverty gap allows us to judge the effectiveness of different transfer instruments in reducing poverty in a much more sensitive fashion than is permitted by the head-count. The change in the size of the poverty gap during the transfer process is also an important factor in the assessment of the efficiency of transfer systems. For example, transfers such as that described above clearly do not contribute to a reduction in poverty. The analysis in Chapter 5 considers the extent to which transfers close the poverty gap, allowing for the spillover of transfers above the poverty line.

3.5. Partial ordering

In the course of the discussion in this and the preceding chapter I have identified two key problems which affect the estimation of poverty in a comparative context: where the poverty line itself is drawn; and the equivalence scale(s) used. As several LIS researchers have shown (Smeeding et al, 1985b; Buhmann et al,1988) poverty estimates are quite sensitive to the way in which these problems are handled. The extensive work of Buhmann et al (1988:140) which produced poverty and inequality estimates for a range of equivalence scales concluded that:

> Choice of equivalence scale can systematically affect comparative absolute and relative levels and rankings of countries (or groups within countries) with respect to measured inequality and poverty. Because of these sensitivities, one must carefully consider summary statements and policy implications derived from cross-national comparisons of poverty and/or inequality.

Indeed, the variation in their results could lead one, as Atkinson (1989a: 2) suggests, to 'conclude that nothing definite can be said.' Atkinson has given this issue - specifically in the context of the LIS data - a great deal of attention and has suggested that **partial ordering** may be the best approach to presenting, analysing and interpreting results from the LIS and similar data sets.[9]

Partial ordering has two aspects as described by Atkinson: the use of rankings rather than numerical values and, over a range of poverty lines or equivalence scales, these rankings may be partial rather than complete. To illustrate Atkinson's argument, consider the example shown in Table 3.5. The first point Atkinson makes is that, given the sensitivity of poverty estimates, we should avoid statements such as 'there is twice as much poverty in Country C than in Country A'. Even if we could agree that Poverty line 1 (PL1) is a measure acceptable to those interested in such comparisons, we know that a slight shift in the poverty line, to positions PL2 and PL3 renders this observation dubious if not inaccurate.

Where there is no agreement on the poverty line(s), Atkinson suggests that rather than using numerical values, it may be that the interested parties might agree on rankings rather than precise estimates. That is, they may agree that there is less poverty in Country A than Country C, but avoid specifying how much less. The figures in Table 3.5 for PL1 and PL2 would suggest that a **complete** ordering is possible for countries A,B and C (A<B<C). However, if we extend the range of observations to include PL3, then only a **partial** ordering becomes possible *ie* Countries A and B < C but Country A has more poverty than Country B, when PL3 is used.

Table 3.5.
Rankings, partial and complete ordering

	Poverty line 1 (PL1)		Poverty line 2 (PL2)		Poverty line 3 (PL3)	
	% poor	rank	% poor	rank	% poor	rank
Country A	8	1	5	1	3	2
Country B	10	2	6	2	2	1
Country C	16	3	8	3	5	3

In the presentation and analysis of the empirical results in the following chapters, it is the ordering of the countries on each measure which is given greatest emphasis. Atkinson (1989b) has proposed that we consider a range of poverty lines $Z^- \leq Z \leq Z^+$ collectively denoted by Z^*. Using the range of results from these alternative lines:

> ... we can make unambiguous comparisons if the number in poverty is lower for all Z in the range ... but we cannot rank two situations if the number in poverty is higher for some Z and lower for other Z in the range Z^*. In other words, for there to be definitely less poverty with one distribution than with another, we require that the cumulative distribution of Y be everywhere below that of the other in the range of possible poverty lines.[10]

In this study the range of poverty lines (Z^*) can be denoted as Z^- (40%); Z (50%); and Z^+ (60%) of median income. Readers familiar with inequality measures will recognise that this ordering approach is analogous to the concept of Lorenz dominance.[11] An ordering of countries in terms of their poverty head-counts (and gaps) can be obtained when the head-count of one country lies entirely below another for all Z in the range Z^*. This situation is shown in Figure 3.5. We see that Germany and Sweden have poverty rates lower than Australia and that Sweden has a lower poverty rate than Germany for all Z in the range Z^*. Thus a complete ordering is possible for these three countries.

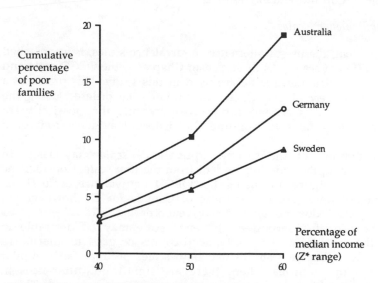

Figure 3.5. Complete ordering of three LIS countries

However, if we add the UK to these observations, this ordering becomes partial. In Figure 3.6 we see that the UK has a lower percentage of persons in poverty at the 40% poverty line than all these countries, but much higher levels than Sweden and Germany at the 50% and 60% levels.

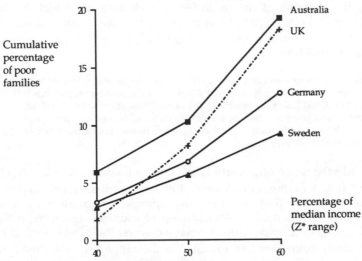

Figure 3.6. Partial ordering of four LIS countries

The ordering approach can also apply to comparisons of the poverty rates of families of different composition between countries and of poverty rates over time within individual countries.

Alternative equivalence scales

The second problem, the use of alternative equivalence scales, is approached by using two different scales. As discussed in Chapter 2, the OECD scale and the Whiteford geometric mean scale are used in this study. This produces a second range of poverty lines which can similarly be ordered using the Atkinson approach. This second range also presents the possibility of comparing the two ranges to examine the ordering evident from both equivalence scales.

The introduction of the second equivalence scale may assist in confirming or denying the ordering evident from the first scale. Consider the ordering shown in Figure 3.7, using the OECD equivalence scale (EQ1) Australia's poverty rates are below those of Canada for Z*; however the Whiteford scale (EQ2), does not allow a complete ordering.

While the use of a second equivalence scale may be desirable in determining the sensitivity of poverty head-counts or gaps to alternative equivalence scales, Chapter 4 shows that both scales produce fairly similar rankings except in countries where there are significant differences in demographic structures, in particular, the number of single persons.[12] This is because of the different weights attached to second adults and children in larger households. In the Whiteford scale these weights are much lower than in the OECD scale, thus the comparative weight of the individual is greater for Whiteford than for the OECD. Therefore we expect the Whiteford scale to measure more individuals in poverty than the OECD scale and conversely, for the Whiteford scale to measure less families in poverty than the OECD scale.

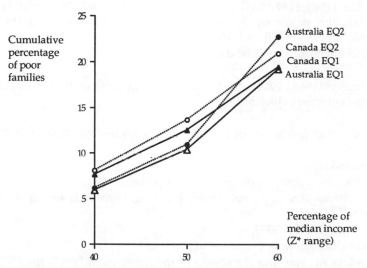

Figure 3.7. Partial ordering using two equivalence scales

3.6. Summary

Assessing the effectiveness of social security transfers in alleviating income poverty requires the establishment of a poverty line as a yardstick against which the transfer systems of various countries can be judged in terms of their ability to reduce poverty rates and poverty gaps.

There is no agreed 'best approach' to setting a poverty line in the comparative context, although the discussion in this chapter suggests that approaches which rely on consumption and expenditure to set and/or measure poverty present greater difficulties in application than do income approaches. For this reason the median income approach suggested by Fuchs is used in the study.

Having selected the poverty standard to be used, there remain a number of measurement problems. Several have been raised here - the sensitivity of estimates to where the poverty line is drawn, the use of alternative equivalence scales, and the presentation and analysis of the results in such an uncertain environment.

The sensitivity problems are tackled in several ways: by using poverty gaps in addition to head-count measures; producing estimates for a series of poverty intervals combined with the use of two equivalence scales; and the presentation and interpretation of the results using the partial ordering approach.

Notes

1 See Sen (1981;1982;1983) ; Townsend (1985) ; and Piachaud (1981). In particular, the paper by Sen and rejoinder by Townsend in the Oxford Economic Papers vols 35 and 37.

2 Cited in Nicholson (1976:80-83).

3 Ibid.

4 Orshansky (1965; 1969). A formalisation of Orshansky's method can be found in Hagenaars (1985:56).

5 Ibid.

6 For a detailed discussion of this approach see Mitchell (1985) and Bradshaw et al (1987).

7 Fuchs (1965:89).

8 See for example, Sen (1979) and Foster's survey (1984).

9 A full discussion of partial ordering in this context is found in Atkinson (1989b:13-15).

10 Atkinson (1989b:13-14).

11 Lorenz dominance is discussed in Chapter 6.

12 Therefore in reporting the results of the analyses in Part I, the OECD scale has generally been used and the text notes where there are significant divergences between the two scales in the ordering of the LIS countries.

4 Poverty reduction in the LIS countries: effectiveness measures

The simplest measures of effectiveness are derived from comparison of the number of units in poverty before and after transfers. In order to make comparisons meaningful across countries it is convenient to express these head-counts as a percentage of the total population. So, for example, we might observe in country A a pre-transfer head-count of 20% and a post-transfer head-count of 10%. The degree of poverty reduction can then be expressed as either a 10 percentage point absolute reduction (*ie* 20%-10%) or as a 50% proportional reduction (100% x 10/20).

The absolute measure is probably less useful for comparative purposes because it takes no account of the size of the pre-transfer poverty population (Smeeding et al,1985b).[1] In country B, for example, the pre-transfer head-count might be 6% and the post-transfer head-count 3%. The absolute measure of poverty reduction would record a 3 percentage point poverty reduction which would appear much smaller than that occurring in country A, even though the proportion of people lifted out of poverty is the same in each country, *ie* 50%. Even if country B were able to completely eliminate poverty, its absolute poverty reduction would be only 6%, still less than the absolute reduction in country A. This hypothetical example demonstrates the advantage of the proportional reduction measure which will be used throughout this chapter.

An alternative measure of poverty which can be used in assessing poverty reduction is the poverty gap, measuring the amount by which each unit falls below the poverty line. The extent of poverty is an important concern for social welfare analysis, for example, a transfer program which lifts a family from dire poverty to an income just below the poverty line would be measured as having no effect on the crude head-count measure but would register a considerable effect using the poverty gap measure (Sen,1979; Beckerman,1979a; Foster,1984; Atkinson,1989b). Furthermore, if we were to use a slightly lower poverty line, the poverty gap measure of poverty reduction would be virtually unchanged, but the head-count measure of poverty reduction would change from zero to one. So the poverty gap should be expected to be both more informative of the extent of poverty reduction and also less sensitive to the choice of poverty line.

One of the aims of this chapter is to use the LIS data to compare the measures of poverty reduction using head-counts with the measures using poverty gaps. Do the two measures rank countries in the same order? Are they equally robust to the choice of poverty line (and also to the choice of equivalence scale)? If both questions are answered in the affirmative, we may conclude that although the poverty gap approach is superior in principle, little information is lost for practical purposes of inter-country comparison by using the simpler head-count approach. If, however, the answers are negative we may conclude that the extra information contained in the poverty gap measures is of operational significance.

The relevance of poverty reduction as an indicator of the effectiveness of a transfer system depends on an implicit assumption that pre-transfer incomes are independent of transfers. In discussing this assumption, O'Higgins et al (1985:6) argue:

> Plainly, this is not the case, particularly when some of the government programs (eg: pensions) have existed for so long that individuals have taken them into account when planning and anticipating their future income needs.

This point can be illustrated in a hypothetical example of countries A and B which start off with identical transfer systems and identical pre- and post- transfer poverty rates of 20% and 10%. Suppose country B expands its state welfare payments to a hitherto neglected group, the aged. Suppose furthermore, that people nearing retirement respond to this policy change by abandoning their private pension and investment plans so that when they reach retirement their market income is lower by the exact amount of the new transfers which they receive from the state. We will then observe that the pre-transfer poverty rate in country B is now, say, 25% whilst the post-transfer poverty rate is still 10%. Measured poverty reduction in country A is still 50% (ie 100% x 10/20), but in country B it has risen to 60% (ie 100% x 15/25), although post-transfer incomes are still identical.

In this hypothetical example substitution between market and state provision makes the poverty reduction measure misleading. How important is this in practice? One way of attempting to answer this question is to compare poverty reduction measures with both pre-transfer and post-transfer poverty rates. If countries with high poverty reduction also have high pre-transfer poverty, there is some evidence that substitution does occur between market and state provision. If the countries with the highest poverty reduction do not have the lowest post-transfer poverty rates, we may conclude that poverty reduction measures are not a good indicator of the overall effectiveness of a transfer system in eliminating poverty. In other words, the post-transfer poverty rate is an alternative indicator of effectiveness which needs to be compared with the poverty reduction measure before we can claim that one country is unambiguously more effective than another in reducing poverty.

There are two further questions concerning the effectiveness of poverty reduction which are addressed in this chapter. First, how is poverty reduction distributed by demographic status? While the aggregate poverty rate and poverty gap measures give an overview of the effectiveness of these systems, they do not tell us whether the outcomes are uniformly spread across the population, or concentrated in a few areas. A recent OECD (1988:6) survey of social security programs noted that poverty amongst the aged has declined dramatically in the OECD countries in the period since 1945:

> The available evidence indicates that the relative income position of the elderly has improved significantly in most countries; in some countries their average level of economic welfare equals or even slightly exceeds that of the non-elderly population.

The survey goes on to point out that among the OECD countries a number of new groups requiring income support have emerged over the past decade (*eg*: sole parents, the young and long-term unemployed). Unlike the aged, these groups do not attract the same level of popular support and have increasingly come to dominate the poor population (OECD,1988:6):

> In those OECD countries which have measures of poverty or low income, the general trend in recent years has been of a static or declining number of elderly poor, with the non-elderly increasingly to be found in the lower parts of the income distribution.

In looking at the disaggregated measures, this chapter considers the effectiveness of these transfer systems in alleviating poverty across a range of groups. Poverty rates are reported for family types as a proportion of each family type and as a proportion of the poor population. Poverty gaps are reported as a proportion of the poverty line for each family type.

Second, to what extent is the poverty reduction of social security transfers offset by taxation? This question has been largely ignored in previous studies which present post-tax (*ie* disposable income) head-counts or gaps without indicating the extent to which the taxation system may reverse the gains made by the social security system.

The empirical analysis has produced a large number of detailed tables which report poverty rates and poverty gaps for: the range of poverty lines (Z*), both equivalence scales, seven family types and for the three stages of the income formation process. Only the key results pertinent to the arguments of this chapter are reported here, additional results are available in Appendix B. Appendix E discusses the statistical significance of the empirical results reported in this, and later, chapters.

Where possible, the results obtained by other researchers using the LIS data will be noted and compared with the results in this study. It is important to note however, that much of the analysis presented in this study covers new ground using the LIS data and comparable findings do not exist.

Moreover, the results here have been obtained from the most recent version of the LIS database (September,1989) which has removed certain anomalies (*eg*: coding errors) from the data. Some of these errors, especially those which affected the income observations, are reflected in existing publications and will contribute to some of the differences between this and other research.

4.1. Aggregate poverty measures: head-counts

Following the methodology set out in Section 3.4, estimates of pre- and post-transfer poverty rates were made by observing the number of families whose pre- and post- transfer incomes are below their respective poverty lines. The post-transfer head-count measure is the most frequently cited statistic in the poverty literature. Despite its well documented flaws (Sen,1979; Foster,1984; Atkinson,1989b), this measure remains a vital statistic for politicians, policy analysts and social welfare lobbies seeking to convey a readily understood 'picture' of the level of poverty in the community.

In the context of comparative research the head-count holds similar attractions, even though LIS researchers have shown that poverty estimates and rankings are extremely sensitive to small variations in the poverty line and equivalence scales (Buhmann et al,1988).

Despite the problems with the head-count measure, these estimates were made for the LIS data for two reasons. First, following the Hill and Bramley model, post-transfer head-counts do represent an immediate outcome of the transfer process. If we concede that poverty alleviation is an aim common to the income transfer systems of the LIS countries then an estimate of the number of families or individuals who remain in poverty post-transfer is an inescapable requirement of the study, irrespective of the methodological flaws associated with head-counts. Second, these estimates can be used as a standpoint to compare other measures used in this study in order to draw conclusions about the most appropriate methods for cross-national comparisons of poverty.

In this section I present post-transfer head-count estimates using the Fuchs' median income approach, but do so with a strong reminder that apart from extreme cases - *eg*: 'there is less poverty in Sweden than in the US' - these head-count rankings need to be backed up by evidence from other measures such as the poverty gap, before any definite conclusions can be drawn about the comparative success of the income transfer systems of the LIS countries in reducing poverty.

Tables 4.1 to 4.3 show the estimates of pre- and post- transfer poverty rates for families in the LIS countries, using both the OECD and Whiteford equivalence scales. The tables also show the proportionate reduction in poverty rates pre- and post- transfer. These findings, in terms of rank orders, are very close to those of Buhmann et al (1988) and Smeeding et al (1989); and generally, are within two percentage points of the head-count estimates in both these studies for similar equivalence scales.[2]

Table 4.1.
Reduction in poverty rates for families , 40% poverty interval

Percentage of families in poverty, pre- and post- transfer:

Country	OECD Equivalence			Whiteford Equivalence		
	Pre-	Post-	Reduction	Pre-	Post-	Reduction
Australia	25.7	5.9	77	26.0	6.1	77
Canada	21.2	7.6	64	21.4	8.1	62
France	31.6	4.9	85	30.9	4.6	85
Germany	29.5	3.3	89	29.4	3.8	87
Netherlands	31.1	5.6	82	31.1	5.5	82
Norway	28.7	3.5	88	29.0	3.8	87
Sweden	33.8	3.8	89	34.1	4.0	88
Switzerland	21.1	6.1	71	21.4	6.8	68
United Kingdom	27.2	1.7	94	27.3	2.7	90
United States	23.4	11.0	53	23.6	11.7	50

Table 4.2.
Reduction in poverty rates for families , 50% poverty interval

Percentage of families in poverty, pre- and post- transfer:

Country	OECD Equivalence			Whiteford Equivalence		
	Pre-	Post-	Reduction	Pre-	Post-	Reduction
Australia	28.0	10.3	63	28.0	10.9	61
Canada	24.9	12.5	50	24.9	13.6	45
France	36.4	7.9	78	35.3	9.0	75
Germany	31.0	6.8	78	31.1	7.2	77
Netherlands	32.5	7.0	78	32.5	6.7	79
Norway	30.6	5.3	83	31.1	5.6	82
Sweden	36.5	5.6	85	36.8	5.5	85
Switzerland	24.3	11.0	55	24.8	11.3	54
United Kingdom	30.0	8.2	73	30.1	11.2	63
United States	27.1	17.0	37	27.1	17.5	35

Table 4.3.
Reduction in poverty rates for families , 60% poverty interval

Percentage of families in poverty, pre- and post- transfer:

Country	OECD Equivalence			Whiteford Equivalence		
	Pre-	Post-	Reduction	Pre-	Post-	Reduction
Australia	30.6	19.2	37	30.4	22.7	25
Canada	28.7	19.4	32	28.4	20.9	26
France	41.2	15.2	63	40.3	16.0	60
Germany	33.6	12.7	62	33.1	13.0	61
Netherlands	33.9	10.6	69	33.9	9.1	73
Norway	32.9	8.8	73	33.1	15.3	54
Sweden	39.5	9.2	77	38.9	9.5	76
Switzerland	28.1	17.8	37	27.7	18.0	35
United Kingdom	33.7	18.2	46	33.1	21.4	35
United States	30.8	23.2	25	30.7	23.5	23

The post-transfer rankings of countries by poverty rates are derived from Tables 4.1-4.3. These rankings are identical for the 40% poverty interval whether we use the OECD or the Whiteford equivalence scales. At the 50% poverty interval the rankings are almost identical except that Norway and Sweden swap places. At the 60% poverty interval, however, there are significant differences between the rankings depending on which equivalence scale we use. Norway's ranking is particularly sensitive: it has the lowest poverty rate using the OECD scale but only the fourth lowest using the Whiteford scale.[3] The explanation for this difference is the combined effect of a 'clustering' of incomes between the 50% and 60% intervals and the larger weighting given to single persons by the Whiteford scale. (The disaggregated analysis in Section 4.5 investigates this difference).

Turning to the differences across the Z* range, several countries change rankings as the poverty line rises. The most notable shift occurs for the UK which has the lowest poverty rate post-transfer at the 40% interval, but this rate rises sharply as the poverty line is increased to 50% and 60% of median income. To a lesser extent, this is also the case for Germany.[4] The explanation for these changes is, again, the clustering of incomes around the various poverty lines. This clustering post-transfer is usually related to particular beneficiary groups who receive uniform levels of benefit and have very little other income.

In the case of the UK, it is aged families which account for virtually all the increase in the poverty rates across the Z* range. For Germany, the clustering is spread across several groups including the aged. In the remaining countries, the post-transfer poverty rates for Sweden, Norway and the Netherlands show no dramatic increases as the poverty line rises (apart from the Norwegian rate at the 60% interval discussed earlier.) While the Netherlands starts off behind the UK and Germany at the 40% interval, its post-transfer rates do not rise substantially; it therefore passes these two countries in the rankings at the higher poverty intervals. At the bottom of the rankings, Australia, Switzerland, Canada and the US have post-transfer poverty rates considerably higher than the other countries, particularly at the 50% and 60% intervals.

Table 4.4 gives the rank correlations for the rankings of post-transfer poverty comparing the 40% and 50% intervals, the 50% and 60% intervals, and the 40% and 60% intervals. The extent to which rankings vary according to the choice of poverty line can be summarised by rank correlation coefficients. A value of 1 would imply that the rankings are identical; a value of zero would imply no relationship between the rankings. In fact, the rank correlation coefficients listed in Table 4.4 indicate that there is little difference between the rankings using the 50% and 60% poverty intervals for the OECD equivalence scale: r=0.95. There is somewhat greater disparity between the rankings using the 40% interval or using the Whiteford equivalence scale. In other words, any assessment of poverty rankings is robust whether we choose the 50% and 60% intervals, but it can vary substantially if we choose the 40% interval, especially with the Whiteford equivalence scale.

Table 4.4.
Rank correlation coefficients for post-transfer head-counts, Z* range

Z correlates	OECD scale	Whiteford scale
40 - 50	0.77	0.65
50 - 60	0.95	0.83
40 - 60	0.62	0.44

Table 4.5 shows the ranking of the LIS countries in terms of the post-transfer poverty rates at each level of the poverty line. As noted earlier there is considerable variation across the Z* range, to the extent that only a limited partial ordering of the countries is possible. In particular the UK shows considerable variation in rank across Z*.[5]

Table 4.5.
Post-transfer head-count rankings for Z* range, OECD scale

Rank	40% line		50% line		60% line	
1	UK	1.7	Norway	5.3	Norway	8.8
2	Germany	3.3	Sweden	5.6	Sweden	9.2
3	Norway	3.5	Germany	6.8	Netherlands	10.6
4	Sweden	3.8	Netherlands	7.0	Germany	12.7
5	France	4.9	France	7.9	France	15.2
6	Netherlands	5.6	UK	8.2	Switzerland	17.8
7	Australia	5.9	Australia	10.3	UK	18.2
8	Switzerland	6.1	Switzerland	11.0	Australia	19.2
9	Canada	7.6	Canada	12.5	Canada	19.4
10	USA	11.0	USA	17.0	USA	23.2

I conclude that, with the exception of countries at the extremes of the rankings ie Sweden and Norway versus Canada and the US, the post-transfer poverty counts do not give a clear picture of anti-poverty effectiveness in the LIS countries. Although the rankings are fairly robust with respect to the choice of equivalence scales, they are highly sensitive to the choice of the poverty line.

The problem is probably best illustrated by Figure 4.1 (based on the data in Table 4.5) which shows that there are a number of countries which crossover ranks as we move from one poverty line to another. Despite the fact that the rankings change as we move from one poverty line to another, we can see from Figure 4.1 that there are some general bands of ordering. At the extremes we see that the US and Canada have higher poverty rates at all levels of the poverty line. Australia and Switzerland follow in the next band. France and Germany form another band, although Germany crosses into the lowest band at the 40% interval. Sweden and Norway have poverty rates lower than all the other bands. The UK and the Netherlands cross these bands, particularly the UK which at each level of the poverty line falls in a different band. It appears that the head-count approach allows a partial, but far from complete, ordering of the level of post-transfer poverty in the LIS countries.

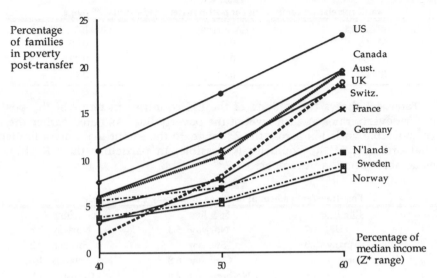

Figure 4.1. Post-transfer head-counts for Z* range, OECD scale

The post-transfer reduction of the poverty head-count

As noted in Chapter 1, an important indicator of the effectiveness of these transfer systems in alleviating poverty is the extent to which the head-count measure is reduced from its pre-transfer level. In Tables 4.1 to 4.3 the proportionate reduction in the head-count has been calculated by the change in the pre-and post- transfer counts, divided by the pre-transfer count.

The results are summarised in Figure 4.2. First, leaving aside the UK, Figure 4.2 shows a strong ordering of the LIS countries in terms of their poverty reduction achievements. The ordering also shows that there are two quite distinct groupings of countries when viewed from this perspective.

Group I consists of the Northern European countries - Sweden, Norway, the Netherlands, France and Germany. As the poverty line rises the poverty reduction achieved by Sweden, Norway and the Netherlands remains fairly constant. In contrast, the poverty reduction achieved by Germany and France tails off between the 50% and 60% intervals, but still remains high relative to Group II.

In the Group II countries, the poverty reduction rates are consistently lower than those for Group I across the Z* range. In addition, the reduction rates are not constant across the range, but fall consistently between Z⁻ and Z⁺. There is a sharp fall in poverty reduction between the 50% and 60% intervals in the Group II countries, and this is particularly true of Australia where the dominance of income-tested programs sharply reduces the level of social security payments over this range.

We see that the UK is quite unlike either of these two groups in terms of its pattern of poverty reduction. At the lowest poverty interval the UK achieves the greatest reduction in the head-count. However, it is unlike the

Northern Europe group in terms of the consistency of poverty reduction - across the Z* range the reduction rate falls quite sharply. At the 60% interval, the UK moves closer to Group II both in terms of the amount of poverty reduction achieved and the tailing off in the rate of reduction.

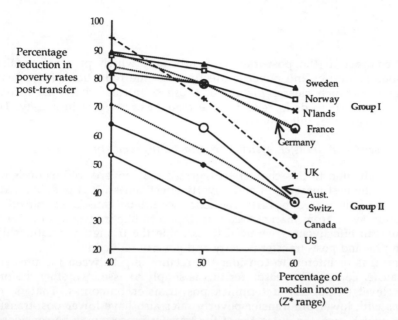

Figure 4.2. Poverty reduction in the LIS countries, OECD equivalence scale

Ranking the effectiveness of the LIS countries in terms of poverty reduction rates, we see that Sweden, Norway and the Netherlands consistently achieve high reductions across the Z* range. France and Germany also achieve large reductions, although these are not as consistent as the former countries as the poverty line rises. The UK is difficult to place in either group as far as the poverty reduction measure is concerned, at lower levels of the poverty line the UK transfer system is extremely effective, but this falls quite sharply as the poverty line rises. However, its effectiveness is clearly superior to the countries in Group II.

At the 40% interval Australia achieves a poverty reduction rate close to that of the Group I countries, but this falls away sharply as the poverty line rises. Switzerland, Canada and the US perform quite poorly even at the lowest poverty interval with poverty reduction rates of around 70% or less. At the 60% interval, poverty reduction is under 40% for this group of countries.

In considering the effectiveness of the countries in reducing poverty across the range Z*, the partial ordering using the results of this study is shown below. This ordering is consistent with the findings of Smeeding et al (1985b).[6]

```
         Sweden ⌐
         Norway │  United Kingdom
    Netherlands └
  = France, Germany
      Australia
     Switzerland
        Canada
     United States
```

In contrast to the post-transfer head-count which presents a fairly ambiguous picture of anti-poverty effectiveness, the reduction of the head-count gives a much clearer picture of those countries where the income transfer system succeeds in reducing the amount of poverty in society. The ordering is, however, still only partial.

The effectiveness of transfer systems in eliminating poverty

In the introduction to this chapter I suggested that poverty reduction is not necessarily the best measure of anti-poverty effectiveness. It is possible that a high level of measured poverty reduction could be caused by offsetting substitution away from market sector saving to public transfers. In order to assess overall effectiveness we need to examine the triangular relationships between pre- and post- transfer poverty and poverty reduction.

First it is of interest to consider the relationship between the pre- and post- transfer counts. The reason for this is simply to assess whether the pre-transfer level of poverty determines post-transfer outcomes. That is, do countries with lower pre-transfer poverty rates also have lower post-transfer rates? In which case, the outcomes of the transfer process may be considered less relevant than say, wages or employment policy in determining the level of poverty in each country.

Figure 4.3 plots the pre- and post- transfer head counts for the LIS countries, we see that in fact there is a moderately strong **inverse** relationship between pre- and post- transfer rates.[7] Those countries with the lowest pre-transfer poverty rates, such as the USA, Canada and Switzerland, tend to have the highest post-transfer poverty rates. The effects of the transfer systems are, in general, strong enough to reverse the poverty rankings.

If market provision of welfare is a substitute for state provision we might expect to find a positive correlation between poverty reduction measures and the level of pre-transfer poverty. This relationship in the LIS countries is illustrated in Figure 4.4.

There is some evidence of a strong positive relationship. In particular, the five Northern European countries with the highest levels of poverty reduction are also the countries with the highest pre-transfer poverty rates. Within Groups I and II, however, there is no obvious relationship between poverty reduction and pre-transfer poverty. This indicates that there may be some degree of substitution between market and state welfare provision. Smeeding et al (1985b:50) have also found this relationship and note that it is particularly pertinent in the case of the elderly.

Further investigation of this question would require the disaggregation of the pre-transfer poor population into those groups whose ability to plan for income support from the state (*eg*: the aged) and those for whom the need for income support would be unplanned (*eg*: sole parents). Comparing such groups may provide clearer evidence of the effects of substitution.[8]

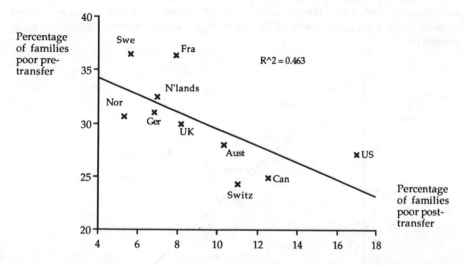

Figure 4.3. Pre- versus post- transfer poverty rates (50% poverty interval, OECD scale)

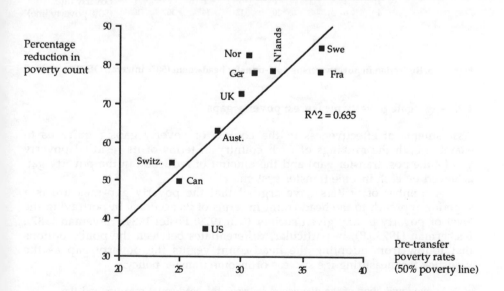

Figure 4.4. Reduction in poverty versus pre-transfer head-count (50% interval, OECD scale)

Most importantly, we want to examine whether there is a correlation between poverty reduction and post-transfer poverty. Figure 4.5 illustrates this relationship. Here the inverse correlation is almost perfect. The countries with the greatest poverty reduction do achieve the lowest poverty rates, and vice versa. This strong relationship indicates that, despite some apparent substitution between state and market provision, poverty reduction does appear to be a good measure of the success a country achieves in eliminating poverty.

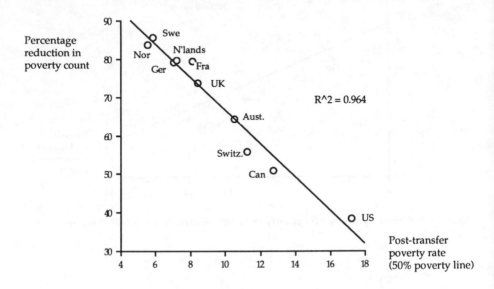

Figure 4.5. Reduction in poverty versus post-transfer head-count (50% interval, OECD scale)

4.2. Aggregate poverty measures: poverty gaps

Assessments of effectiveness in the context of poverty gaps require us to examine both the rankings of each country in terms of its residual poverty gap (*ie* the post-transfer gap) and the amount of reduction in the poverty gap achieved by each income transfer system.

A number of writers have argued that the poverty gap measure is a superior approach to the head-count in terms of its accuracy in portraying the level of poverty in any given society (Sen,1979; Foster,1984; Haveman,1987). Beckerman (1979b:8), in particular, differentiates between the policy options that follow from adopting the head-count versus the poverty gap as the yardstick for measuring the success of income transfer policy:

> ... one implication of the distinction between the head-count measure and the poverty gap measure that is important for policy analysis is that ... if the total amount of funds to be transferred to the poor is given, and if policy objectives were conceived (as they often seem to be) in terms of a reduction in the numbers below

the poverty line (a head-count measure), the best procedure might appear to be to concentrate the transfers on those people who fall below the poverty line by a relatively small amount, for in this way the greatest number of people could be raised up to the poverty line... If, by contrast, the objective were to reduce the most acute poverty, then it would be preferable to concentrate the transfers on those with the largest poverty gaps, and not to reduce the numbers in poverty at all until everybody had been raised up to the poverty line.

Beckerman's observation is of critical importance in the context of making judgements about the relative success of the LIS transfer systems and will be returned to in the conclusions of this chapter.

While the size of the poverty gap is relatively straightforward to measure (summing the gaps between family income and the poverty line) the yardstick against which the poverty gap should be compared at the aggregate level presents a number of possibilities. Generally, the poverty gap is presented as a percentage of the poverty line - ie each family's gap is separately calculated as a percentage of its poverty line and the resulting estimates averaged (Smeeding et al,1985b; Buhmann et al,1988). This approach has not been adopted here because, as the discussion on the disaggregated measures in Section 4.6 will show, there is considerable variation in the size of the poverty gaps of different family types and these variations are disguised when averages are taken across the poor population.

An alternative to this approach is presented by Beckerman (1979b) who used total social security expenditure as the comparative yardstick in his four country study for the ILO. In national contexts where social security expenditure, as a percentage of government outlays, is fairly stable over time this may be a useful yardstick to indicate whether income transfer programs are maintaining their impetus and it may suggest how much social security outlays would need to grow to close the poverty gap. In cross-sectional comparisons however, the value of such a measure is dubious.

A more informative measure in the comparative context may be that adopted by Beckerman (1982) in his later work which compares the size of the poverty gap to GDP. This captures the extent of poverty in relation to a country's total economic resources. This may give a more consonant picture of aggregate outcomes in relation to the resources which could be devoted to income transfers.

It is of interest to look at the relationship between the poverty gap and GDP to assess the extent to which the size of the poverty gap is related to the income of a country. We might expect that the richer nations would be in a position to devote a greater proportion of their resources to poverty alleviation, hence they might exhibit greater reductions in poverty. Figure 4.6 plots GDP per capita (expressed in 1980 $US)[9] against the poverty gap as a percentage of GDP, for the 50% interval.

The figure shows that although we might expect the richer countries to have a lower poverty gap, there is in fact a tendency for the richer countries, notably the US and Canada, to have the highest post-transfer poverty gaps. At the other extreme the UK, which is the poorest country in the sample, has the lowest poverty gap. This has also been observed by Smeeding et al (1985b:43) who note that 'the UK does remarkably well in reducing the pre-transfer post-tax poverty gap given their relatively low percentage of GDP spent on income transfers.' To a lesser extent, this is also true of Australia and Sweden.

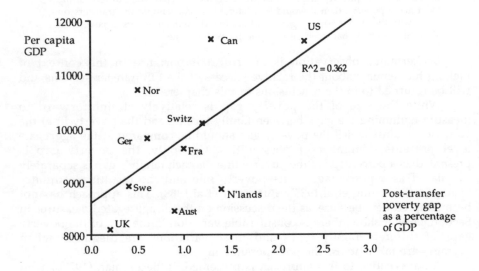

Figure 4.6. Comparison of post-transfer gap and per capita GDP, 1980

Overall the relationship is, on this evidence, rather weak. It should be noted that this question has been tackled here in a fairly preliminary way and therefore the results should be read accordingly. A more detailed analysis, breaking down the aggregate poverty gap into the gaps of different family types and comparing these with the resources devoted to each group may reveal a more definite picture of this relationship.

Post-transfer poverty gaps

In Tables 4.6 to 4.8 the aggregate poverty gap pre- and post- transfer is expressed as a percentage of GDP for each poverty interval. The proportional reduction in the poverty gap is also shown. The tables show these estimates for family income adjusted by both the OECD and Whiteford equivalence scales.[10]

A first point to note is that at each poverty interval, the estimates of the size of the poverty gap post-transfer for each of the equivalence scales are virtually identical in both absolute terms and in the rankings of countries based on these estimates. In addition, the poverty gap produces a fairly stable set of rankings across the Z^* range. The rank correlation coefficients shown in Table 4.9 are all above 0.94.

Table 4.6.

Reduction in poverty gaps for families, 40% poverty interval

Poverty gap as a percentage of GDP, pre- and post- transfer:

	OECD Equivalence			Whiteford Equivalence		
	Pre-	Post-	Reduction	Pre-	Post-	Reduction
Australia	3.4	0.5	85	3.5	0.5	86
Canada	2.9	0.6	78	3.0	0.6	80
France	4.7	0.5	89	4.8	0.5	90
Germany	4.9	0.3	95	5.2	0.3	95
Netherlands	5.0	1.0	80	5.1	1.0	81
Norway	3.4	0.3	92	3.7	0.3	92
Sweden	3.0	0.2	94	3.1	0.2	94
Switzerland	3.4	0.7	81	3.6	0.7	80
United Kingdom	2.4	0.1	97	2.6	0.1	97
United States	4.0	1.2	69	4.0	1.2	69

Table 4.7.

Reduction in poverty gaps for families, 50% poverty interval

Poverty gap as a percentage of GDP, pre- and post- transfer:

	OECD Equivalence			Whiteford Equivalence		
	Pre-	Post-	Reduction	Pre-	Post-	Reduction
Australia	4.5	0.9	79	4.7	0.9	81
Canada	4.2	1.3	70	4.2	1.2	72
France	6.7	1.0	85	6.6	0.9	87
Germany	6.4	0.6	91	6.7	0.6	92
Netherlands	6.5	1.4	79	6.6	1.3	80
Norway	4.6	0.5	90	5.0	0.5	90
Sweden	4.1	0.4	91	4.2	0.3	92
Switzerland	4.9	1.2	75	5.2	1.3	75
United Kingdom	3.3	0.2	93	3.5	0.3	92
United States	5.6	2.3	60	5.6	2.1	60

Table 4.8.

Reduction in poverty gaps for families, 60% poverty interval

Poverty gap as a percentage of GDP, pre- and post- transfer:

	OECD Equivalence			Whiteford Equivalence		
	Pre-	Post-	Reduction	Pre-	Post-	Reduction
Australia	5.8	1.6	72	6.0	1.7	72
Canada	5.7	2.2	61	5.7	2.2	62
France	9.0	1.8	80	8.8	1.6	82
Germany	8.0	1.2	85	8.3	1.1	87
Netherlands	8.1	1.9	76	8.1	1.8	78
Norway	5.9	0.8	86	6.4	0.9	86
Sweden	5.3	0.6	88	5.4	0.6	89
Switzerland	6.7	2.4	65	7.0	2.3	67
United Kingdom	4.3	0.7	84	4.5	0.8	82
United States	7.6	3.7	51	7.5	3.5	50

Table 4.9.
Correlation coefficients for post-transfer poverty gap ranks for Z* range

Z correlates	OECD scale	Whiteford scale
40 - 50	0.98	0.99
50 - 60	0.94	0.97
40 - 60	0.95	0.95

In contrast to the substantial variations in the post-transfer poverty head-counts, the poverty gap measure gives a virtually identical picture whichever equivalence scale is used, and whichever poverty line is used. It is clear from these results that the poverty gap is a far more robust measure of poverty for cross-national comparisons than is the head-count. Because of the stability of these rankings the discussion in the following sections uses the OECD scale results for the 50% poverty interval.

Table 4.10.
Ranks on size of the poverty gap at the 40,50 and 60 % intervals, OECD scale

Rank	40% line		50% line		60% line	
1	UK	0.1	UK	0.2	Sweden	0.6
2	Sweden	0.2	Sweden	0.4	UK	0.7
3	Germany	0.3	Norway	0.5	Norway	0.8
4	Norway	0.3	Germany	0.6	Germany	1.2
5	Australia	0.5	Australia	0.9	Australia	1.6
6	France	0.5	France	1.0	France	1.8
7	Canada	0.6	Switzerland	1.2	Netherlands	1.9
8	Switzerland	0.7	Canada	1.3	Canada	2.2
9	Netherlands	1.0	Netherlands	1.4	Switzerland	2.4
10	USA	1.2	USA	2.3	USA	3.7

Table 4.10 shows the ranking of the LIS countries across the Z* range based on the poverty gap as a percentage of GDP. Comparison with Table 4.5 shows that the poverty gap produces a significantly different ranking to the head-count measure. In particular the UK, Netherlands and Australia, are ranked quite differently on the post-transfer poverty gap.

The effects of the clustering of incomes in the UK around the poverty lines - which causes the head-count to vary dramatically across Z* - is removed and we see that in the UK, income transfer policies result in the majority of the beneficiary population receiving incomes which are around the 40% poverty interval.

The reverse of this case is the Netherlands which has a low head-count but a sizeable poverty gap, indicating that those who are not lifted out of poverty remain some distance from the poverty line.[11]

Of the remaining countries, Sweden and Norway feature in the top ranks consistent with their head-count ranks. In the upper-middle ranks Germany and France are joined by Australia, while the Netherlands falls to the lower- middle rank with Switzerland and Canada. The US runs a long way last, consistent with its poverty head-count.

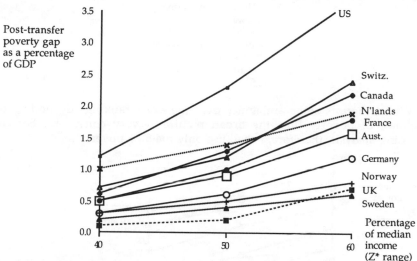

Figure 4.7. Partial ordering using poverty gap measure, OECD scale

A visual representation of the post-transfer poverty gap rankings is given in Figure 4.7. Three distinct groups are evident: the lowest poverty gaps are found in Sweden, UK, Norway and Germany. In a fairly large middle group are Australia, France, Netherlands, Canada and Switzerland. Of this group, Australia and France have a lower poverty gap across the Z* range than the other three countries. At the upper extreme, the US has a poverty gap far greater than all these countries which is accentuated by the fact that it is one of the wealthiest countries in this group in GDP per capita terms.

The post-transfer reduction of the poverty gap

The ordering of the countries based on the reduction in the poverty gap achieved by the transfer system is illustrated in Figure 4.8. In the upper group Sweden, UK, Germany and Norway achieve the greatest reductions in the poverty gap, although the rate of reduction for the UK falls considerably between the 50% and 60% poverty line.[12]

The large middle group evident in the size measures - France, the Netherlands, Australia, Switzerland and Canada - breaks into two distinctive groups on the reduction measure. An upper-middle group composed of France, the Netherlands and Australia achieve reductions in the poverty gap of greater than 70% across the Z* range, whereas Switzerland and Canada fall well below this level of reduction at the 60% interval. As with the size measure of the poverty gap, the US falls a long way behind the other countries in terms of reduction.

In considering the effectiveness of the countries in reducing the poverty gap across the range Z*, the overall ranking would be:

```
= UK, Sweden, Germany
Norway
France
= Netherlands, Australia
Switzerland
Canada
US
```

Whilst there is some ambiguity over the exact rankings depending on the choice of poverty line, the broad picture is very consistent. For the succeeding analysis, therefore, I shall use only the 50% poverty line.

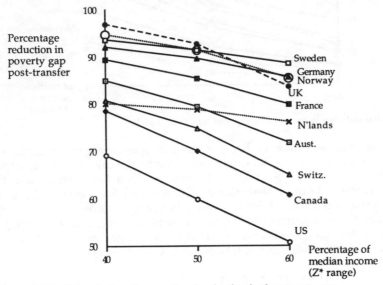

Figure 4.8. Partial ordering of proportional reduction in the poverty gap

Assessing effectiveness in eliminating the poverty gap

The triangular relationships between the pre-transfer, post-transfer and proportional reduction in the poverty gap measures are illustrated in Figures 4.9 and 4.10. This complements the analysis for the head-count measure which was presented in Section 4.1.

It is evident from Figure 4.9 that there is no clear relationship between poverty reduction and the extent of pre-transfer poverty when we use the gap measure of poverty. This result, which stands in contrast to the positive relationship found using the head-count measure of poverty (see Figure 4.4), implies that any substitution between state and private welfare provision is not substantial in relation to the poverty gap.

From Figure 4.10 it is evident that there is a strongly negative linear relationship between poverty reduction and the extent of the post-transfer poverty gap. Moreover, the rankings of countries by these two measures are almost identical and confirm the post-transfer gap analysis in sorting the countries into three distinct groups. The countries which are most effective in alleviating poverty are, unambiguously, the UK, Sweden, Norway and Germany. An intermediate group is composed of France, Australia, the Netherlands, Switzerland and Canada. The US is clearly the least effective in eliminating poverty whether we judge in terms of the proportional reduction of the poverty gap or in terms of the size of the post-transfer gap.

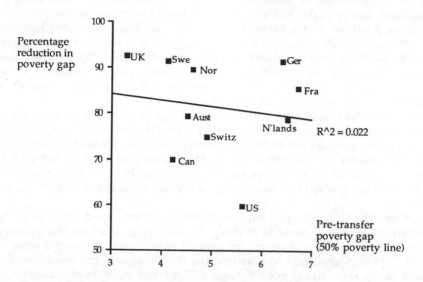

Figure 4.9. Reduction in poverty gap versus size of pre-transfer gap

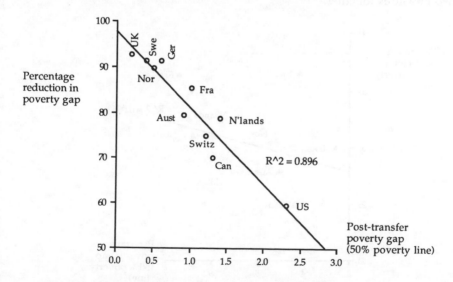

Figure 4.10. Reduction in poverty gap versus size of post-transfer gap

4.3. Comparing aggregate poverty levels: head-counts versus poverty gaps

I noted earlier that key theorists in the poverty measurement literature consider that the poverty gap is, in principle, superior to the head-count as a measure of poverty because it takes account of the extent of poverty and is less likely to be influenced by arbitrariness in the choice of a particular poverty line or equivalence scale. The empirical analysis presented in the previous two sections supports this view. Whereas the rankings using head-counts vary substantially depending on the choice of equivalence scale and, in particular, on the choice of poverty line, the rankings using the gap measure are almost identical whichever set of choices one makes. Buhmann et al (1988:133) also note that: 'interestingly, average poverty gaps are not often greatly affected by choice of equivalence scale.'

An important implication of these findings is that the analyst using poverty gap measures need be far less concerned with the problem of defining the appropriate equivalence scale and poverty line than the analyst who uses head-count measures. A well defined set of measures such as the OECD equivalence scale and the 50% poverty interval can be used in conjunction with the poverty gap with a high degree of confidence that the results will be robust.

Given that the head-count has often been used for poverty measurement it is of interest to investigate the extent to which the poverty gap measure provides a different picture of cross-national comparisons of poverty. It is also important to note that the information in the head-count is relevant in its own right, even though it does not indicate the degree of poverty. It may prove useful for some purposes to use the information in the two measures together.

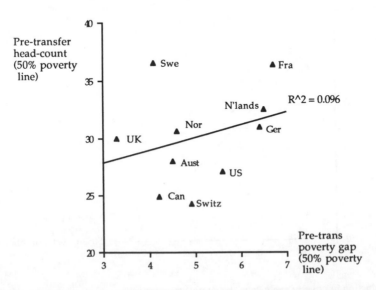

Figure 4.11. Head-count versus poverty gap measures of pre-transfer poverty

The relationship between the pre-transfer head-count and gap is plotted in Figure 4.11 for the 50% poverty line. Examining Figure 4.11, we see that Switzerland ranks lowest in pre-transfer poverty on the head-count measure, but is in the middle of the poverty gap rankings. Sweden on the other hand, ranks highest on the head-count, but is one of the lowest on the poverty gap measure. These differences reflect very different distributions of income amongst the pre-transfer poor. In Sweden, there are a large number of poor families relatively close to the poverty line whereas in Switzerland, many of the poor are a long way below the poverty line. It appears that the head-count measure by itself gives a very misleading picture of the extent of pre-transfer poverty.

The rank correlations for the head-count and gap measures of post-transfer poverty are given in Table 4.11 and Figure 4.12. Here we observe a much stronger, though far from perfect, correlation between the head-count and gap measures of poverty.

Table 4.11.
Rank correlations for post-transfer head-count and poverty gap, Z* range

Count versus gap	40% interval	50% interval	60% interval
OECD	0.87	0.67	0.60
Whiteford	0.87	0.59	0.43

From Figure 4.12 we can see that the head-count measure tells a very similar story to the gap measure of post-transfer poverty except in the case of the Netherlands which has relatively few people in poverty on the head-count but exhibits a relatively large amount of poverty in terms of the poverty gap.[13]

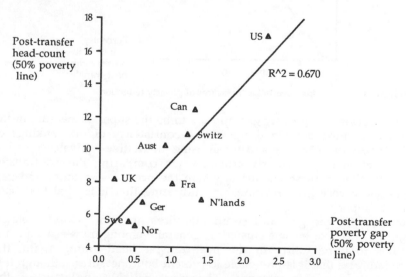

Figure 4.12. Head-count versus poverty gap measures of post-transfer poverty

Equivalent comparisons in relation to measurement of poverty reduction are displayed in Table 4.12 and Figure 4.13. The comparative stories of poverty reduction as told by the two measures are now virtually identical except for the Netherlands - where poverty reduction is exaggerated by the head-count; and the UK - where poverty reduction is understated by the head-count. The inference we can draw from these comparisons is that the transfer system in the Netherlands leaves a relatively few families a long way below the poverty line whereas the UK system raises a relatively large number of families close to, but not above, the line.

Table 4.12.
Rank correlations for reduction in the head-count and poverty gap, Z* range

Count versus gap	40% interval	50% interval	60% interval
OECD	0.96	0.84	0.89
Whiteford	0.96	0.84	0.80

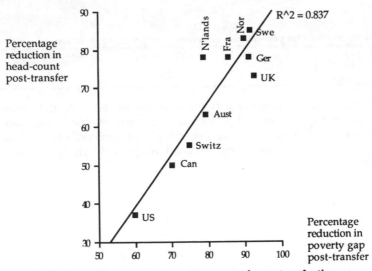

Figure 4.13. Head-count versus poverty gap measures of poverty reduction

In conclusion, the poverty gap appears to be the superior measure in the comparative context both in terms of the consistency of the rankings of countries across the Z* range and when using alternative equivalence scales. This observation is particularly crucial when comparing the pre-transfer poverty situation in these countries, where the pre-transfer count and gap measures show very little relationship; indicating that it is vital that both measures be reported.

Post-transfer the gap and count measures are more closely related although the effects of income clustering, generally among transfer recipients, contributes to unreliability in the post-transfer head-count. Again, the evidence indicates that it is preferable to present both measures, although it is less imperative in this instance. The most reliable indicator of the effectiveness of the transfer system (where data is confined to head-count measures) is the reduction measure. This is evidenced here by the strong positive relationship between the reduction in the head-count and gap measures ($R^2=0.84$).

4.4. Disaggregated poverty measures: head-counts

This section examines the pre- and post- transfer head-counts for the family types identified in Chapter 2. The head-counts are analysed in three ways. First, the 'poor' population is disaggregated into family types. Second, a 'representation' index is used to indicate the relative presence of each family type within the poor population. Third, the percentage of each family type defined as poor pre- and post- transfer and the percentage reduction for each family type is estimated.

In this section I report the results based on the 50% poverty interval and the OECD scale adjusted incomes. The results from this scale are fairly representative of the findings and patterns of the Whiteford scale and similar trends emerge at the 50% interval as at the 60% interval. The results diverge from the 40% interval because of the clustering of incomes in the UK and German data which was identified at the aggregate level for the 40% interval.

Disaggregation of the post-transfer head-count

Table 4.13 breaks down the pre-transfer poor population into family types. These percentages are compared with the composition of families in the overall population to produce a representation index in Table 4.14. The representation tables are interpreted as follows: if a family type comprises 10% of the poor population but only 5% of the total population, its representation index is 2 (*ie* 10/5). The weighted average of the representation index must, by definition, equal 1. We see that in all countries the aged are over-represented in the pre-transfer poor population by a factor of 2 to 3. The other significant group in the pre-transfer poor population are lone parents. In Australia, Canada, the Netherlands, the UK and US lone parents are over-represented in the poor population by a factor of two.

Table 4.13.
The composition of the pre-transfer poor at 50% poverty interval, OECD scale

	Aged (S)	Aged (C)	Single (NC)	Couple (NC)	Lone Parent	Couple (CH)	Other	Total
Australia	22.7	20.3	19.5	8.7	11.2	14.3	3.3	100
Canada	22.5	17.6	19.1	6.5	11.4	18.5	4.5	100
France	29.4	24.1	6.9	10.6	3.1	21.6	4.3	100
Germany	43.3	25.8	14.6	7.1	2.1	4.3	2.7	100
Netherlands	22.2	19.0	17.2	14.3	7.6	15.0	4.7	100
Norway	45.3	21.1	15.7	2.8	9.9	5.2	*	100
Sweden	41.1	20.9	26.5	3.9	4.0	3.6	*	100
Switzerland	42.6	19.9	27.3	3.3	3.9	3.0	*	100
UK	35.9	26.1	10.9	4.3	7.8	9.6	5.4	100
USA	24.8	18.3	16.9	5.5	16.3	12.5	5.7	100

Table 4.14.
Representation of family types in poor population pre-transfer

	Aged (S)	Aged (C)	Single (NC)	Couple (NC)	Lone Parent	Couple (CH)	Other
Australia	2.9	2.5	0.9	0.4	2.1	0.4	0.9
Canada	2.9	2.2	0.9	0.3	2.0	0.5	1.1
France	2.4	2.1	0.6	0.5	1.1	0.6	1.0
Germany	2.8	2.3	0.8	0.4	0.7	0.1	0.8
Netherlands	2.2	2.0	1.4	0.6	2.2	0.4	1.3
Norway	2.7	2.0	0.9	0.3	1.2	0.1	*
Sweden	2.5	2.2	0.8	0.3	0.9	0.2	*
Switzerland	3.0	2.5	0.8	0.2	1.0	0.1	*
UK	2.9	2.3	0.9	0.2	1.8	0.3	1.0
USA	2.7	2.1	0.8	0.3	2.0	0.4	1.3

Table 4.15.
Composition of the post-transfer poor at 50% poverty interval, OECD scale

	Aged (S)	Aged (C)	Single (NC)	Couple (NC)	Lone Parent	Couple (CH)	Other	Total
Australia	2.9	5.3	28.0	7.5	20.4	34.0	1.9	100
Canada	7.1	5.6	28.1	8.3	17.4	29.0	4.6	100
France	2.1	4.8	14.8	20.5	7.2	43.4	7.3	100
Germany	23.8	14.6	21.7	11.0	3.9	20.3	6.2	100
Netherlands	6.9	4.2	25.9	19.4	3.0	34.7	5.9	100
Norway	21.8	3.7	31.0	4.6	14.9	21.8	*	100
Sweden	0.0	0.8	66.7	8.2	5.8	18.5	*	100
Switzerland	24.1	8.7	45.6	3.2	6.1	12.2	*	100
UK	23.7	24.2	13.5	6.3	9.9	20.2	2.3	100
USA	17.3	8.4	21.3	5.8	22.2	20.2	4.7	100

Table 4.16.
Representation of family types in poor population post-transfer

	Aged (S)	Aged (C)	Single (NC)	Couple (NC)	Lone Parent	Couple (CH)	Other
Australia	0.4	0.7	1.4	0.4	3.8	1.0	0.5
Canada	0.9	0.7	1.4	0.4	3.1	0.9	1.1
France	0.2	0.4	1.4	1.0	2.5	1.2	1.6
Germany	1.5	1.3	1.2	0.6	1.3	0.7	1.9
Netherlands	0.7	0.4	2.1	0.8	0.9	1.0	1.6
Norway	1.3	0.4	1.7	0.4	1.8	0.6	*
Sweden	0.0	0.1	2.0	0.5	1.3	0.9	*
Switzerland	1.7	1.1	1.3	0.2	1.5	0.5	*
UK	1.9	2.2	1.2	0.3	2.3	0.6	0.4
USA	1.9	1.0	1.0	0.3	2.7	0.7	1.1

Post-transfer, Tables 4.15 and 4.16 show that poverty among the aged has significantly declined in most countries, although single aged persons remain over-represented in the UK, US, Germany and Norway.

Aged couples fare better in these countries, except for the UK where they remain over-represented by a factor of 2. In Germany, Switzerland and the US they remain in the post-transfer population in about the same proportion as their composition in the overall population.

In all these countries the representation index for the aged generally falls below 1 at the 40% interval, suggesting that the statutory incomes for the aged are fixed at around this level. This clustering is most notable in the UK, Germany and the US.

The significant group which emerges as over-represented in the post-transfer poor is the lone parent group, which is over-represented in all countries except the Netherlands. The disproportionate representation of lone parents in the post-transfer poor population is greatest in Australia, Canada, US, France and the UK where they are over-represented by factors ranging from around 2.5 (UK, France) to almost 4 (Australia).

Single persons are also disproportionately over-represented although in Sweden, the Netherlands and Norway the unit of analysis problem discussed in Chapter 2 contributes to the level of poverty recorded among this group in these countries. A significant percentage of this group are residing in multi-family households - most likely living with parents - and their poverty status may be questionable.

Smeeding et al (1989) also identify families with children as a significant group in the poor population. In this study these families do form a significant proportion of the post-transfer poor population (Table 4.16), however only in France are these families disproportionately present in the post-transfer poor population. In Australia, Canada, Sweden and the Netherlands their presence in the post-transfer poor population is close to proportional.

To summarise, the pattern which emerges across these countries is one of the predominance of the aged and lone parents in the pre- and post-transfer poor populations. While the income transfer systems considerably reduce poverty among aged families, lone parents (and to a lesser extent couple-headed families with children) do not fare as well and dominate the post-transfer poor population; along with young single persons in a number of countries. This pattern confirms the observations made in the OECD report discussed earlier.

Disaggregation of the post-transfer reduction of the poverty head-count

To give a clearer picture of the impact of transfers across these family types, Tables 4.17 and 4.18 show the percentage of each family type defined as poor pre- and post- transfer. The reduction in the poverty rate of each family type is shown in Table 4.19. Poverty reduction is highest among aged families. Apart from Switzerland, the UK and US all the LIS countries achieve reductions in the poverty rates for aged families in excess of 85%. Aged persons appear to fare worst in the US.

Table 4.17.
Pre-transfer head-count at the 50% poverty interval, OECD scale.

	Aged (S)	Aged (C)	Single (NC)	Couple (NC)	Lone Parent	Couple (CH)	Other
Australia	82.1	70.2	26.6	12.1	59.3	11.6	25.5
Canada	71.5	55.2	23.5	8.0	50.4	13.5	26.3
France	87.5	77.7	23.2	17.9	39.4	21.5	34.1
Germany	85.8	70.6	24.8	11.5	22.8	4.5	25.1
Netherlands	72.9	64.0	45.2	18.6	73.0	13.5	41.5
Norway	82.7	61.8	26.7	8.1	35.7	4.4	*
Sweden	92.0	81.1	28.2	9.3	33.0	6.4	*
Switzerland	72.8	59.9	18.7	5.2	23.8	3.1	*
UK	86.2	70.1	27.9	6.1	54.3	8.5	29.8
USA	72.6	57.4	21.6	7.9	53.3	11.5	35.0

Table 4.18.
Post-transfer head-count at the 50% poverty interval, OECD scale.

	Aged (S)	Aged (C)	Single (NC)	Couple (NC)	Lone Parent	Couple (CH)	Other
Australia	3.8	6.9	13.9	3.8	39.5	10.2	5.1
Canada	11.3	8.7	17.3	5.2	38.7	10.6	13.3
France	1.4	3.4	10.8	7.5	19.4	9.3	12.6
Germany	10.4	8.8	8.2	3.4	9.4	4.7	12.9
Netherlands	4.9	3.0	14.6	5.5	6.0	6.8	11.2
Norway	7.0	2.6	9.1	2.8	9.5	3.2	*
Sweden	0.0	0.0	8.5	1.0	5.4	1.6	*
Switzerland	18.6	11.9	14.2	2.3	17.1	5.8	*
UK	15.6	17.8	9.4	2.4	18.8	4.8	3.4
USA	31.9	16.4	17.3	5.3	45.7	11.7	18.4

Table 4.19.
Reduction in the head-count at the 50% poverty interval, OECD scale.

	Aged (S)	Aged (C)	Single (NC)	Couple (NC)	Lone Parent	Couple (CH)	Other
Australia	95	90	48	69	33	12	80
Canada	84	84	26	35	23	21	49
France	98	96	53	58	51	57	63
Germany	88	88	67	70	59	-4	49
Netherlands	93	95	68	70	92	50	73
Norway	92	96	66	65	73	27	*
Sweden	100	100	70	89	84	75	*
Switzerland	74	80	24	56	28	-87	*
UK	82	75	66	61	65	44	89
USA	56	71	20	33	14	-2	47

In general, poverty rate reductions are least in families with children. Couples with children fare worst in Australia, Canada, Norway, Switzerland, US and to a lesser extent the UK. Lone parent poverty is least reduced in Australia, Canada, Switzerland and the US.

In broad terms, these findings are similar to Smeeding et al (1989), however there are differences in the rankings and levels of reduction estimated here. These differences may be attributed to equivalence scales and changes to the LIS database.[14]

The pattern of the consistency in poverty reduction across these countries is also interesting in assessing the effectiveness of each transfer system in meeting a range of needs. For example, in Sweden the reduction in poverty rates across the board is relatively balanced with the highest poverty reductions for most family types; ranging from 100% for aged families to 70% for single persons. By contrast, Australia's poverty reduction is fairly unbalanced, ranging from 95% for single aged persons to only 12% for couples with children. A number of other countries also have an imbalance in their effectiveness across these family types. In addition to Australia, Germany, Switzerland, and the US have a large variation in their reductions across the family types. The most balanced reductions occur in Sweden, UK, France and the Netherlands. Canada and Norway lie somewhere in between these groups.

4.5. Disaggregated poverty measures: poverty gaps

The estimates of the poverty gap for each family type have been calculated by summing the difference between each individual family's income and its poverty line.[15] The total gap is then averaged across the families defined as poor in each group and expressed as a percentage of the poverty line. The full results of these estimates are reported in Appendix B.

Like the aggregate estimates of the poverty gap, the disaggregated estimates of the poverty gap are virtually identical, whether the OECD or Whiteford scale adjusted incomes are used. Unlike the aggregate measures however, there is considerable variation in the average post-transfer poverty gap across the Z* range for each family type. There are two main causes of this variation. First, the very small cell counts for some family types (especially the aged) at the 40% and 50% intervals exaggerate the average size of the poverty gap. In particular, it is families which report negative or zero disposable incomes which affect the results at these lower levels.[16] Second, countries which successfully reduce the poverty gap and/or have a relatively small number of families in their surveys, have lower cell counts across the Z* range which again contributes to the unreliability of the poverty gap estimates.

For these reasons, the disaggregated poverty gap measures are reported for the 60% **poverty interval**, using the OECD equivalence scale. At this level of the Z* range, the greatest number of observations are captured for each family type in each country. Generally, the number of observations at this interval is sufficient to offset any unreliability arising from sampling error and the under-reporting of income.

Table 4.20.
Average pre-transfer poverty gap at the 60% interval, OECD scale

	Aged (S)	Aged (C)	Single (NC)	Couple (NC)	Lone Parent	Couple (CH)	Other
	Poverty gaps for families as a percentage of the poverty line.						
Australia	87	81	76	71	82	51	66
Canada	79	65	68	50	74	40	59
France	91	82	75	60	57	36	61
Germany	93	87	85	71	60	33	72
Netherlands	80	78	96	87	92	80	84
Norway	84	72	79	70	69	39	*
Sweden	82	76	65	56	56	35	*
Switzerland	69	56	63	61	60	20	*
UK	84	73	78	61	74	34	70
USA	80	65	65	53	70	39	65

Table 4.21.
Average post-transfer poverty gap at the 60% interval, OECD scale

	Aged (S)	Aged (C)	Single (NC)	Couple (NC)	Lone Parent	Couple (CH)	Other
	Poverty gaps for families as a percentage of the poverty line.						
Australia	8	13	41	29	33	30	30
Canada	16	18	44	34	41	28	29
France	10	19	47	36	38	25	35
Germany	25	21	35	38	24	16	34
Netherlands	66	26	89	53	17	39	34
Norway	48	16	48	40	24	24	*
Sweden	5	10	43	31	30	24	*
Switzerland	22	18	50	31	39	16	*
UK	14	15	25	22	21	20	14
USA	31	30	48	37	43	29	42

Table 4.22.
Reduction in the poverty gap at the 60% interval, OECD scale

	Aged (S)	Aged (C)	Single (NC)	Couple (NC)	Lone Parent	Couple (CH)	Other
	Percentage reduction in the poverty gap						
Australia	91	84	46	59	60	41	55
Canada	80	72	35	32	45	30	51
France	89	77	37	40	33	31	43
Germany	73	76	59	46	60	52	53
Netherlands	18	67	7	39	82	51	60
Norway	43	78	39	43	65	38	*
Sweden	94	87	34	45	46	31	*
Switzerland	68	68	21	49	35	20	*
UK	83	79	68	64	72	41	80
USA	61	54	26	30	39	26	35

Disaggregation of the post-transfer poverty gap

Tables 4.20 to 4.22 report the average poverty gap estimates for each family type pre- and post- transfer and the reduction in the poverty gap for each family type. Pre-transfer, the poverty gap estimates show that the average size of the poverty gap is fairly similar across the family types, with the exception of couple-headed families with children whose pre-transfer gaps are generally less than those of other families. The one exception to this is the Netherlands, where the pre-transfer gap for this family type is similar to other types of families. Thus although the composition of the pre-transfer poor population is dominated by aged families, the poverty gap estimates show that other families who are poor have poverty gaps of a similar magnitude to the aged.

Post-transfer, the poverty gap measures tell a similar story to the head-count. As noted earlier, the results are generally unaffected by the equivalence scale used, the main exception being single aged persons who are reported in larger numbers by the Whiteford scale. Table 4.23 shows the rank correlation coefficients between the two scales for each family type.

Table 4.23.
Correlation coefficients post-transfer gap at the 60% interval

	Aged (S)	Aged(C)	Single (NC)	Couple (NC)	Lone Parent	Couple (CH)	Other
OECD - W'ford	0.80	0.95	0.85	0.94	0.96	0.98	0.98

Generally, the poverty gaps for aged families are considerably reduced after social security transfers. In the case of the Netherlands it should be noted that the estimate is based on an extremely small cell count (28 cases), the majority of which report a zero disposable income.

The largest poverty gaps are reported for single people without children. Apart from the UK, the average post-transfer poverty gap for this group is greater than 35% of the poverty line for all countries. Detailed investigation of this group in the course of the study indicated that the prevalence of poverty among this group may be mitigated by intra-family transfers (upwards of 30% of this group reside with their parents in all countries). In several countries - Australia, US and Canada - there is a significant number of unemployed persons in this group. The heterogeneity of this group makes it difficult to ascribe any strong explanatory causes for the post-transfer position of single persons, other than the arguments advanced in the OECD study discussed at the outset of this chapter, namely that young adults are not viewed with the same legitimacy as other groups in terms of their claims on the transfer system.

This latter point is also applicable to lone parents who are another group with a large post-transfer poverty gap, reflecting a dependence on income transfers as the major source of income.

Couples without children also record large poverty gaps. In head-count terms, this group is relatively small in all countries - excepting Australia, Canada, France and the US[17] - and the averages are affected by the incidence of zero incomes for this group.

The post-transfer position of families with children, as evidenced in the LIS data, has been extensively discussed by Smeeding et al (1989:110-115). The estimates of the poverty gap for these families concur with Smeeding's findings.

Disaggregation of the post-transfer reduction in the poverty gap

The reduction in the poverty gap for each family type is again similar to the picture presented by the head-count measure. Generally, it is aged families whose poverty gaps are most reduced by the transfer system and single persons the least. Surprisingly, lone parents poverty gaps are considerably reduced even though they are more likely to be poor post-transfer than any other group. Part of the explanation for this is simply that this group starts from a low pre-transfer position. But it also indicates that income support programs for lone parents, however modest, are in place in all of the LIS countries.

Unlike lone parents, the couple-headed families with children have far less reduction in their poverty gaps. In particular, families with unemployed household heads and the 'working poor' with three or more children are a significant among this group. This issue was again raised in the OECD report - discussed in the introduction to this chapter - which noted that the necessity for program coverage for this group of the 'new poor' was only beginning to be recognised in the 1980s. Thus in countries such as Australia and the UK, Family Income Supplement programs were introduced in the course of the decade in response to evidence similar to the estimates presented here for 1980. For the remaining family types, the reductions measures are generally not worth comment mainly due to cell count problems.

Comparing disaggregated poverty levels: head-counts versus poverty gaps

At the disaggregated level, the poverty head-count appears to be a more informative measure than the poverty gap. This is largely due to the effect of of small cell counts post-transfer, so that just one or two families with zero incomes are sufficient to distort the average poverty gap when measured against the poverty line income. For further discussion of this point see Appendix E.

The head-count can be disaggregated in two ways to show: the composition of the poor; and indicate the representation of each family type in the poor population. The reduction in the head-count for each family type also provides critical information about the effectiveness of the transfer system. Each of these measures gives a slightly different perspective on the numbers, and significance, of different family types in poverty and the impact of transfers on this poverty.

Although the poverty gap is less useful in this context, it does add some important information to the head-count picture. For example, although the pre- and post- transfer poverty populations in most of the LIS countries are dominated by one or two groups in terms of numbers, there is considerable variation between, and within, these countries in terms of the direction of transfers to different family types to close these gaps.

While the head-count appears to be an unreliable measure at the aggregate level, it is a necessary starting point for disaggregated analyses. The poverty gap measure adds information to the head-count picture, but cannot stand alone as a summary measure in this context.

4.6. The role of social security and taxation in reducing poverty

In the Introduction I noted that most studies of poverty and inequality estimate the net changes accruing to transfers without breaking down the transfer system into its direct and indirect components. In this section I examine the role which taxation plays in poverty reduction.[18]

Table 4.24 shows the poverty head-counts across the Z* range after social security and taxes. The table shows that, with the exception of France at the lowest poverty interval, the taxation systems in all these countries reduce the incomes of some near-poor families to the extent that these families are brought below the poverty line.

Table 4.24.
Effect of taxation on poverty counts at the aggregate level, OECD scale

Z*:	Poverty count at 40%			Poverty count at 50%			Poverty count at 60%		
Country:	Post-social sec.	Post-tax	Percent change	Post-social sec.	Post-tax	Percent change	Post-social sec.	Post-tax	Percent change
Australia	5.7	5.9	4	9.6	10.3	7	17.7	19.2	8
Canada	7.3	7.6	4	11.8	12.5	6	18.0	19.4	8
France	4.9	4.9	0	7.7	7.9	3	14.8	15.2	3
Germany	2.5	3.3	32	5.3	6.8	28	8.9	12.7	43
Netherlands	5.1	5.6	10	5.8	7	21	6.7	10.6	58
Norway	3.2	3.5	9	4.6	5.3	15	6.7	8.8	31
Sweden	2.7	3.8	41	3.6	5.6	56	5.4	9.2	70
Switzerland	5.3	6.1	15	9.0	11	22	14.3	17.8	24
UK	1.4	1.7	21	7.3	8.2	12	16.2	18.2	12
USA	10.4	11.0	6	15.9	17.0	7	20.8	23.2	12

Leaving aside the changes at the 40% interval, where relatively small changes in the post-tax counts produce dramatic percentage changes between the post- social security and tax head-counts, we see that at the 50% and 60% intervals the countries form two distinct groups with respect to the impact of taxes on family poverty status.

A first group of countries comprising Australia, Canada, France, UK and US have taxation systems which have a marginal effect on the incomes of the poor and near-poor. In these countries, a combination of tax deductions, concessions and rebates reduces the impact of taxes on the incomes of many households. The size and importance of these indirect transfers is discussed further in Chapter 11.

France, in particular, keeps its lower income earners out of the taxation net. This is largely due to the relatively small amount of taxation revenue collected through income taxes, combined with tax expenditures, thresholds and a progressive structure.[19]

In the remaining countries the poor and near-poor are brought into the taxation system at comparatively low levels of income. However, it should be noted that although the taxation systems in this group of countries significantly offsets the poverty reduction achieved by social security transfers, they still remain (with the exception of Switzerland) the countries which most reduce the poverty count overall.

In the LIS countries, the tax burden does not fall evenly across the poor population. Tables 4.25 and 4.26 show the composition of the poor population post- social security and tax. Apart from the Netherlands, where the impact of taxation is fairly evenly spread, it is couple-headed families with children and to a lesser extent, couples without children, who disproportionately bear the burden of taxes on the low income population.

Table 4.25.
Poor population post- social security, 50% interval OECD scale

	Aged (S)	Aged (C)	Single (NC)	Couple (NC)	Lone Parent	Couple (CH)	Other	Total
Australia	3.1	5.6	29.6	8.0	19.9	31.9	1.8	100
Canada	7.5	5.8	29.2	8.6	18.1	26.4	4.3	100
France	2.0	4.7	14.8	20.2	7.1	43.7	7.4	100
Germany	30.7	18.1	26.4	6.2	3.4	7.7	7.4	100
Netherlands	8.3	3.2	29.5	20.1	1.5	32.2	5.3	100
Norway	25.3	5.3	32.0	5.3	14.7	17.3	*	100
Sweden	0.0	0.0	80.5	3.8	6.9	8.8	*	100
Switzerland	26.7	7.8	50.5	2.5	6.4	6.0	*	100
UK	25.5	26.0	13.5	6.1	11.0	15.3	2.6	100
USA	18.5	8.9	21.4	5.8	22.9	17.6	5.0	100

Table 4.26.
Poor population post- taxation, 50% interval OECD scale

	Aged (S)	Aged (C)	Single (NC)	Couple (NC)	Lone Parent	Couple (CH)	Other	Total
Australia	2.9	5.3	28.0	7.5	20.4	34.0	1.9	100
Canada	7.1	5.6	28.1	8.3	17.4	29.0	4.6	100
France	2.1	4.8	14.8	20.5	7.2	43.4	7.3	100
Germany	23.8	14.6	21.7	11.0	3.9	20.3	6.2	100
Netherlands	6.9	4.2	25.9	19.4	3.0	34.7	5.9	100
Norway	21.8	3.7	31.0	4.6	14.9	21.8	*	100
Sweden	0.0	0.8	66.7	8.2	5.8	18.5	*	100
Switzerland	24.1	8.7	45.6	3.2	6.1	12.2	*	100
UK	23.7	24.2	13.5	6.3	9.9	20.2	2.3	100
USA	17.3	8.4	21.3	5.8	22.2	20.2	4.7	100

The effect of taxation on the poverty gap is summarised in Table 4.27. We see that in all countries the taxation system generally re-opens a small part of the gap closed by the social security system, particularly for families with incomes just above the 60% poverty interval.

The size of the changes for Germany, Sweden, Norway and Switzerland suggest that the taxation system claws-back transfers from social security recipients just above the 50% poverty interval.[20]   A point which will be considered further in the following chapter and Chapter 11 is that aggregate transfer measures which take account only of direct transfers will overstate the amount of welfare effort made by the transfer systems in these countries, while not taking account of the role of taxes which clawback these expenditures at relatively low income levels.

Table 4.27.
Effect of taxation on the size of the poverty gap across Z* range

| | Gaps as a percentage of GDP | | | | | | Percentage change | | |
| | Post-ss transfers | | | Post-tax | | | between ss and taxes | | |
Z*:	40	50	60	40	50	60	40	50	60
Australia	0.50	0.90	1.53	0.51	0.93	1.65	-2	-4	-8
Canada	0.62	1.21	2.10	0.63	1.25	2.24	-2	-4	-7
France	0.50	0.96	1.79	0.50	0.97	1.82	-2	-2	-2
Germany	0.19	0.39	0.75	0.26	0.56	1.17	-37	-43	-56
Netherlands	0.94	1.27	1.66	1.00	1.39	1.94	-6	-9	-17
Norway	0.25	0.42	0.70	0.27	0.47	0.85	-8	-11	-20
Sweden	0.14	0.24	0.37	0.19	0.35	0.61	-33	-50	-64
Switzerland	0.59	1.06	1.87	0.66	1.24	2.36	-11	-17	-26
UK	0.06	0.20	0.59	0.07	0.24	0.71	-29	-21	-19
USA	1.17	2.12	3.42	1.24	2.27	3.74	-6	-7	-9

4.7. Summary

In all the LIS countries income transfers do have a significant impact on poverty. Whether the existence of state transfers is partly responsible for the creation of some portion of pre-transfer poverty - as suggested by O'Higgins (1985) and Smeeding et al (1985b) - is a moot point on the evidence presented here. In Section 4.1, the relationship between pre-transfer poverty rates and levels of reduction was moderately strong (R^2=0.64), while the relationship between the pre-transfer poverty gap and the reduction in the poverty gap was virtually non-existent (R^2=0.02). One interpretation of these observations could be that while there may be some offsetting behaviour - according to the head-count - the poverty gap suggests that this reliance may be confined to the 'topping-up', rather than supplanting, of private provision. Additionally it has been shown that in the LIS countries, the extent of poverty alleviation is independent of the income of a country.

The detailed empirical research confirms that, at the aggregate level, the poverty gap measure is more robust than the head-count measure; in particular, it is less sensitive to where the poverty line is drawn and the equivalence scale used. The poverty gap measure presents quite a different picture to the head-count of the effectiveness of several countries in alleviating poverty. Most notably, the UK and Australia appear more effective in closing the poverty gap and move up the effectiveness rankings, while the Netherlands and France leave a smaller number of families a long way below the poverty line and in aggregate terms, move down the rankings.

In disaggregated analyses the head-count is probably a more informative approach: the composition and representation of different demographic groups as a proportion of the poor population provides more detail about those in poverty than does the average poverty gap measure which may be unreliable and/or misleading where there are small cell counts for different family types. The disaggregated analysis shows that while the head-count estimates of post-transfer poverty vary from around 5% to 17% in the LIS countries, the composition of the post-transfer poor population is fairly similar. Lone parents and single adults are the two groups most likely to be in poverty in all these countries.

This suggests that cross-national comparisons of poverty requires both aggregated and disaggregated estimates of the head-count and gap in order to give a balanced picture of the effectiveness of transfers in reducing poverty. For example, the aggregate size of the poverty gap gives a fairly clear picture of the magnitude of the poverty problem pre- and post- transfer, while the disaggregated head-count adds detail on which groups are most/least affected by the transfer system. In the absence of aggregate poverty gap information, the degree of correlation between the reduction in the head-count and the poverty gap suggests that effectiveness (using only head-count data) may be best gauged by the reduction of the head-count pre- and post- transfer, rather than using the raw head-count.

Notes

[1] Smeeding et al (1985b:4) note that the proportionate reduction in the head-count is 'an important dimension of inter-country comparisons of poverty.'

[2] The equivalence scale closest to those used here, is the PROG scale used by Buhmann et al (1988). The only country which differs in rank order and actual count terms is Switzerland which is one of the countries where incomes have been adjusted since earlier versions of the database.

[3] This is also observed in Buhmann et al (1988:131).

[4] These patterns have also been identified by Buhmann et al (1988:133).

[5] See also, Buhmann et al (1988:133).

[6] Only six of the countries examined here were studied by Smeeding et al (1985b). In addition to identical rankings of the common set of countries, the actual estimates of reduction presented here are within five percentage points of the Smeeding study.

[7] The R^2 statistic shown in the diagram indicates the strength of the linear association between the two variables and the straight line is the Ordinary Least Squares (OLS) regression line indicating the direction and magnitude of the linear association. The actual notation, R^2, in the diagrams is due to software constraints. It is, of course, identical to the R^2 notation used in the text. The statistical significance of these regressions is discussed in Appendix E.

[8] Some preliminary analysis using the data from this study shows that comparisons similar to those in Diagram 4.5 for the aged and sole parents, yields OLS regression results of $R^2=0.69$ for the aged and $R^2=0.01$ for sole parents.

[9] Data from Summers and Heston, 1988.

[10] There have been no comparable studies comparing the poverty gap with GDP using the LIS data.

[11] This may partly reflect an under-reporting of transfer income and/or the business cycle effects which were discussed in Chapter 2.

[12] Using a different measure of the poverty gap (ie as a percentage of the poverty line), Smeeding et al (1989b:34) rank identically, the six countries in common with this study.

[13] This finding should be considered carefully given the large number of zero and negative incomes observed in the Netherlands' data set. Cf the discussion in Section 2.4.

[14] See also the findings reported in Smeeding et al (1990).

[15] The methodology for calculating the poverty line for each family is discussed in Chapter 2.

[16] Families which report negative incomes are recoded to zero as discussed in Chapter 2.

[17] In these countries this group is present in the poor population in roughly the same numbers as the overall population.

[18] Taxes refers to income taxes as well as payroll deductions for social insurance contributions.

[19] The structure of the French taxation system is discussed in the following chapter in Section 5.7.

[20] In the following chapter the question of taxation clawback is investigated further.

5 Poverty reduction in the LIS countries: efficiency measures

Chapter 1 discussed the ways in which efficiency can be considered in relation to the goals of income transfer policies. It was suggested in the context of the poverty alleviation goal, that targeting efficiency and poverty reduction efficiency are two measures which reflect the efficiency with which transfer systems convert inputs (social security expenditures) into outputs (size and incidence of expenditure). These measures attempt to provide answers to the following questions: what percentage of social security expenditure accrues to the pre-transfer poor (targeting efficiency)? How much poverty does each unit of social security expenditure alleviate (poverty reduction efficiency)?

This approach implies that, in a highly efficient social security system, all expenditures would go to the poor. It should be noted however, that this underlying assumption may conflict with other objectives of the social security systems in this study. For example, the preservation of horizontal equity which motivates transfers to families with children may require 'inefficient' transfers in order to be 'effective'. In many of the countries in this study, the status-preserving element of retirement benefits may also introduce desired inefficiencies to the social security system. For these reasons, interpretation of the measures reported here must be tempered by such considerations. In this chapter I propose only to report the measures and discuss the results at face value; the policy implications and interpretation of the results are considered more fully in Part II of the study.

This chapter distinguishes two aspects of the efficiency of social security expenditure. Primary expenditure efficiency refers to the percentage of expenditure which goes to those who were poor prior to transfers. Secondary expenditure efficiency refers to the proportion of the social security transfers received by the poor which is sufficient to take them up to a pre-defined level of poverty income; transfers in excess of the poverty line are referred to in the literature as 'spillover'. Combining these two aspects of efficiency, the study provides an overview of the efficiency with which the income transfer systems of the LIS countries reduce their poverty gaps.

5.1. Beckerman's efficiency model

Beckerman (1979a,b;1982) provides a framework which formalises these concepts.[1] To illustrate Beckerman's approach, Figure 5.1 shows the components of the analysis and the derivation of his efficiency measures. An important point to note is that Beckerman's measures are driven by the poverty gap, and as the analysis in the previous chapter demonstrated, this is a reliable means of addressing poverty issues at the aggregate level.

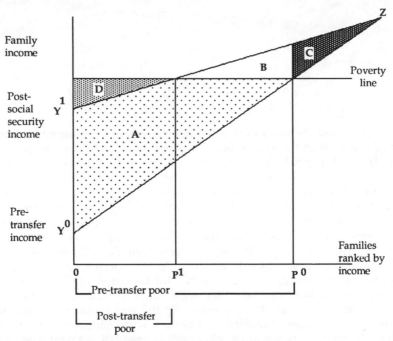

Figure 5.1. Beckerman's efficiency model post social security transfers

Families classified as poor, prior to transfers, are found in the range 0 to P^0; the size of their poverty gaps being the distance from the line Y^0Z to the poverty line. Thus the areas marked A and D represent the total pre-transfer poverty gap.

After transfers, the poor are found in the range 0 to P^1; the size of their poverty gaps being the distance between Y^1Z and the poverty line. The area D represents the total post-transfer poverty gap.

Families raised above the poverty line are those in the range P^1 to P^0; and their distance above the poverty line is the distance between Y^1Z and the poverty line. The area B represents the extent to which transfers have taken these families above the poverty line. If we were to assume that the most efficient way of directing expenditures was to take families to the poverty line but not beyond, the area B represents some level of inefficiency, that is, where expenditures spillover. A more telling measure of targeting efficiency however is the size of the area C - the sum of the transfers which accrue to the non-poor.

Using these concepts, Beckerman defines three targeting efficiency measures: vertical expenditure efficiency (VEE) or the proportion of transfers accruing to those who were poor prior to transfer; spillover (S); and poverty reduction efficiency (PRE) which combines the VEE and spillover measures. To summarise, the areas defined in Figure 5.1 correspond to the following magnitudes:

$$A + B + C = \text{total social security transfer expenditure}$$
$$A + B = \text{total transfers received by the pre-transfer poor}$$
$$A + D = \text{pre-transfer poverty gap}$$
$$D = \text{post-transfer poverty gap}$$

Beckerman's efficiency measures are given by:

$$VEE = (A + B) / (A + B + C)$$
$$S = B / (A + B)$$
$$PRE = A / (A + B + C) = (1\text{-}S) \times VEE$$

Beckerman's approach has previously been applied only in aggregate. Here it is disaggregated in two stages: first, targeting and poverty reduction efficiency are estimated post- social security; second, to allow for 'clawback' through the taxation system, these estimates are repeated post-tax. This approach allows the study to establish the overall efficiency of the income transfer system by observing the interaction of the social security and taxation systems in each country.

In addition, this chapter further disaggregates the results to discover which families in each of these countries comprise: the non-poor who receive transfers; those whose transfers spillover the poverty line; and those who receive transfers and are subject to clawback through the tax system.

5.2. Efficiency of aggregate social security expenditure

Tables 5.1 to 5.3 summarise the targeting efficiency of the LIS countries' social security systems for the Z* range. The results are reported only for OECD scale adjusted incomes since the poverty gap measures which drive the estimates are virtually identical for both scales (see Chapter 4).

81

Table 5.1.
Targeting efficiency measures (40% interval, OECD scale)

	Vertical expenditure efficiency %	Spillover %	Poverty reduction efficiency %
Australia	65.6	37.1	41.3
Canada	46.0	34.6	30.1
France	65.7	61.3	25.4
Germany	63.0	54.6	28.6
Netherlands	61.6	65.5	21.3
Norway	63.6	55.8	28.1
Sweden	57.6	69.4	17.6
Switzerland	56.4	46.7	30.1
UK	40.1	38.8	24.5
USA	54.0	38.0	33.5

Table 5.2.
Targeting efficiency measures (50% interval, OECD scale)

	Vertical expenditure efficiency %	Spillover %	Poverty reduction efficiency %
Australia	68.4	24.1	51.8
Canada	51.7	25.2	38.7
France	69.4	50.6	34.3
Germany	65.1	44.4	36.2
Netherlands	64.0	57.3	27.3
Norway	67.0	44.8	37.0
Sweden	61.5	61.2	23.9
Switzerland	63.2	35.3	40.9
UK	44.3	27.6	32.1
USA	59.8	30.7	41.4

Table 5.3.
Targeting efficiency measures (60% interval, OECD scale)

	Vertical expenditure efficiency %	Spillover %	Poverty reduction efficiency %
Australia	71.4	14.6	60.9
Canada	56.8	17.8	46.7
France	75.8	40.9	44.8
Germany	69.6	37.0	43.9
Netherlands	65.9	49.1	33.5
Norway	70.6	35.0	45.9
Sweden	65.5	53.3	30.6
Switzerland	69.9	27.4	50.7
UK	49.4	22.1	38.5
USA	64.1	24.4	48.5

First, in terms of the proportion of expenditure accruing to the pre-transfer poor (VEE), we might expect systems with elements of income testing (*eg:* Australia, US) to be more efficient than universal systems (*eg:* Sweden, Norway). As the tables show, the results are fairly mixed; generally the universal and social insurance systems tend to be more efficient than income-tested systems on this criterion, with the exception of Australia which is second to France in terms of primary efficiency.

The implication of this finding is that the universal and social insurance social security systems do transfer the bulk of their social security expenditures to the pre-transfer poor, relying on mechanisms other than income tests to establish who is in need. The notable exception to this is the UK, which has the lowest VEE ratio across the Z* range.

Figure 5.2 shows the VEE ratios for the LIS countries across the Z* range. Apart from Switzerland, the ordering is fairly complete at each level of Z. We see that it is not until the 60% interval that at least two-thirds of social security transfers are accruing to the poor in all countries except Canada and the UK. On the evidence of the VEE measure, France is the most efficient country in targeting the poor followed by Australia. At the other extreme, Canada and the UK are transferring around half their social security expenditures to the poor at this interval.

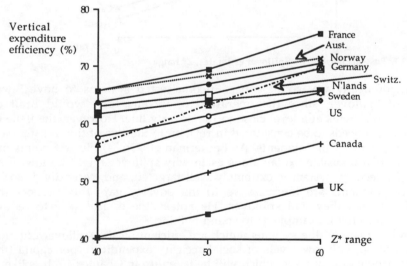

Figure 5.2. Post- social security VEE estimates, Z* range

Where the non income-tested versus income-tested systems differ substantially is in the area of spillover. The results show that those countries with elements of income-testing in their programs (Australia, US, UK, Canada and Switzerland) have the lowest levels of spillover. Figure 5.3 shows that there is a distinct break between the spillover levels of these countries and the rest. There is also a second break in the spillover in the remaining countries. The highest levels of spillover are found in Sweden and the

Netherlands, where around half of the transfers accruing to the pre-transfer poor take them above the poverty line at the 60% interval. In the middle range France, Germany and Norway have spillover levels of between 35-40%.

In the Group III countries, we see that Canada and the UK have low levels of spillover at the 60% interval. Recalling the VEE results, we see that of the 50% of transfers which do accrue to the pre-transfer poor, around 20% of these contribute to spillover.

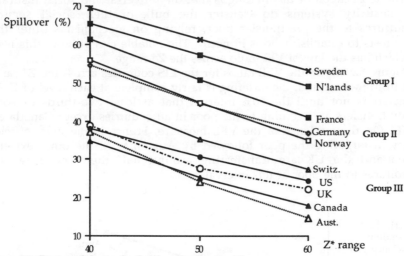

Figure 5.3. Post- social security Spillover estimates, Z* range

Theoretically we would expect income-tested systems to have lower levels of spillover, since the operation of income tests would limit or withdraw payments at a level close to the poverty line. However, the issue of spillover also needs to be considered in relation to the size of the transfer base and the generosity of payments. As Beckerman (1979b:54) himself points out there are two plausible explanations as to why spillover might be low: first, the social security system is extremely well targeted, and, secondly, if social security payments are low relative to the poverty gap, this reduces the probability that they will spillover. He notes: 'the easiest way to reduce spillover to zero, for example, is to spend nothing.'[2]

In fact many of the systems which are efficient on the spillover criterion are also those with low levels of social security expenditure per capita (the welfare 'laggards'), an issue which will be taken up in Chapter 10. It is likely, therefore, that this measure of efficiency reflects a combination of, on the one hand, low levels of expenditure and, on the other, the effects of targeting through income tests. Section 5.4 investigates the number and type of families which receive transfers in the spillover area and how far above the poverty line the spillover extends. The more generous levels of payments in some countries result in high levels of spillover at this stage of the redistribution process. In a later section I investigate the possibility that these countries' tax systems may clawback social security transfers, thereby acting as a de facto form of income test. If this is the case, we would expect to see the spillover measures post-tax to be considerably lower than those post- social security. Taking the VEE and spillover results together one puzzling finding is that the US, Canada and the UK appear to have poor targeting in the primary sense, *ie* in distinguishing the poor and non-poor while at the same time being target efficient on the secondary measure, *ie* limiting payments to those who receive transfers. In Section 5.9 this apparent anomaly is investigated and it is suggested that these results are in large part due to the universal availability of some transfers, notably child benefits, while other basic income supports are income-tested.

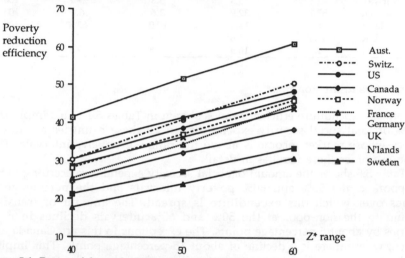

Figure 5.4. Post- social security PRE estimates, Z* range

The third of Beckerman's measures, poverty reduction efficiency, is a summary measure which captures the overall efficiency of social security transfers by first, reducing aggregate social security expenditures by the amount which spillover the poverty line; and second, proportionately reducing the remaining expenditures by the ratio of transfers received by the non-poor. Thus: PRE = (1-Spillover) x VEE. Figure 5.4 shows the ordering based on the PRE estimates across the Z* range. It is interesting to note that this summary measure produces an ordering which conforms to the conventional wisdom that income-tested systems are more efficient, even though the components of the measure (VEE and spillover), examined individually produce mixed results.

Australia's position as the most efficient country is unambiguous and reflects the extensive income-testing elements of its social security system. At the other extreme, Sweden, the Netherlands and the UK are the least efficient systems on the post- social security estimates of poverty reduction efficiency. The intervening countries show no strong ordering with several countries changing ranks across Z*. Table 5.4 shows the distribution of families in the Beckerman model for each country. These groups are discussed in the following sections.

Table 5.4.
Distribution of families in the Beckerman model post-social security, 50% interval

	Non-poor who receive trans. %	Families in spillover area %	Post-transfer poor %	Receive no transfers %	Total
Australia	42.7	17.8	10.2	29.3	100
Canada	56.6	12.4	12.5	18.5	100
France	32.3	28.7	7.7	31.3	100
Germany	42.5	25.3	5.7	26.5	100
Netherlands	43.8	26.5	6.1	23.7	100
Norway	42.1	25.3	5.3	27.2	100
Sweden	57.1	32.9	3.6	6.4	100
Switzerland	11.8	14.3	10.0	63.8	100
UK	52.6	21.6	8.3	17.3	100
USA	20.1	10.3	16.8	52.8	100

5.3. Transfers to the non-poor

The vertical expenditure efficiency ratios shown in Tables 5.1 to 5.3 imply that 30-40% of total social security expenditure in all these countries accrues to families whose market income is above the range of poverty intervals. This section examines these families in detail.

Table 5.5 shows the amount of social security expenditure accruing to the 'non-poor' at the 50% and 60% poverty intervals and the percentage of families over which this expenditure is spread. The amount of transfers accruing to the non-poor at the 50% and 60% intervals declines in most countries by about 5 percentage points. The exceptions to this are Canada and Sweden, where there is a decline of about 15 percentage points. This implies that there is a cluster of low income families - just above the 50% poverty interval - who receive substantial social security benefits in these two countries. In discussing the non-poor who receive transfers, I will concentrate on those above the 60% interval as it is more likely that at this level we are capturing the non-poor (rather than the 'near-poor', ie those just above the 50% interval).

Table 5.5.
Transfers to families with market income above the 50% and 60% intervals

	Amount of transfers to non-poor as a percentage of social security		Percentage of non-poor who receive social security transfers	
	50% interval	60% interval	50% interval	60% interval
Australia	32	29	43	40
Canada	48	33	57	53
France	31	24	32	28
Germany	35	30	43	40
Netherlands	36	34	44	42
Norway	33	29	42	40
Sweden	38	24	57	54
Switzerland	37	30	12	10
UK	56	51	53	49
USA	40	36	20	18

Comparing the amount of transfers received by the non-poor and the percentage of families which receive these transfers four tendencies can be discerned as shown in Figure 5.5. In this figure, the diagonal represents proportionality between the percentage of transfers accruing to the non-poor and the percentage of (all) families receiving these transfers. It serves to illustrate whether the transfers are: spread across a small number of families (above and to the left of the diagonal); closely proportional (on or near the diagonal); roughly proportional (fairly close on either side of the diagonal); or spread across a large number of families (below and to the right of the diagonal).

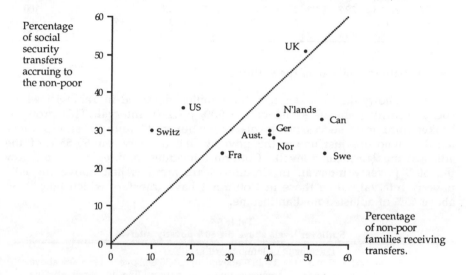

Figure 5.5. The spread of transfers among the non-poor (60% interval).

First, in Switzerland and the US, transfers to the non-poor are concentrated on a relatively small percentage of families. Table 5.6 shows that it is the non-poor aged which dominate this group in both countries, followed by couples with children in the US. In France and the UK, the percentage of transfers accruing to the non-poor is proportionate to the percentage of families. In these countries, it is couple-headed families with children who benefit most from these transfers.

Countries where there is rough proportionality are the Netherlands, Germany, Australia and Norway. The tendency in these countries is for the transfers to be spread across a slightly larger than proportionate number of families and again it is couple-headed families with children who are the predominant non-poor recipients of transfers. In Norway, the other significant group is lone parents. In Canada and Sweden, the spread of transfers to the non-poor is even larger, dominated to a lesser extent by couple-headed families with children.

Table 5.6.
Composition of non-poor families receiving social security (60% interval)

	Aged (S)	Aged (C)	Single (NC)	Couple (NC)	Lone Parent	Couple (CH)	Other	Total
Australia	2.4	2.6	4.9	11.5	4.3	69.7	4.6	100
Canada	3.7	4.5	13.2	17.8	4.9	51.6	4.4	100
France	4.3	3.8	3.2	16.6	3.8	62.7	5.6	100
Germany	3.7	4.2	3.1	13.1	4.8	67.1	4.0	100
Netherlands	5.9	5.4	0.6	11.9	1.9	71.2	3.2	100
Norway	4.4	6.2	3.3	5.3	10.3	70.4	*	100
Sweden	1.9	7.6	34.6	17.7	4.9	33.4	*	100
Switzerland	29.7	26.1	18.7	15.5	3.9	6.1	*	100
UK	2.6	3.9	5.9	19.3	3.3	58.7	6.3	100
USA	10.4	23.1	12.0	14.7	4.0	28.2	7.6	100

5.4. The pattern and size of the spillover

Table 5.7 shows the breakdown of the families identified in Table 5.4 whose social security transfers spillover the 50% poverty interval. This group is broken into four successive levels of spillover. Column 1 shows those families who are just above the poverty line (*ie* between 50-55% of the adjusted median income level). Column 2 includes families who are below the 60% poverty interval. In Column 3 are families just above the 60% poverty interval, while those in Column 4 have transfers which take them above 65% of adjusted median income.

Table 5.7.
Spillover levels above the 50% poverty interval

	Percentage of families with spillover:			
	<10% above poverty line	10-20% above poverty line	20-30% above poverty line	>30% above poverty line
Australia	10.9	29.1	20.7	39.3
Canada	12.5	10.3	7.7	69.4
France	11.9	14.9	11.8	61.4
Germany	6.0	9.1	9.4	75.5
Netherlands	2.3	5.3	7.9	84.5
Norway	5.6	26.2	13.3	54.8
Sweden	1.0	0.7	3.5	94.7
Switzerland	2.7	3.8	7.6	85.9
UK	26.8	21.1	15.2	36.9
USA	14.3	11.0	9.0	65.7

Figure 5.6 shows three patterns of spillover which emerge after social security transfers. In the UK and Australia around 60% of families whose transfers do spillover, do so at a level less than 30% above the poverty line. At the other extreme, in Sweden, Switzerland and the Netherlands, around 85% of families in the spillover range receive transfers which take them more than 30% above the poverty line. In the remaining countries the percentage of families receiving transfers which take them more than 30% above the poverty line is between 50% and 70%.

Table 5.8 shows the composition, by family type, of those whose social security transfers spillover. While these countries vary in respect of the size of their spillover, there is high degree of similarity in the spread of the spillover amongst family types. In all countries, the aged account for upwards of 60% of families whose transfers spillover (except the Netherlands where the aged account for around 50%). The predominance of the aged is explained by a number of factors which operate variably across these countries for example, the relative generosity of transfers to this group, universal payments, or more relaxed income tests. In France, the Netherlands and the UK another sizeable group whose payments spillover are families with children. This is probably due to child related benefits which are non income-tested. The extent of the spillover amongst these two groups supports the observation made at the outset of this chapter concerning 'desirable inefficiencies' to achieve effective outcomes among some sections of the population. Many of the countries also have a significant number of single persons whose benefits spillover. In these countries the transfers received by this group spillover by only a small margin, predominantly at a level of less than 20% above the poverty line.

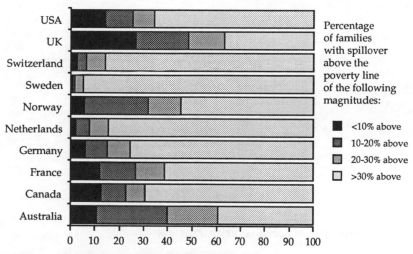

Figure 5.6. Pattern of the spillover above the 50% poverty interval

Table 5.8.
Breakdown of the spillover by family type, 50% poverty interval

	Aged (S)	Aged (C)	Single (NC)	Couple (NC)	Lone Parent	Couple (CH)	Other	Total
Australia	33.8	26.6	13.9	11.1	5.4	5.0	4.1	100
Canada	36.1	23.9	12.5	6.8	7.1	9.0	4.6	100
France	33.9	28.0	4.7	11.4	2.2	16.2	3.6	100
Germany	46.4	26.1	11.2	8.1	3.8	1.6	3.2	100
Netherlands	25.7	22.4	14.3	14.4	8.6	11.0	3.8	100
Norway	50.9	24.8	13.3	2.3	5.7	3.1	*	100
Sweden	45.7	23.5	21.2	3.6	3.4	2.7	*	100
Switzerland	56.4	25.3	12.7	2.8	1.5	0.9	*	100
UK	37.4	21.6	9.1	6.8	4.1	14.4	6.5	100
USA	39.1	27.3	8.5	8.0	6.6	4.2	6.4	100

5.5. The poor who don't receive transfers

Table 5.9 shows the percentage of families whose pre-transfer incomes are below the 50% poverty interval and who do not receive social security transfers. The reasons for this include: intra-family transfers to support students or other young dependents without income; non take-up of benefits; ineligibility; or non-reporting of social security income. It is not possible to discern which of these causes may be operating in each instance.

It is important to recall here the discussion of Chapter 2 concerning the number of families with zero and negative incomes and the possible connection of the incidence of these observations and the business cycle, this may partly explain the unexpectedly high percentage of apparent non-receipt of transfers in the Netherlands.

Apart from the US (and perhaps the Netherlands) the percentage of the poor not receiving some form of government assistance is fairly small in relation to the population as a whole. Examining this group in greater detail is difficult since, in most countries, the cell sizes are too small to pursue any meaningful analysis.

Table 5.9.
'Poor' who receive no transfers

Percentage of pre-transfer poor families	
Australia	2.4
Canada	1.5
France	3.2
Germany	0.9
Netherlands	4.5
Norway	1.6
Sweden	0.7
Switzerland	3.7
UK	0.9
USA	5.1

5.6. The efficiency of social security transfers

Using the PRE measure, the approximate ordering of the LIS countries across the Z^* range is:

> Australia
> United States
> = Canada, Norway   Switzerland
> = France, Germany
> United Kingdom
> Netherlands
> Sweden

As Figure 5.4 illustrated, Australia's overall efficiency is around 20% greater than the nearest country across the Z^* range, clearly indicative of the impact of both the categorical eligibility criteria and the extensive income-testing in the Australian system. The US and Canada follow and the evidence here suggests that the results for these two countries is largely determined by secondary efficiency in limiting payments to poor recipients, rather than distinguishing between the poor and non-poor.

France, Norway, Germany and Switzerland all achieve high levels of primary efficiency, so that these systems transfer the bulk of their payments (65-70%) to the poor and at the same time these payments take recipients above the poverty line. This level of spillover pulls the PRE measure for these countries to around 35-40%.

The UK exhibits a pattern similar to the US and Canada in that its transfer system is very inefficient in terms of distinguishing between the poor and non-poor, ie even at the highest poverty interval less than 45% of transfers accrue to the poor; while at the same time the size of the spillover is also quite low. Sweden and the Netherlands are moderately efficient on the primary criterion but have spillover levels far in excess of all the other LIS countries. It is the size of the spillover which dominates the PRE results for these two countries.

The major source of 'inefficiency' in these social security systems may be gauged from the ratio of the proportion of transfers accruing to the poor to the proportion which does not spillover. This ratio is shown in Table 5.10.

Table 5.10.
Ratio of primary and secondary
expenditure efficiency, 60% poverty interval

	Ratio of VEE:1-S
Sweden	1.4
Netherlands	1.3
France	1.3
Germany	1.1
Norway	1.1
Switzerland	1.0
USA	0.8
Australia	0.8
Canada	0.7
UK	0.6

The table shows that for those countries above Switzerland, the major source of inefficiency is transfers which spillover the poverty line. In Switzerland, inefficiency is equally attributable to both transfers to the non-poor and transfers which spillover. While in those countries below Switzerland, it is the transfers to the non-poor which are the major source of inefficiency. In the following section I examine the impact of taxes on the overall efficiency of the income transfer systems in the LIS countries.

5.7. 'Clawback' through taxation: an extension of the Beckerman model

Table 5.11 shows estimates of the percentage of social security transfers which are clawed back through the taxation system. The clawback has been calculated for each family by subtracting taxes (payroll and mandatory social insurance contributions) from social security transfers to give a net transfer figure. If net transfers are negative then the net transfer variable has been set to zero, *ie* the model assumes that at the point where the taxation system has clawed back 100% of social security transfers, the negative amount represents the taxation of other income sources.

As would be expected, the more generous social security systems in Sweden and the Netherlands clawback a large percentage (around 43%) of social security payments through the tax system. The clawback in Canada and the UK is also considerable, at around one-third. Of the remaining countries Germany, the US, Switzerland, Australia and Norway clawback in increasing order 20% to 30% of transfers. The figure for Australia is surprisingly high since we would expect that benefits would have been clawed back through the operation of the income test on benefits.[3]

France has the lowest clawback of all these countries. This is partly due to the structure of tax revenue raising in France. OECD revenue statistics show that personal income taxes in France comprise only 12% of total taxation revenues and Pechman (1987:88) estimated that, in 1983, the share of personal income tax revenue in the tax base in France was 20% less than the OECD average.[4]

Table 5.11.
Clawback of social security transfers through the tax system

	Clawback
Australia	26.5
Canada	33.3
France	11.7
Germany	19.3
Netherlands	43.3
Norway	28.5
Sweden	42.9
Switzerland	24.6
UK	36.9
USA	22.4

The next stage of the analysis modifies Beckerman's approach by substituting net transfers for total social security expenditure. In Figure 5.7, the line Y^1Z bounds the post- social security income levels. After taxes, disposable income is pushed back to the area bounded by Y^2Z. As the figure shows, the effect of clawback (darker shading) through the tax system is to reduce the percentage of transfers which spillover (B) and which accrue to the non-poor (C). In some countries, the tax system may even clawback transfers from those who are below the Z^* range of poverty lines post- social security (D).

The efficiency measures are calculated using the same formulae set out in Section 5.1 with the proviso that net transfers, rather than total social security transfers, are used as the denominator. Using this approach, Tables 5.12 to 5.14 summarise the results of the post-tax efficiency measures across the Z^* range. The following sections use these results to examine: the net efficiency of transfers; which families are most affected by taxation clawback; the level of transfers which accrue to the non-poor after taxes; and the amount of the spillover clawed back through the tax system. The final section compares the changes in the efficiency measures post- social security and tax.

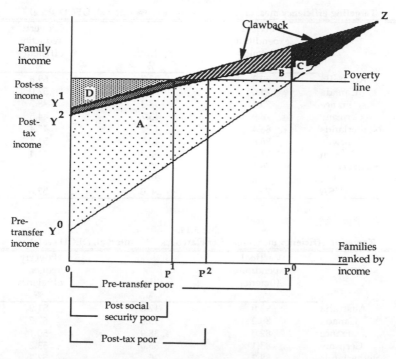

Figure 5.7. The extension of the transfer efficiency model post-tax

To summarise, the areas defined in Figure 5.7 correspond to the following magnitudes:

$$(A+B+C) - \text{Clawback} = \text{net transfer expenditure}$$
$$(A+B) - \text{Clawback} = \text{net transfers received by the pre transfer poor}$$
$$A+D = \text{pre-transfer poverty gap}$$
$$D + \text{Clawback} = \text{post-tax poverty gap}$$

Table 5.12.
Targeting efficiency measures after clawback (40% interval, OECD scale)

	Vertical expenditure efficiency %	Spillover %	Poverty reduction efficiency %
Australia	87.4	36.1	55.9
Canada	67.7	33.8	44.8
France	70.1	59.0	28.7
Germany	77.1	54.3	35.3
Netherlands	83.4	55.5	37.1
Norway	82.9	52.8	39.1
Sweden	79.9	61.6	30.7
Switzerland	69.4	43.0	39.6
UK	62.3	37.7	38.8
USA	68.4	37.5	42.8

Table 5.13.
Targeting efficiency measures after clawback (50% interval, OECD scale)

	Vertical expenditure efficiency %	Spillover %	Poverty reduction efficiency %
Australia	90.3	22.7	69.8
Canada	74.6	23.7	57.0
France	75.6	48.8	38.7
Germany	78.9	43.7	44.5
Netherlands	86.4	45.1	47.4
Norway	86.6	40.7	51.4
Sweden	84.2	50.8	41.4
Switzerland	76.6	30.6	53.1
UK	67.6	25.4	50.4
USA	75.1	30.0	52.6

Table 5.14.
Targeting efficiency measures after clawback(60% interval, OECD scale)

	Vertical expenditure efficiency %	Spillover %	Poverty reduction efficiency %
Australia	93.0	12.6	81.2
Canada	80.2	15.6	67.7
France	82.0	38.9	50.1
Germany	83.1	36.0	53.2
Netherlands	88.2	35.0	57.3
Norway	90.0	29.6	63.4
Sweden	87.9	40.1	52.7
Switzerland	83.5	22.3	64.9
UK	73.6	18.6	59.9
USA	79.7	23.3	61.2

5.8. The impact of taxation clawback

Figure 5.8 shows the post-tax vertical expenditure efficiency ratios for the LIS countries across the Z* range. In general, the VEE ratios of these countries increases markedly after the clawback by the tax system. Comparing the countries with their post- social security positions we see that Australia moves to the top of the efficiency table with around 90% of net social security expenditure accruing to the pre-transfer poor. In Norway, the Netherlands and Sweden more than 85% of net expenditure accrues to the pre-transfer poor. This confirms earlier observations concerning the importance of the interaction of the tax and social security systems in countries where universal and/or generous social insurance programs predominate. It is interesting to note that such radically different patterns of provision can produce fairly similar outcomes. The bracketing of Australia with Norway, the Netherlands and Sweden in Group I may support Ringen's (1987:12) contention that progressive taxes are a form of *de facto* income test.

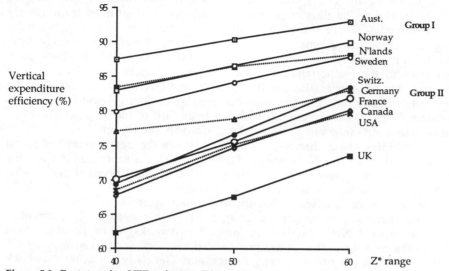

Figure 5.8. Post- taxation VEE estimates, Z* range

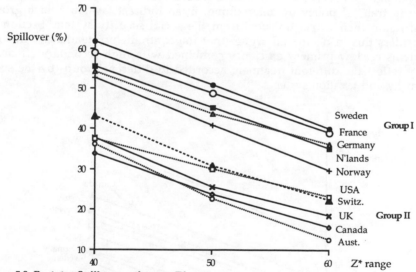

Figure 5.9. Post- tax Spillover estimates, Z* range

In the Group II countries, Switzerland, Germany and France have moved down the rankings post-tax and this is mainly due to a combination of less progressive tax structures and lower levels of the tax 'take'. The latter is a particularly prominent feature of the French system, as noted earlier. The ranks of Canada, the US and the UK are virtually unchanged from the post-social security position; although the VEE increases, in absolute terms, by around 20 to 25 percentage points.

Once again, the spillover presents quite a different grouping of countries. Figure 5.9 illustrates that the spillover distinguishes quite clearly those countries where the combination of income tests, now supported by taxation, limit the extent to which transfers spillover the poverty line. Comparing Figures 5.9 and 5.3, we see that the effect of the clawback pulls Sweden and the Netherlands into the same group as France, Germany and Norway. The steeper gradient of the spillover plots across the Z* range in the Group I countries indicates that considerable clawback of generous transfers is occurring. This can be contrasted with the tailing off of the clawback between the 50% and 60% intervals in Switzerland, Canada, the US and UK.

Combining these changes, Figure 5.10 shows the net poverty reduction efficiency of these transfer systems. There is considerable re-ranking on this measure, as a comparison with Figure 5.4 will confirm. I noted in Section 5.2 that the PRE rankings post- social security conformed to the pattern predicted by the conventional wisdom that income-tested systems are more efficient. Post-tax, there are some notable exceptions to this pattern. In particular, Norway and the Netherlands have jumped two ranks, while France, which was in the middle of this group post- social security, is last on the post-tax rankings. In all countries, except France and Germany, taxation clawback enhances poverty reduction efficiency (at the 50% interval) by more than 10 percentage points. We see from these results that taxation plays an important part in transfer policy by determining, in an indirect fashion, which groups will retain their direct transfers from the social security system. Section 5.9 considers this in detail and argues that the contradictory tendencies in some systems *eg*: low primary efficiency combined with high secondary efficiency may reflect the different treatment accorded to different groups by the social security and taxation systems.

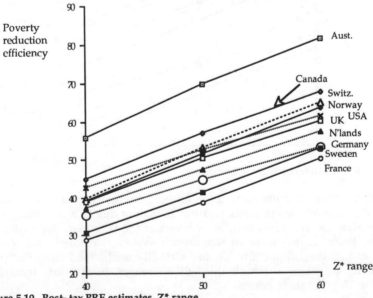

Figure 5.10. Post- tax PRE estimates, Z* range

96

5.9. Who is affected by clawback?

Table 5.15 shows how much of the tax clawback of social security transfers comes from families located in different parts of the Beckerman model. The balance between clawback from the spillover and transfers to the non-poor varies considerably, with half the countries clawing back the bulk of transfers from the non-poor (Australia, Canada, Germany, UK) and others predominantly clawing back from those in the spillover range (France, the Netherlands, Sweden and Switzerland). In Norway and the US, the balance is roughly equal. In all countries except France, the clawback also affects the pre-transfer poor, most notably in Switzerland and the US.

Table 5.15.
Distribution of the clawback (50% interval,OECD scale)

	Breakdown of the clawback of social security transfers from those:		
	In spillover range after social security	Non-poor who received transfers	Who were poor pre-transfer
Australia	32	66	2
Canada	35	63	2
France	76	24	0
Germany	37	61	2
Netherlands	59	40	1
Norway	49	50	1
Sweden	61	39	1
Switzerland	67	30	3
UK	44	55	1
USA	49	48	3

It is interesting to compare this table with Table 5.10 which shows the ratios of the VEE and Spillover measures. In the top half of that table were the countries whose major source of inefficiency is the spillover of transfers. We see from Table 5.15 that this is where more than 60% of the clawback occurs for these countries. Conversely, Australia, Canada and the UK predominantly clawback social security transfers from the non-poor.

On either side of the division of Table 5.10, are Norway and the US, and this is matched in Table 5.15 by fairly equal clawback of transfers from both sources of inefficiency. In Switzerland, where inefficient transfers were evenly spread between the spillover and transfers to the non-poor, the taxation system operates most strongly on the spillover. This suggests that the taxation system is either weakly progressive or that there are a series of tax exemptions, rebates or concession which leave social security transfers untaxed for specific groups.

While the distribution of the clawback in terms of **volume** varies markedly in these countries, the taxation system radically changes the **spread** of the clawback such that the percentage of non-poor families who receive net positive transfers declines dramatically. This is illustrated in Tables 5.16 and 5.17. This information, together with that contained in Table 5.15, suggests that in most countries the transfers received by the non-poor are relatively small and widely spread. So that in volume terms, the clawback is smaller than the clawback from the spillover, but larger in terms of the numbers of families affected. These families are re-located in the model to 'non-recipient' status. Families in the spillover area post- social security and who are affected by clawback tend to remain in the spillover area post-tax, but often at a lower level of spillover (in some countries the clawback moves a small percentage of these families below the poverty line).

Table 5.16.
Distribution of families in the model after clawback (50% interval)

	Percentage of families				
	Non-poor who receive trans.	Families in spillover area	Post-transfer poor	Receive zero net transfers	
	%	%	%	%	Total
Australia	6.0	17.3	10.7	65.9	100
Canada	14.6	11.8	13.1	60.5	100
France	22.9	28.6	7.8	40.7	100
Germany	10.6	24.8	6.2	58.4	100
Netherlands	8.1	25.6	6.9	59.4	100
Norway	7.9	24.9	5.7	61.5	100
Sweden	13.1	32.3	4.2	50.4	100
Switzerland	8.4	13.4	11.0	67.2	100
UK	21.0	21.1	8.9	49.0	100
USA	8.7	10.1	17.0	64.2	100

Table 5.17.
Absolute differences in the distribution after clawback (50% interval)

	Differences after clawback			
	Non-poor who receive trans.	Families in spillover area	Post-transfer poor	Receive zero net transfers
Australia	-36	-1	0	37
Canada	-42	-1	1	42
France	-9	0	0	9
Germany	-32	-1	0	32
Netherlands	-36	-1	1	36
Norway	-34	0	0	34
Sweden	-44	-1	1	44
Switzerland	-3	-1	1	3
UK	-32	-1	1	32
USA	-11	-1	0	12

Table 5.18.
Net transfers to families with pre-transfer income
above the 50% and 60% poverty intervals, OECD scale

	Amount of transfers to non-poor as a percentage of net transfers		Percentage of non-poor who receive positive net transfers	
	50% interval	60% interval	50% interval	60% interval
Australia	19.2	15.6	6.0	4.7
Canada	40.9	33.8	14.6	11.8
France	31.5	25.9	22.9	19.2
Germany	28.6	23.5	10.6	8.8
Netherlands	32.8	29.8	8.1	7.3
Norway	26.1	21.5	7.9	6.5
Sweden	38.3	31.5	13.1	10.8
Switzerland	39.2	30.3	8.4	6.5
UK	55.7	48.2	21.0	18.1
USA	37.9	32.5	8.7	7.2

Non-poor families affected by clawback

Table 5.18 compares the volume and spread of net transfers to the non-poor. This information is displayed visually in Figure 5.11. Comparing this figure with Figure 5.5 we see a dramatic shift in the proportionality between the volume and spread of net transfers. In Figure 5.5 only two countries (US, Switzerland) were above and to the left of the proportional diagonal indicating a large volume of transfers being spread across a small number of families. After clawback, all countries are found above the diagonal, indicating that the spread of transfers to the non-poor is tightly restricted in all these countries. However, there are substantial differences in the volume. The exceptions to this are France and the UK whose positions change very little in either volume or spread terms.

With less than 20% of net transfers accruing to the non-poor, Australia is the most efficient in vertical distribution terms. In the next band are Norway, Germany and France where between 20-30% of net transfers accrue to the non-poor, although here there is considerable differences in the spread. In a tight cluster above this group are Sweden, the Netherlands, Canada, the US and Switzerland where 30-40% of transfers accrue to around 5-15% of the non-poor population. Least efficient in vertical distribution terms is the UK, where around 50% of net transfers accrue to 20% of the non-poor population.

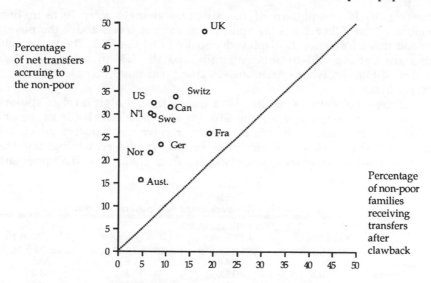

Figure 5.11. The spread of net transfers to the non-poor (60% interval)

The composition of non-poor families receiving positive net transfers also changes significantly after the taxation clawback. Comparing Table 5.19 with Table 5.6, we see that with the exception of France, Sweden and the UK, it is couples with children who are most affected by the clawback and their relative presence in this group declines by as much as 80% in some countries (Australia, Norway) to around 50% in the US. The results for Sweden and the

UK indicate that tax allowances operate to protect universal transfers for children from clawback, in the UK in particular approximately 25% of net transfers accrue to non-poor couples with children. In the Netherlands, Norway, Switzerland and the US the aged become the predominant non-poor transfer recipients comprising around 50% of this group.

Table 5.19.
Non-poor families receiving positive net transfers, 60% interval

	Aged (S)	Aged (C)	Single (NC)	Couple (NC)	Lone Parent	Couple (CH)	Other	Total
Australia	11.5	15.6	10.4	19.3	7.8	14.4	21.1	100
Canada	12.6	20.0	11.7	16.5	5.3	24.9	9.1	100
France	6.2	8.4	3.1	12.7	4.8	57.7	7.0	100
Germany	15.9	20.4	11.0	15.2	5.5	20.4	11.6	100
Netherlands	28.1	28.1	2.1	19.9	2.6	9.9	9.2	100
Norway	22.6	23.6	6.6	13.2	19.8	14.2	*	100
Sweden	8.3	9.4	28.8	17.3	10.2	26.0	*	100
Switzerland	38.4	29.6	19.2	7.9	2.5	2.5	*	100
UK	5.5	10.3	8.9	17.9	4.3	43.5	9.5	100
USA	22.5	31.6	7.8	13.5	3.4	11.7	9.5	100

Pattern and size of the spillover after clawback

After clawback, the pattern of the spillover changes very little in these countries. Table 5.20 reports the spillover at various levels above the poverty line and this information is displayed visually in Figure 5.12. The two notable shifts are Canada which joins Australia and the UK in having the least number of families whose net transfers take them more than 30% above the poverty line.

At the other extreme, Switzerland moves from a high level of spillover into the intermediate range leaving Sweden and the Netherlands as the only countries where more than 80% of families receive net transfers which take them more than 30% above the poverty line. In the remaining countries there are small incremental changes which reduce spillover at the upper end.

Table 5.20.
Spillover levels after clawback at the 50% poverty interval

	Percentage of families with spillover:			
	<10% above poverty line	10-20% above poverty line	20-30% above poverty line	>30% above poverty line
Australia	9.8	29.8	21.8	38.6
Canada	20.6	19.0	17.2	43.2
France	9.4	10.5	12.4	67.7
Germany	6.2	6.6	8.9	78.3
Netherlands	3.0	5.1	5.1	86.8
Norway	3.9	3.0	22.4	70.6
Sweden	1.3	4.8	5.6	88.4
Switzerland	14.6	15.8	16.5	53.0
UK	22.2	17.5	16.7	43.5
USA	14.2	12.8	13.0	59.9

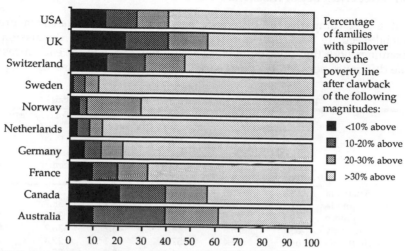

Figure 5.12. Pattern of the spillover after clawback (50% interval)

Table 5.21 shows the composition of the families whose net transfers spillover the poverty line. Comparing this table with Table 5.8, we see that there is virtually no difference in the composition of spillover families. This information, together with the volume measures, suggests that the taxation systems in these countries are clawing back fairly small amounts from a large number of transfer recipients and doing so in a fairly equitable fashion *ie* there is no evidence of groups which are exempted from tax on their non-transfer incomes.

The one exception to this is Switzerland, where there is a rise in the percentage of the aged, suggesting that there may be some tax exemption of benefits for this group.

Table 5.21.
Breakdown of the spillover after clawback (50% poverty interval)

	Aged (S)	Aged (C)	Single (NC)	Couple (NC)	Lone Parent	Couple (CH)	Other	Total
Australia	33.5	28.7	13.7	9.0	5.3	3.8	6.0	100
Canada	39.2	30.8	8.8	4.5	4.1	8.0	4.6	100
France	36.9	29.3	4.8	7.9	2.0	15.7	3.4	100
Germany	46.9	28.2	11.5	7.0	1.7	2.1	2.6	100
Netherlands	26.2	23.0	14.8	12.9	8.5	10.3	4.3	100
Norway	50.7	24.9	13.2	2.4	6.3	2.4	*	100
Sweden	46.4	23.6	20.2	3.8	3.5	2.5	*	100
Switzerland	57.4	36.2	4.0	0.7	1.2	0.5	*	100
UK	41.2	27.4	8.9	3.8	4.5	7.0	7.2	100
USA	36.5	34.4	7.7	5.2	3.9	4.1	8.2	100

5.10. Net efficiency of transfers: a summary

Table 5.22 compares the difference between the Beckerman measures post-social security and post-tax at the 50% interval. The discussion below examines both the ordering evident across the Z* range for each measure and the difference between the post- social security and tax measures.

Table 5.22.
Targeting efficiency measures (50% interval, OECD scale)

	Vertical expenditure efficiency		Spillover		Poverty reduction efficiency	
	Post social security %	Post tax %	Post social security %	Post tax %	Post social security %	Post tax %
Australia	68.4	90.3	24.1	22.7	51.8	69.8
Canada	51.7	74.6	25.2	23.7	38.7	57.0
France	69.4	75.6	50.6	48.8	34.3	38.7
Germany	65.1	78.9	44.4	43.7	36.2	44.5
Netherlands	64.0	86.4	57.3	45.1	27.3	47.4
Norway	67.0	86.6	44.8	40.7	37.0	51.4
Sweden	61.5	84.2	61.2	50.8	23.9	41.4
Switzerland	63.2	76.6	35.3	30.6	40.9	53.1
UK	44.3	67.6	27.6	25.4	32.1	50.4
USA	59.8	75.1	30.7	30.0	41.4	52.6

Table 5.22 shows that the tax clawback has a marked effect on the percentage of social security transfers which finally accrue to the non-poor as demonstrated by the vertical expenditure efficiency measure. Through the operation of the tax system, Australia, Canada, the Netherlands, Norway, Sweden and the UK effectively reduce the percentage of transfers accruing to the non-poor by around 20 percentage points. In Germany, Switzerland and the US the reduction is around 15 points. France has the least clawback with a reduction of around 5 percentage points, although this is from a much higher starting position than a number of other countries.

Large reductions in the spillover are confined to Sweden (11 percentage points) and the Netherlands (8 percentage points). There are smaller reductions in Norway and Switzerland of around 5 percentage points, with the remaining countries having little clawback from pre-transfer poor recipients.

The overall affect of the tax clawback is to make substantial efficiency gains in all countries with the exception of France, and to a lesser extent Germany. In absolute terms, there are gains of around 20 percentage points in Australia, Canada, the Netherlands, Sweden and the UK. Gains of around 12 points are made in Norway, Switzerland and the US.

The rankings on overall poverty reduction efficiency alter considerably once the tax clawback is taken into consideration. Notably Canada,the UK and Netherlands move up two ranks, while Sweden is promoted one rank. Australia retains its position at the top of the table with the gap between it and the remaining countries substantially reduced, as compared with the post social security measures.

Finally, Table 5.23 presents the ratio of primary to secondary expenditure efficiency for net transfers. The ratios for social security expenditures are also shown. It is evident that in all countries, except the UK, net spillovers are the major source of inefficiency. This is further evidence that the taxation systems in many of these countries operate to restrict the level of transfers which finally accrue to the pre-transfer non-poor.

Table 5.23.
Ratio of primary and secondary expenditure efficiency, 60% poverty interval

	Ratio of VEE:1-S post - SS		Ratio of VEE:1-S post - Tax
Sweden	1.4	Sweden	1.5
Netherlands	1.3	Netherlands	1.4
France	1.3	France	1.3
Germany	1.1	Germany	1.3
Norway	1.1	Norway	1.3
Switzerland	1.0	Switzerland	1.1
USA	0.8	Australia	1.1
Australia	0.8	USA	1.0
Canada	0.7	Canada	1.0
UK	0.6	UK	0.9

5.11. Summary

This chapter has analysed poverty reduction efficiency, defined as the percentage of transfers which accrue to the poor but do not spillover the poverty line. It has been shown that taxation can play an important role in reducing the spillover in countries where universal transfers predominate. Taxation is even more significant in increasing primary targeting efficiency, that is to say in reducing the size of net transfers to the non-poor.

The evidence presented here raises doubts about the commonly held view that income-tested social security systems are necessarily more efficient in targeting the poor rather than the non-poor. Indeed, primary expenditure efficiency in the universal or social insurance systems is at least as high on social security transfers and tends to be higher with respect to net transfers. This evidence lends some credence to the claim that taxation can act as a *de facto* income test in non income-tested systems. The one country with widespread income testing which does stand out as the most efficiently targeted on the poor is Australia.

The area in which income-tested systems do appear to be more efficient is in relation to transfers which spillover the poverty line. Taxation plays an important role in reducing the size of the spillover in some of the non income-tested systems, especially in Sweden and the Netherlands, but even on net transfers spillover is less in the income-tested systems.

In aggregate, poverty reduction efficiency, which is the product of the primary and secondary efficiency measures, bears some relation to income-testing, especially after taking account of the role of taxation. The income-tested systems tend to be more efficient but, with the exception of Australia, the efficiency differences are minor.

This chapter has presented an extension to the Beckerman model to take account of the 'clawback' of benefits through taxation. Clawback is especially significant in reducing the proportion of non-poor families who receive net transfers (except in the case of France).

Disaggregation of the clawback of spillover benefits indicates, however, that in almost all countries the clawback is both small and evenly distributed across family types. The principal exception to this is Switzerland, where clawback does not appear to affect the aged as much as other family types.

Analysis of the clawback of transfers to the non-poor by family type indicates that in almost all countries it is predominantly targeted on couples with children.

The aged, on the other hand, are much less affected by clawback in these countries. This suggests that in the LIS countries there are substantial taxation provisions to keep the incomes of aged persons out of the taxation net and therefore that indirect transfers, in addition to improved social security provisions, are an important part of the improvement of the relative incomes of the aged in the post-war period.

Notes

1 Similar methodologies have been developed by several writers in the US, for example Weisbrod (1970), Plotnick and Skidmore (1975). Beckerman's approach is used here as it represents the most fully worked out model of these efficiency issues.

2 Beckerman (1979b:54). Although he identified these possibilities in the four country study conducted for the ILO, Beckerman did not indicate which of these factors dominated the spillover in each country.

3 Although it should be recalled that at the time of the data collection, there were two universal elements in the Australian social security system: Family Allowances and the over-70s age pension.

4 The structure of taxation raises important questions for comparative studies of well-being. In Part II of the study, I examine the implications of the balance between direct and indirect taxes and how this may modify our view of the evidence presented in microdata, as well as some further observations concerning the limitations of income measures.

6 The measurement of inequality

The measurement of inequality, like the measurement of poverty, presents researchers with a wide range of potential analytical tools and approaches. Unlike the poverty methodology, however, it is not possible to preclude any of the inequality approaches on the basis of their suitability in the comparative context or on the type of data required to support the measures: each method is driven by the same type of data (income) and each is equally applicable in a comparative context. In this respect, the choice of an appropriate inequality measure is less apparent than the choice of the poverty measure. Moreover, various writers (*eg*: Champernowne,1974) have pointed out that alternative measures of inequality do not provide the same ranking of distributions and that these rankings can be quite contradictory. Essentially the choice of approach comes down to what is appropriate in terms of the focus of this study. In the following section I discuss the main approaches to the measurement of inequality in order to illustrate the properties of each measure. Later sections discuss the choice of perspective for this study and the reasons for this choice.

The literature dealing with the description and measurement of income inequality is largely associated with the disciplines of economics and econometrics. The discussion below begins with the description of the Lorenz curve and the Gini coefficient which, together, form the main conceptual bases for the inequality methodology. Since the mid-70s this work has broken into a number of branches and I provide a brief guide to the main theories in the field.

6.1. The Lorenz curve and Gini coefficient

Cowell (1977) describes a number of methods which chart inequality. The best known of these is the Lorenz curve (Figure 6.1), which is derived by arranging the observations of the incomes of the recipient units in ascending order. The cumulative population of these units is then plotted against the cumulative incomes received by the recipient population. If income were equally distributed, that is if each of n recipient units receives $1/n$ of total income, we would find that the diagonal described by OA represents the income distribution. Thus in Figure 6.1 we see that the bottom 20% of the population receives 20% of total income, the bottom 40% of the population receives 40% of total income and so on. The diagonal OA is referred to as the "line of equality" because cumulative income increases in direct proportion to cumulative population. The closer the Lorenz curve is to this line, the more equitable the income distribution.

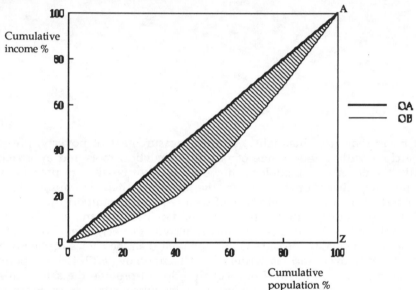

Figure 6.1. Lorenz curve and line of equality

If income is not equally distributed we find distributions described by the curves OB, OC and OD in Figure 6.2. These curves have been derived from the hypothetical data contained in Table 6.1. Note that these are four alternative ways of distributing the same amount of income. If we wished to compare two distributions to make statements about the degree of income inequality it is sometimes possible to deduce from the Lorenz curves whether one distribution is less unequal than another. For example, distribution A is clearly the most equitable and C the least equitable, since at all points OA lies above the other Lorenz curves and OC, below.

But what of the other distributions? It is possible to say that distribution B is more equitable than distribution C. This is apparent from both the cumulative total of income accruing to the ordered population and from the fact that the Lorenz curve for B (OB) lies wholly inside of the Lorenz curve for C (OC) and closer to the line of equality. This is a condition referred to in the literature as 'Lorenz dominance' as there is no ambiguity in the ranking of the two distributions.[1] Problems arise in interpreting Lorenz curves when the curves intersect, *ie* where there is no Lorenz dominance, as is the case for distributions B and D.

Table 6.1.
Four examples of income distributions

Distribution	Person 1	Person 2	Person 3	Person 4	Person 5	Gini
A	5	5	5	5	5	0.000
Cum. distrib'n	5	10	15	20	25	
B	2	3	5	7	8	0.256
Cum. distrib'n	2	5	10	17	25	
C	1	2	2	4	16	0.512
Cum. distrib'n	2	5	10	17	25	
D	3	3	3	6	10	0.272
Cum. distrib'n	2	5	10	17	25	

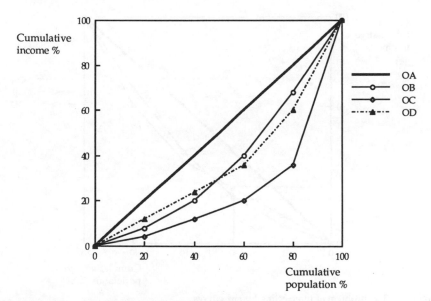

Figure 6.2. Lorenz curves for income distributions A-D

Statements comparing distributions B and D are less easy to make, visual inspection allows some comparisons to be made about parts of the distribution but these do not make an overall statement possible.

Comparisons of this kind are left to summary measures such as the Gini coefficient. The Gini coefficient is a summary measure which compares the ratio of the area between the line of equality and the Lorenz curve (the shaded area) with the area bounded by OAZ as shown in Figure 6.1. Thus the closer the Lorenz curve lies to the line of equality, the smaller the ratio of the two areas and hence the lower the Gini coefficient. Using the Gini coefficient we may now rank the distributions shown in Table 6.1 from lesser to greater inequality as A, B, D and C.

The ranking of income distributions using the Gini coefficient as described above, has been subject to several criticisms. If we inspect Figure 6.2 more closely, the reasons for this will become clearer. While distribution B is ranked on the Gini coefficient as being more equal than distribution D, closer inspection raises a very important issue. Figure 6.3 reproduces distributions B and D, notice that the bottom two quintiles (*ie* the bottom 40% of income earners) have a larger share of income under distribution D than for B.

Thus if we are concerned with income inequality among low income households, we may consider distribution D to be preferable to distribution B even though, overall, the latter distribution according to the Gini coefficient is the more equal. How does this result occur? It should be recognised that the Gini coefficient (as with all summary measures) is concerned with all parts of the income distribution, thus a more equal distribution at the top end of the distribution can offset a less equal one at the lower end. This is the situation described in Figure 6.3.

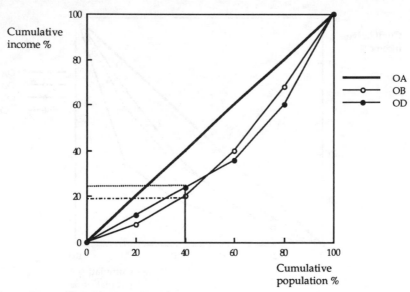

Figure 6.3. The problem of intersecting Lorenz curves

The Atkinson measure

A second critical problem in using and interpreting Gini coefficients, referred to as transfer sensitivity, was demonstrated by Atkinson (1970) who showed that changes in the Gini coefficient are sensitive to where transfers accrue. Atkinson noted that the Gini coefficient usually attaches more weight to transfers affecting middle income earners.[2] To illustrate this point, consider the income distributions shown in Table 6.2. Y^0 represents an initial income distribution which is concentrated around the median income. In Y^1, a transfer of 10 units occurs between two individuals (B and A) who are initially separated by an income gap of 25 units, at the lower end of the distribution. As a result of this transfer, the Gini coefficient falls from 0.4363 to 0.4336, implying a reduction in inequality of 0.6%

Table 6.2.
Income redistributions around the median

Distr.	A	B	C	D	E	F	G	H	I	Gini
Y^0	5	30	40	45	50	65	180	200	205	0.4363
Y^1	15	20	40	45	50	65	180	200	205	0.4336
Y^2	5	30	50	45	50	55	180	200	205	0.4295
Y^3	5	30	40	45	50	65	190	200	195	0.4322

In Y^2 a transfer of 10 units is again effected across a similar income gap, but this time in the middle of the distribution (between individuals F and C). As a result of this transfer, the Gini coefficient falls to 0.4295, representing a reduction in inequality of 1.6%. Thus for a transfer of a similar magnitude of that in Y^1, in Y^2 there is a much greater fall in the Gini coefficient and a redistribution estimated which is more than double that of the redistribution estimated for the transfer in the lower income range.

In Y^3 a similar transfer takes place at the upper end of the income distribution, between individuals I and G. The resultant Gini coefficient is 0.4322, representing a redistribution of 0.9%.

To overcome this bias Atkinson (1970) proposed the use of an inequality aversion parameter 'ε', which would reflect the relative sensitivity to transfers at different income levels. As ε rises, more weight is attached to transfers at the lower end of the distribution and less weight to transfers at the top. The limiting cases for this measure are where $\varepsilon \to \infty$ which takes account of transfers only to the very lowest income group; and at the other extreme, where $\varepsilon = 0$, which is completely insensitive to transfers and ranks distributions solely according to aggregate income.

Atkinson's approach can be best illustrated by the following example. We start with two individuals A and B, where B has an income four times greater than A. If we are inequality averse we would approve of a redistribution of $1 from B to A with no net loss of income (ie the redistribution process is 'cost-less'). In reality, the transfer process is in fact not cost-less, so that we may still approve of a transfer even if it is going to take more than $1 from B in order to give $1 to A. How much more we are prepared to take from B will be reflected in the weighting given to ε. Let us suppose that we are prepared to take up to $(\$4)^\varepsilon$ from B in order to give $1 to A. So that:

$\varepsilon = 0$ implies a transfer of $1 from B to provide $1 to A;
$\varepsilon = 0.5$ implies a transfer of $2 from B to provide $1 to A;
$\varepsilon = 1$ implies a transfer of $4 from B to provide $1 to A; and
$\varepsilon = 2$ implies a transfer of $16 from B to provide $1 to A.

If we return to the problem raised earlier in relation to the preferred ranking of distributions B and D, Table 6.3 shows that for higher values of ε

(ie attaching greater weight to the lower end of the income distribution), the Atkinson measure reverses the inequality ranking of the Gini coefficient, so that distribution D is to be preferred to distribution B.

Table 6.3.
Atkinson's inequality aversion ranking of income distributions

Atkinson parameter	Distribution B	Distribution D
0.5	0.0571	0.0655
1.0	0.1167	0.1231
1.5	0.1760	0.1714
2.0	0.2315	0.2105
5.0	0.4324	0.3222
Gini coefficient	0.2560	0.2720

An even more marked result is demonstrated for distributions Y^0 to Y^3 in Tables 6.4 and 6.5, where for all values of $\varepsilon > 0$ the given transfer reduces inequality most when it occurs at the lower end of the distribution (*ie* Y^1) and reduces inequality least at the upper end (*ie* Y^3). For values of $\varepsilon > 2$, the transfer at the upper end of the distribution (Y^3) is given such a low weighting that the impact on inequality is considered negligible and thus the inequality index is identical to the original distribution Y^0.

Table 6.4.
Atkinson's inequality aversion index for distributions Y^0 to Y^3

Atkinson parameter	Y^0	Y^1	Y^2	Y^3
0.5	0.1808	0.1674	0.1786	0.1805
1.0	0.3730	0.3228	0.3691	0.3728
1.5	0.5576	0.4484	0.5539	0.5574
2.0	0.7019	0.5399	0.6999	0.7019
5.0	0.9050	0.7359	0.9050	0.9050
Gini coefficient	0.4364	0.4336	0.4295	0.4322

Table 6.5.
Rank of distributions Y^0 to Y^3 based on the Atkinson index

Distrib'n	Gini	0.5	1.0	1.5	2.0	5.0
Y^0	4	4	4	4	=3	=2
Y^1	3	1	1	1	1	1
Y^2	1	2	2	2	2	=2
Y^3	2	3	3	3	=3	=2

Additively decomposable inequality measures

A third group of inequality measures, deriving from the work of Theil (1967), concerns the extent to which inequality in the total population can be attributed to income differences within and between sub-groups in the population. These sub-groups may be defined by income (*eg*: the lowest quintile of income earners) or by demographic characteristics (*eg*: age, sex, race, occupation, level of education and so on).[3]

A well-known contribution in this area is the work of Shorrocks (1980), who derives a class of additively decomposable inequality measures. Briefly, Shorrocks' approach shows that an aggregate distribution can be decomposed into distributions for a number of sub-populations and inequality indices derived for the 'within group' inequality index and a 'between group' index. Thus:

Aggregate inequality = inequality amongst sub-group 1 X proportion of population in sub-group 1
+ inequality amongst sub-group 2 X proportion of population in sub-group 2
+ inequality between the average incomes of sub-groups 1 and 2.

In theory, any number of sub-populations may be decomposed. To illustrate the use of Shorrocks' work consider the income distributions Y^0 to Y^3 described in Table 6.2. These distributions are replicated in Table 6.6, showing the sex of the income recipient.

Table 6.6.
Decomposition of inequality by population sub-groups

Person	A	B	C	D	E	F	G	H	I	Gini
SEX	female	female	female	male	male	male	male	male	male	
Y^0	5	30	40	45	50	65	180	200	205	0.4363
Y^1	15	20	40	45	50	65	180	200	205	0.4336
Y^2	5	30	50	45	50	55	180	200	205	0.4295
Y^3	5	30	40	45	50	65	190	200	195	0.4322

In distribution Y^1, a transfer occurs within the group of female income earners (from B to A). In Y^2, a transfer occurs between a male income earner (F) and a female income earner (C). In Y^3, a transfer occurs within the group of male earners (from I to G). The effects on inequality of these transfers for the sub-populations (females and males) is shown in Table 6.7.

For distribution Y^1, where there is a transfer within the female sub-group only the within group indices for females (Columns ii and iii) and the aggregate index (Column i) change. There is no change in inequality among the male sub-population (Columns iv and v) or between the two sub-populations (Column vi) since the total income for each sub-population remains the same. The fall in aggregate inequality (Column i) is 0.0770 which is equal to the fall in inequality among the female group as shown in Column iii.

In distribution Y^2, a transfer occurs between the male and female populations, thus inequality between the two groups falls (from 0.2247 to 0.1920). In this case, inequality within the male group rises and since the transfer accrued to the top income earner within the female group, inequality within this group also rises. (If the transfer accrued to the bottom income earner we would expect a decrease in inequality within the female population). While the fall in inequality between the male and female groups is measured as 0.0327 (Column vi) this is off set by a rise in inequality amongst both the female (0.169) and male (0.96) groups and thus aggregate inequality falls only slightly (0.063).

Table 6.7.

Table 6.7.
Shorrocks' inequality indices for distributions Y^0 to Y^3

Distrib'n	[i] Aggregate inequality (total pop'n)	[ii] Inequality index for females Total	[iii] /N of females	[iv] Inequality index for males Total	[v] /N of males	[vi] Inequality between sub-pop'ns
Y^0	0.4669	0.3190	0.1064	0.2037	0.1358	0.2247
Y^1	0.3899	0.0879	0.0294	0.2037	0.1358	0.2247
Y^2	0.4606	0.3698	0.1233	0.2181	0.1454	0.1920
Y^3	0.4664	0.3190	0.1064	0.2031	0.1354	0.2247

Notes to table: Aggregate inequality= iii+v+vi
Inequality within female pop'n= iii
Inequality within male population= v

In Y^3, a similar result to distribution Y^1 obtains *ie* there is no change to the between group index (Column vi) there is no change to the female group index and inequality within the male group falls slightly, resulting in a fall of equal magnitude in the aggregate index.

It is also worth noting that the Shorrock's measure ranks these distributions differently to the Gini coefficient. Like the Atkinson measure, the Shorrock's measure orders these distributions (from lower to higher levels of inequality) as Y^1, Y^2, Y^3, Y^0.

Decomposition of the redistribution process

The three methods described above examine income distribution and inequality from a **static** perspective. That is, the methods reveal the extent of inequality before and after redistribution. The work of Kakwani (1980;1986) departs from these measures by introducing a **dynamic** perspective to redistribution. His work attempts to capture the intermediate processes by which one income distribution is transformed into another. These 'intermediate processes' are of course, social security and taxation transfers. The logic of Kakwani's approach is summarised below.

An initial distribution may be labelled A, representing the set of initial incomes a^i for each unit i (typically a person, family or household):

$A \equiv (a^1, a^2, a^3 \ldots a^n)$ where n is the total number of units
or $A \equiv \{a^i\}$ i= 1 ... n

The transfer system is a set of net transfers B, where each unit receives a net transfer b^i which may be positive or negative:

$B \equiv \{b^i\}$ i= 1... n

Each net transfer may be composed of a number of positive transfers (benefits) and negative transfers (taxes) indexed by j:

$b^i = \sum_j b^i_j$

where b^i_j represents the jth transfer paid to (or by) the ith unit:

$B = \{\sum b^i_j\}.$

After the transfers, each unit has income c_i:

$c_i = a_i + b_i$

and we can define the post-transfer income distribution as C:

$C = A + B.$

Kakwani's analysis focuses on the properties of B, *ie* how a decrease (or increase) in inequality is brought about by the transfer system. Moreover, Kakwani's approach enables the researcher to analyse separately the effects of the social security and taxation systems, as well as their net effects. If we have some inequality measure $I(x)$ which reduces any income distribution to a single-value index of inequality, the redistributive effect, R, of the transfer system can be measured as the proportional change in the index:

$$R(B) \equiv \frac{I(A) - I(B)}{I(A)}$$

Note that the redistributive effect is defined in proportional terms so as to make it independent of the scale of the inequality index. Thus R=0.2 measures, for instance, a 20% reduction in the inequality measure.

In principle, any inequality index could be used. If for example, we use an Atkinson inequality measure, the index might be $I^{At\ 0.5}$ (where 0.5 is a chosen value for the Atkinson inequality-aversion parameter) in which case we can define the Atkinson redistributive effect of a given transfer system as:

$$R^{At\ 0.5}(B) = \frac{I^{At\ 0.5}(A) - I^{At\ 0.5}(C)}{I^{At\ 0.5}(A)}$$

The difference between Kakwani's approach and others is that rather than simply calculating redistribution based on the changes between A and C, he uses the characteristics of B - the transfer mechanisms - to highlight the separate effects of social security and taxes on redistribution.

Kakwani uses a particular inequality index, the Gini coefficient (G). As noted earlier the Gini coefficient has two main limitations: its relative insensitivity to changes at the upper and lower ends of the distribution, and the fact that it cannot be decomposed simply across constituent groups of income units (whereas the Shorrocks measure, for example, can be decomposed into inequality within each group, and inequality between groups).[4]

Kakwani's major contribution is to show that, despite the limitations of Gini as a base measure of **inequality**, its use in the analysis of **redistribution** makes possible a decomposition of redistribution into the effects of three key features of transfer systems: the progressivity of social security transfers and income taxes; the average rate of benefit received, or taxes extracted from, the income unit; and the inefficiencies introduced into the transfer system by the 'leap-frogging' of equivalent income units.

Progressivity is defined as a concentration measure and is most easily understood when applied to analysing taxes. By superimposing on the Lorenz curve for the initial income distribution, the concentration curve of taxes,

113

where each point on the concentration curve plots the cumulative proportion of total taxes paid by the bottom ith proportion of income units. It is, in effect, the Lorenz curve for tax payments, with the vital proviso that the units are ranked not by tax payments but by income. In Figure 6.4, the concentration curve for taxes has been plotted with the Lorenz curve for income. The figure shows that the poorest 20% receive 10% of total income and pay no taxes, while the poorest 70% of income units receive 50% of total income and pay 30% of total taxes.

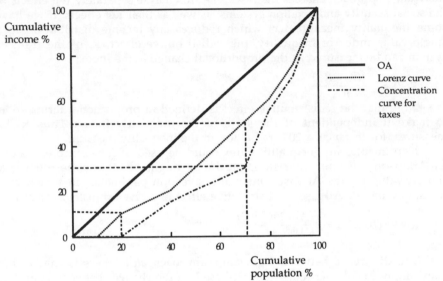

Figure 6.4. The concentration curve for taxes

A tax system is defined as progressive (under the liability definition) if the average tax rate (the ratio of tax to income) rises with income. In other words, if income rises by a given proportion, tax rises by a greater proportion *ie,* the tax elasticity is greater than unity. Under a progressive tax system the concentration curve must lie below the Lorenz curve; under a proportional tax system, where everyone pays the same proportion of income in tax, the two curves must coincide; under a regressive system the tax concentration curve will lie above the Lorenz curve. Kakwani's measure of progressivity (P) is twice the area between the two curves.[5] (The area is doubled to make it consistent with the Gini index which is twice the area between the diagonal and the Lorenz curve.) Thus: $P \equiv C-G$, where C is the concentration index of taxes, computed in the same way as the Gini coefficient, taking tax payments as the basic measure, and ranking by income.

From Figure 6.4, it is obvious that the maximum value of P is (1-G), which occurs if all taxes are paid by the richest unit, and its minimum value is -(1+G) if all taxes are paid by the poorest unit. P is positive if the tax is progressive and negative if it is regressive.

114

Although Kakwani (1986) analyses only taxes, his formulae are extended in this study and applied to social security benefits, thus: $P \equiv G - C$. The application of this extension is illustrated in Figure 6.5.

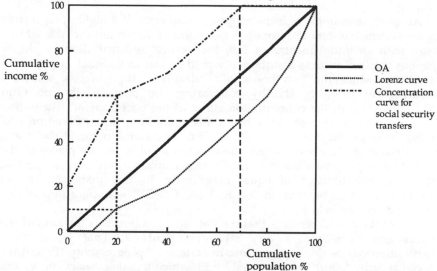

Figure 6.5. The concentration curve for social security transfers

Here the poorest 20% receive 10% of pre-transfer income and 60% of benefits, whilst the poorest 70% receive 50% of income and all the benefits. A progressive benefit system, as shown, must have a concentration curve above the Lorenz curve. Again, the progressivity can be measured as twice the area between the curves - with a maximum value of G+1 (if all benefits go to the poorest individual) and a minimum value of G-1 (if all benefits go to the richest individual); as noted above, P is positive if the benefit is progressive and negative if it is regressive. Knowing the progressivity of a tax or social security benefit does not in itself tell us how much redistribution will occur. A system might be highly progressive, taking taxes only from the rich and giving benefits only to the poor; but if the tax and benefit rates are small, little redistribution will occur. The average transfer rate 'E' (the ratio of total taxes or benefits to total income), is clearly an important element of redistribution. Thus Kakwani defines a measure of gross vertical redistribution 'V': $V \equiv PE/(1^{\pm}E)G$.[6] So as V increases the more progressive the redistribution and/or the greater the average tax or benefit rate.

Kakwani points out that, even though a transfer system may bring about significant vertical redistribution, it is possible that the Gini coefficient for the post-transfer distribution (G*) may still be close to the initial Gini coefficient (G). That is, the net redistribution R (=[G-G*]/G) may be smaller than the vertical redistribution. This will occur if the transfers result in some (equivalent) income units being re-ranked, which Kakwani refers to as 'horizontal inequity.' Kakwani's terminology should not be confused with the general concept of horizontal inequity used by taxation policy analysts to refer to the differential treatment of tax units. To avoid confusion I retain Kakwani's notation (H) but refer to this aspect of the transfer process as 'leap-frogging' or 're-ranking' which is exactly what Kakwani's measure is capturing.[7]

An extreme example of leap-frogging would occur if a highly progressive transfer system transfers $90 from a person with an initial income of $100 to a person with an initial income of $10; the vertical redistribution would be large, but the final income distribution would be just as unequal as the initial distribution, since the two households simply change places. Kakwani measures leap-frogging (H) by comparing the post-distribution Gini coefficient (G*) with the concentration curve of the post-transfer distribution (Cd). Cd can be thought of as the post-transfer Gini coefficient based on pre-transfer rankings, thus: $H \equiv (Cd - G^*)/G$. If no re-ranking occurs, Cd=G* and H=0. In the example above, where the two households change places in the distribution, a positive vertical redistribution would be offset by a negative horizontal redistribution of equal magnitude. In this instance the net redistribution would be zero, so that R=0 and G*=G. The implications of this result are discussed below.

Kakwani's crucial result is that the net redistribution R is the sum of the vertical and horizontal equity measures: R=H+V. That is, the net redistribution can be decomposed into the effects of progressivity (P) and tax or social security 'effort' (as measured by E), which together determine V; and the re-ranking of income units (as measured by H). The merits of this decomposition are illustrated in Table 6.8, which shows an initial income distribution, a set of taxes and the resultant redistribution (disposable income).

Table 6.8.
Kakwani's decomposition of the income distribution process.

Household	Equivalent gross income	Equivalent tax liability	Equiv.disp. income	Kakwani measures
1	5	0	5	G =0.3465
2	20	0	20	G*=0.3164
3	30	5	25	P =0.1285
4	40	5	35	R =0.0869
5	50	5	45	H =0.0000
6	70	20	50	V =0.0869
7	80	20	60	E =0.4750
8	100	20	80	C =0.4167
				Cd=0.3258

Kakwani's measures as shown are interpreted as follows: the Gini coefficient for the original income distribution falls from G=0.3465 to G*=0.3164 after taxes, producing a net redistribution (R) of 8.69%. This can be decomposed as follows: the concentration index of taxes (C=0.4750) is only slightly higher than the initial Gini coefficient, so the progressivity measure (P=0.1285) is low. The tax effort (E=0.1899) is combined with the progressivity measure to give the vertical redistribution V:

$$V = \frac{0.1285 \times 0.1899}{(1 - 0.1899) \times 0.3465} = 0.0869$$

No leap-frogging occurs, *ie* each income unit retains its ranking in the post- tax distribution, so H=0. In this case the net redistribution ,R, is identical to the vertical redistribution, V.

Table 6.9 analyses the effects of a shift in the tax threshold which pushes household 5 - in the original distribution in Table 6.8 - into the upper tax bracket. Initially this household paid 5 units in tax and now pays 20 units. The tax effort (E=0.2278) is now higher, but is also less progressive for the middle income range, so P falls from 0.1285 to 0.0701. As a result, vertical redistribution falls to 0.0597. Household 5 in the initial distribution, is now ranked 4th, in the post-tax distribution and this re-ranking is measured as a loss of horizontal equity, H= -0.0118 (-1.18%). So the net redistribution is lower than V, thus R= 0.0479 (4.79%). Thus the result of this change to the tax threshold is a decrease in the progressivity of the incidence of the tax and a decrease in the redistributive effect of the tax system.

Table 6.9.
Kakwani's analysis of a change to the tax threshold

Household	Equivalent gross income	Equivalent tax liability	Equiv.disp. income	Kakwani measures
1	5	0	5	G =0.3465
2	20	0	20	G*=0.3299
3	30	5	25	P =0.0701
4	40	5	35]	R =0.0479
5	50	20	30]	H= -0.0118
6	70	20	50	V =0.0597
7	80	20	60	E =0.2278
8	100	20	80	C =0.4167
				Cd=0.3258

A corresponding example of a change in a social security transfer payment is shown in Table 6.10. We see that, although the average benefit level is low (E=0.0633) -*ie*, on average transfers account for 6.3 cents of each $1 of household income - it is targeted exclusively on low income earners, so the progressivity measure is very high (P=0.9215).[8] As a result, the vertical redistribution is much higher than for the tax system, with V=0.1583. Since no re-ranking occurs, H=0 and the post-transfer Gini is substantially lower (G*=0.2917), with a net redistribution of around 16%.

Table 6.10.
Kakwani's analysis of a change in the targeting of social security payments

Household	Equivalent Market income	Social security payments	Gross income	Kakwani measures
1	5	10	15	G =0.3465
2	20	10	30	G*=0.2917
3	30	5	35	P =0.9215
4	40	5	45	R =0.1583
5	50	0	50	H =0.0000
6	70	0	70	V =0.1583
7	80	0	80	E =0.0633
8	100	0	100	C =0.5750
				Cd=0.2917

The distribution presented in Table 6.10 is now modified in Table 6.11 to illustrate the effects of targeting benefits on a narrow income range. In this new redistribution, households 3 and 4 lose their benefits to households 1 and 2, so that only the poorest households receive benefits. With a higher average benefit (E=0.0759) and a more progressive system (P=1.0965), the vertical redistribution rises to V=0.2234. However, the increased targeting results in some re-ranking - household 3 loses its benefits and is now the 2nd poorest household in the post-transfer distribution - so there is some leap-frogging (H=-0.0085) and the net redistribution is 21.49%.

Table 6.11.
Kakwani's analysis of further targeting of social security payments

Household	Equivalent Market income	Equiv. SS payments	Equiv. gross income	Kakwani measures
1	5	15	20	G =0.3465
2	20	15	35]	G*=0.2721
3	30	0	30]	P =1.0965
4	40	0	40	R =0.2149
5	50	0	50	H= -0.0085
6	70	0	70	V =0.2234
7	80	0	80	E =0.0759
8	100	0	100	C =0.7500
				Cd=0.2691

6.2. Using inequality measures to assess efficiency and effectiveness

The measures discussed in the previous section all provide useful and quite different perspectives on the effectiveness of income transfer systems in reducing inequality. The simple Gini coefficient estimates how much redistribution occurs between the pre- and post- transfer states; the Atkinson measure improves on the Gini estimate by increasing sensitivity to transfers at lower income levels; the Shorrocks measures examine changes among different sub-populations; and the Kakwani measures allow the effects of the transfer instruments to be analysed separately.

In addition, there are also a number of simple descriptive statistics such as the analysis of the distribution based on deciles or quintiles of household units which describe in a broad brush fashion, the cumulative proportion of income accruing to each decile/quintile. Much of this basic descriptive material for the LIS data has been presented in a number of papers prepared by LIS researchers (see O'Higgins et al,1985; Smeeding et al,1985b; Saunders,1989b). The information conveyed by these measures is fairly similar to that of the poverty gap data and for this reason is not reported here.

To some extent the information conveyed by the Atkinson and Shorrocks measures is also covered by the poverty analysis. For example, the poverty measures concentrate exclusively on that section of the population with which the Atkinson measure is most concerned and the disaggregated analysis of family types in the poverty head-count and gaps sections gives an overview of how different family units fare in the transfer process.

The poverty head-count and gap measures, however, are not entirely satisfactory in giving a view of the taxation side of the transfer process - other than to indicate the extent to which taxation affects those below the poverty line. The size and distribution of the clawback of social security transfers through taxation (Chapter 5) indicated that the interaction of the transfer mechanisms is quite important in the LIS countries. The findings of Chapter 5 suggest that further investigation of taxation is critical to a more complete understanding of how the patterns of final disposable income in these countries are shaped.

On the efficiency side, only the Kakwani measures provide any substantive means by which efficiency questions can be addressed. The leap-frogging index (H) is a Pareto type efficiency measure which indicates whether the transfer instruments are redistributing the inputs in such a fashion as to cause households to swap places without any actual addition to aggregate welfare. The progressivity index (P) reflects the incidence of transfers across the distribution, providing a view of the transfer instruments akin to the targeting measure (VEE) discussed in Chapter 5.

In the context of this study, the Kakwani approach offers a number of distinctive features. In particular, the ability to decompose the redistribution process into its social security and taxation components supplements the picture of the effectiveness of the social security system presented in the poverty analysis; while the derivation of the progressivity and leap-frogging indices allow the efficiency aspects of these systems to be addressed.

6.3. The application of Kakwani's methodology

Kakwani's main indices - as derived in Section 6.1 - form the focus of the efficiency and effectiveness discussions in the following chapters. In these chapters, I report: the Gini coefficients pre- and post- transfer; the redistribution achieved by each transfer instrument, and the vertical and horizontal components of this redistribution; the progressivity of the transfer instrument; and the average rate of tax extraction/benefit receipt for the income unit. In each chapter, the analysis decomposes the redistribution process into the post- social security and post-tax position, allowing the effects of each instrument to be viewed.

In applying the Kakwani methodology to the LIS data, two operational issues arise in respect of: the appropriate measure of unit income; and the weighting of the income unit prior to rank-ordering the observations. These issues have been discussed by Atkinson (1983) and O'Higgins (1985a,b). The approach adopted here is that favoured by O'Higgins *ie* family equivalent income per person.

On the effectiveness side, the post-transfer Gini coefficient and the redistribution measure form the indicators of effectiveness for each transfer instrument. The amount of redistribution achieved by the social security and taxation components as a percentage of total redistribution is also presented. These are discussed in Chapter 7.

In Chapter 8 the efficiency of these systems is gauged by: the amount of redistribution achieved for the given tax and social security inputs; the relationship between the redistribution and progressivity; and the amount of leap-frogging associated with each instrument.

The abbreviated forms of Kakwani's measures to be used in the following chapters are:

G = pre-transfer Gini coefficient
G* = post-transfer Gini coefficient
P = progressivity index of the benefit or tax
R = net redistribution achieved by the social security or tax system
H = re-ranking index
V = vertical (or gross) redistribution
E = average incidence of benefits and taxes for the income unit
C = concentration index of benefit/tax received/paid by the unit ranked by pre-transfer position
CD = concentration index of post-transfer income.

Notes

1 See Cowell (1977) for a fuller discussion of Lorenz dominance.

2 Kakwani (1986) more specifically notes that it is transfers around the modal classes to which the Gini coefficient is most sensitive. These views do not necessarily conflict, it is a matter of recognising whether the middle income range coincides with the modal income class.

3 A discussion of the various forms of decomposition can be found in Nygard and Sandstrom (1981).

4 Although Kakwani (1986:94) describes the decomposition of G by *factor* components (eg: wage income, property income etc).

5 More precisely, twice the area between the two curves where the concentration curve lies below the Lorenz curve, and **minus** twice the area where the concentration curve lies above.

6 1+E in the case of social security transfers and 1-E in the case of taxes.

7 The phenomenon of 'leap-frogging' was first discussed by Plotnick and Skidmore (1975: Chapter 6). Their approach to measuring the extent of 'leap-frogging' is fairly similar to that of Kakwani. However Kakwani's approach has the advantage, for this study, of being able to provide a summary index.

8 When applied to other countries, the units will change. Thus E=0.063 in the UK means an average benefit of 6.3 pence per £1 of household income etc.

7 Inequality reduction in the LIS countries: effectiveness measures

The effectiveness of an income transfer system may be judged by the extent to which indices of inequality, such as the Gini coefficient, decrease (or increase) during the transfer process. As the previous chapter demonstrated, such a change measures the amount of redistribution achieved by the transfer system. The analysis to be presented in this chapter uses Kakwani's methodology to focus on the social security and taxation components of the redistribution process as well as on the net outcome of these transfers. Section 7.1 reports the Gini coefficients for the pre-transfer distribution (*ie* the distribution of market incomes) and the post-tax distribution (*ie* the distribution of disposable income). The net redistributive effects of the transfer systems are compared with both the pre-transfer and post-transfer measures of inequality in order to determine whether transfer systems are actually effective in reducing inequality.

In Section 7.2 the relationship between the wealth of a country (measured in terms of GDP per capita) and the level of inequality is examined. The question here is whether richer/poorer countries achieve a greater/lesser degree of redistribution and whether they achieve a more/less equal final distribution of income. Put simply, is the degree of reduction in inequality a function of a country's income or is it the result of autonomous policy decisions? Section 7.3 compares both the redistribution achieved by the social security and taxation instruments in each country, and how much of the net redistribution accrues to each instrument in each country. Section 7.4 focuses on the determinants of redistribution, in particular, the progressivity of the transfer instruments in each country and the amount of inputs to the transfer process.

7.1. The impact of transfer systems on income inequality

The purpose of this section is twofold: first, to establish which countries achieve the greatest reduction in inequality through their transfer systems (social security and taxation taken together); second, to investigate whether the post-transfer degree of inequality is determined by the amount of redistribution, or whether it is determined by the market distribution of income.

It is usually assumed in the social policy literature that a high level of redistribution will achieve the aim of a low level of post-transfer inequality.[1] This should indeed be so if pre-transfer inequality is independent of the transfer system. It is possible, however, that market incomes might react to the transfer system so as to nullify its effect. For instance, highly progressive taxation might simply have the effect of increasing wage differentials, resulting in exactly the same dispersion of disposable incomes as would result from a less progressive taxation system. We need, therefore, to establish empirically whether redistributive instruments are actually effective in lowering inequality.

Chapter 6 described the operational aspects of adapting the Kakwani measures to the LIS data. Like the poverty measures, both the OECD and Whiteford equivalence scales were used to adjust family incomes prior to weighting and ranking the files. Both scales produced virtually identical results for all the computed Kakwani indices, as evidenced by the correlation coefficients shown in Table 7.1. For this reason only the OECD results are reported in this chapter. A full tabulation of the inequality indices using both equivalence scales is reported in Appendix C.

Table 7.1.
Correlation coefficients for Kakwani indices, OECD and Whiteford scales

Distribution	G	G*	P	R	H	V	E
Post-ss	0.99	1.0	0.98	0.99	0.99	0.99	1.0
Post-tax	1.0	0.99	0.99	0.99	1.0	0.99	1.0

Table 7.2 shows the Gini coefficients computed for the pre-transfer and post-transfer distributions (G and G* respectively) and the associated measure of redistribution (R = [G - G*]/G). Countries where the income transfer system has the least impact on the distribution of disposable income are Switzerland, Canada and the US, where the overall change in the Gini coefficient is 25% or less. In France, the UK and Australia the transfer system achieves a 30-35% decrease in inequality; while in Norway, Germany and the Netherlands the decrease is around 40%. There is a large gap to Sweden at the top of the table, where income transfers effect a 53% reduction in inequality.

In the poverty analysis presented in Chapter 4, I examined the extent to which the level of pre-transfer poverty was related to the post-transfer outcome. In this section I present a similar analysis in the context of inequality. The purpose here is to establish whether the degree of inequality evident from the market distribution of income is consistently related to the degree of inequality in disposable incomes.

Table 7.2.
Gini coefficients and estimated redistribution post- transfers

	G = Gini (pre-transfer)	G* = Gini (post-transfer)	R = net redistrib'n
Australia	0.4143	0.2872	0.31
Canada	0.3865	0.2931	0.24
France	0.4707	0.3065	0.35
Germany	0.4066	0.2517	0.38
Netherlands	0.4672	0.2932	0.37
Norway	0.3848	0.2342	0.39
Sweden	0.4168	0.1967	0.53
Switzerland	0.4142	0.3355	0.19
UK	0.3928	0.2638	0.33
US	0.4252	0.3168	0.25

Figure 7.1 plots the post-transfer Gini coefficients against the pre-transfer Gini coefficients. We see that the relationship between the market distribution and the distribution of disposable income is very weak (and statistically insignificant). This result indicates that redistribution can in practice sever the relationship between market distribution of income and the final distribution of disposable income.

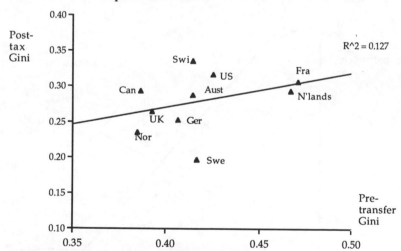

Figure 7.1. Pre- and post- transfer income distributions

Figures 7.2 and 7.3 plot the degree of redistribution (R) against the pre-transfer Gini and the post-transfer Gini respectively. We find first that there is no relationship at all between the level of inequality in market incomes and the degree of redistribution. This suggests that, in aggregate, market incomes do not adjust in any systematic and significant way to nullify attempts at redistribution.[2] On the other hand, there is a strong, statistically significant and negative relationship between redistribution and the post-transfer level of inequality. In other words, countries such as Sweden which redistribute strongly through their transfer systems are in practice effective at reducing the level of inequality in disposable incomes.

123

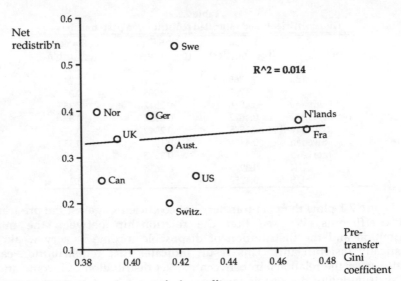

Figure 7.2. Redistribution and pre-transfer inequality

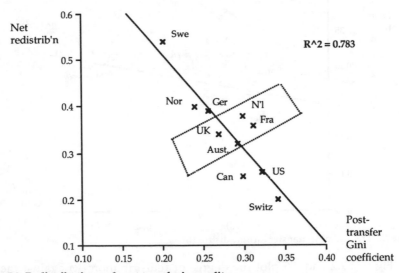

Figure 7.3. Redistribution and post-transfer inequality

It appears from these cross-country comparisons that transfer systems are effective in reducing income inequality, they are not nullified by counter-acting changes in the dispersion of market incomes. In particular, I note that the amount of redistribution is a good indicator of the inequality of disposable income. On the basis of this result, it is possible to define a partial ordering of LIS countries in terms of their effectiveness in reducing inequality. The criteria for the ranking are that a country has both a higher degree of redistribution (R) and a lower level of inequality in disposable income (G*). The relevant country groupings are shown in Figure 7.3.

Sweden
Norway
Germany
=Netherlands, France, UK, Australia,
Canada, USA
Switzerland

Sweden, Norway and Germany are unambiguously the most effective, in that order, in reducing inequality, whether one judges in terms of redistribution or inequality in disposable income. The group of four countries shown next cannot be unambiguously ranked. The UK, for instance, achieves lower inequality (G*) but has less net redistribution (R) than France or the Netherlands; Australia has the lowest redistribution of the group, but achieves lower inequality than either France or the Netherlands. Canada and the USA achieve substantially lower redistribution than the group of four placed above them in the rankings. (Strictly speaking, however, they should be grouped together because Canadian inequality is less than that for France; but the substantial gap in redistribution justifies ranking them below). Finally, Switzerland is unambiguously the least effective in reducing inequality.

7.2. Aggregate income and redistribution

In this section I examine whether income distribution is related to the income of a country, in particular, do richer countries have less inequality than poor countries and/or do they achieve more redistribution than poorer countries? Two hypotheses might predict a relationship between inequality and income. First, reducing inequality might be seen as a 'luxury good', which only the well-off countries can afford. If so, we should expect to find a positive relationship between aggregate income and the amount of redistribution carried out. On the other hand, supply-side economists might argue that substantial income differentials are a necessary pre-condition for an economy to generate the appropriate incentives required for economic efficiency and growth. In this case, we might expect to find a positive relationship between post-transfer inequality (a proxy for the level of economic incentives) and income (a proxy for economic efficiency). Income is approximated here by GDP per capita.[3] Figure 7.4 shows that there is virtually no relationship between a country's wealth and the distribution of income in the LIS countries from the market. (R^2= 0.06).

Post-transfer, Figure 7.5 shows that this relationship remains virtually unchanged (R^2= 0.09). We can conclude, therefore, that amongst the LIS countries, the aggregate income of a country does not predispose it to a more or less equal distribution of income whether we examine market or disposable incomes. There is little support here for the 'economic incentives' argument.

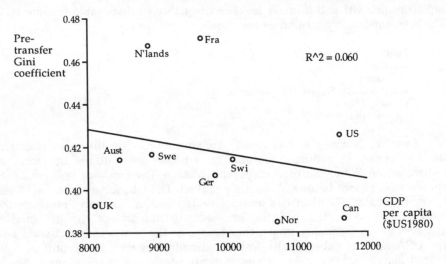

Figure 7.4. GDP per capita and pre-transfer inequality

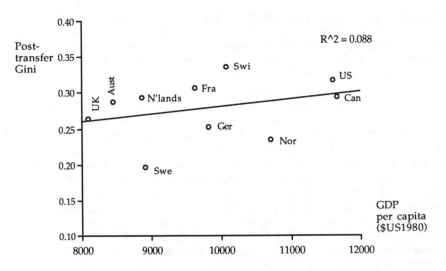

Figure 7.5. GDP per capita and post-transfer inequality

126

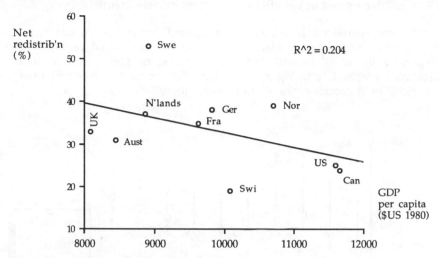

Figure 7.6. Relationship between GDP per capita and net redistribution

The amount of redistribution achieved does, however, have a slightly stronger relationship with GDP per capita. In contradiction to the 'luxury good' hypothesis, however, the relationship is weakly negative. That is, the poorer countries (*eg* :the UK) achieve larger redistributions than some of the richer countries (*eg:* the US and Canada). This relationship is shown in Figure 7.6.

We can conclude that there is virtually no systematic relationship in the LIS sample between a country's wealth on the one hand and either inequality or redistribution on the other. It appears, therefore, that neither the 'economic incentives' nor the 'luxury good' arguments apply. Instead, it seems that a country's policy towards inequality and redistribution can be regarded as an autonomous policy decision.

Table 7.3.
Gini coefficients and estimated redistribution post- social security and taxes

	Gini (pre-transfer)	Gini (post-soc sec)	Redistrib'n (soc. sec)	Gini (post-tax)	Redistrib'n (tax)
Australia	0.4143	0.3359	0.1892	0.2872	0.1426
Canada	0.3865	0.3245	0.1605	0.2931	0.0899
France	0.4707	0.3435	0.2703	0.3065	0.1085
Germany	0.4066	0.2796	0.3125	0.2517	0.0946
Netherlands	0.4672	0.3291	0.2957	0.2932	0.1074
Norway	0.3848	0.2854	0.2583	0.2342	0.1682
Sweden	0.4168	0.2407	0.4225	0.1967	0.1829
Switzerland	0.4142	0.3574	0.1373	0.3355	0.0504
UK	0.3928	0.2933	0.2532	0.2638	0.0841
US	0.4252	0.3690	0.1322	0.3168	0.1307

7.3. The relative impact of benefits and taxes on income inequality

Table 7.3 shows the Gini coefficients computed for the pre-transfer, post-social security and post-tax distributions and the associated redistribution measures for the social security and taxation transfers. The same information is displayed graphically in Figure 7.7, where the countries are ordered (from left to right) by decreasing size of net redistribution.

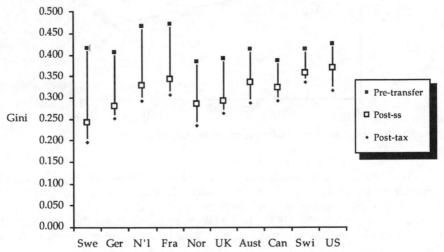

Figure 7.7. Gini coefficients pre-transfer, post- social security and post-tax

In Table 7.4 the countries are ranked from lesser to greater inequality at each stage of the income formation process. There is considerable change in ranks between the pre-transfer (market income) distribution and the post-social security (gross income) distributions; the rank correlation coefficient, r=0.49. The rank changes post-tax are minor, generally one rank switches and r=0.93.

Before examining these changes in detail, it is worth noting whether the LIS countries diverge or converge in the distribution of income during the transfer process. At the market income stage, the difference between the Gini coefficients of the top country (Norway) and the bottom (France) is .086, and the coefficient of variation (the sample standard deviation divided by the sample mean) is 7.2%. After social security transfers, the difference between the Gini coefficients for the top and bottom of the range increases to .128, coefficient of variation is 12.6%; and post-tax the range increases to .139, coefficient of variation is 15.0%.[4]

This indicates that while social security and taxation systems do reduce the level of inequality within each country, the amount of reduction achieved varies considerably across countries and has the effect of increasing the inter-country differences in inequality.

Table 7.4.
Ranks based on Gini coefficients pre- and post- transfers

Rank	Pre-transfer Gini	Post- social security Gini	Post-tax Gini
1	Norway .385	Sweden .241	Sweden .197
2	Canada .387	Germany .280	Norway .234
3	UK .393	Norway .285	Germany .252
4	Germany .407	UK .293	UK .264
5	Switzerland .414	Canada .325	Australia .287
6	Australia .414	Netherlands .329	Canada .293
7	Sweden .417	Australia .336	Netherlands .293
8	US .425	France .344	France .307
9	Netherlands .467	Switzerland .357	US .317
10	France .471	US .369	Switzerland .336
	range .086	*.128*	*.139*
coefficient of variation	*7.19%*	*12.64%*	*14.97%*

The next question of interest is whether it is the social security or the taxation system which has the greatest impact in reducing inequality. In principle, social security and taxation are alternative (or complementary) instruments for lowering inequality. For example, support to low income parents can be achieved either through child benefit payments or through child tax allowances.

In Table 7.5 the net redistribution effected by the total transfer system is shown in the first column (net R). The second column shows the redistribution which occurs between market and gross incomes, *ie* the redistributive effect of the social security system (R post-ss). The final column shows the redistribution which occurs between pre-tax income and disposable income, *ie* the redistributive effect of taxation (R post-tax). Note that the second and third columns do not sum to equal the first because they have different denominators.

Table 7.5.
Redistributive effects of social security and taxation systems (%)

Net R	R post-ss	R post-tax
Sweden 53	Sweden 42	Sweden 18
Norway 39	Germany 31	Norway 17
Germany 38	Netherlands 30	Australia 14
Netherlands 37	France 27	US 13
France 35	Norway 26	France 11
UK 33	UK 25	Netherlands 11
Australia 31	Australia 19	Germany 9
US 25	Canada 16	Canada 9
Canada 24	Switzerland 14	UK 8
Switzerland 19	US 13	Switzerland 5

While social security transfers have the greatest impact on inequality, there are several countries whose taxation systems generate a significant amount of the overall redistribution most notably, the US, Australia, Canada and Norway. In Table 7.6 the net redistribution is broken down into the proportions carried out by the social security and taxation instruments. The social security share of net redistribution (R to SS) is calculated as [(R post SS)/net R] and the taxation share (R to taxes) is calculated as [1 - (R to SS)]. In all countries except the US social security transfers account for more than 60% of the net redistribution. In Germany, the Netherlands and Sweden the social security system is responsible for over 80% of the net redistribution.

Table 7.6.
Percentage share of redistribution accruing to social security and taxation

	R to SS	R to taxes	Net R
Australia	62	38	100
Canada	66	34	100
France	77	23	100
Germany	82	18	100
Netherlands	79	21	100
Norway	66	34	100
Sweden	80	20	100
Switzerland	72	28	100
UK	77	23	100
US	52	48	100

In general, it is the countries which achieve the largest amount of redistribution through social security transfers which are the most successful in reducing income inequality. There is a positive correlation between Net R and R to SS, the simple correlation coefficient is r=0.54. An important exception to this relationship is Norway, which is ranked 2nd both in terms of amount of redistribution achieved and post-tax inequality. Unlike the other countries which are most effective in reducing inequality, Norway achieves sizeable redistribution through its tax instruments.

It appears, therefore, that although social security is the principal instrument for reducing inequality taxation can play an important and independent role.

7.4. The determinants of redistribution

In the previous sections I have discounted the effects of the initial market distribution of incomes and the aggregate wealth of a country in explaining the post-transfer outcome (*ie* the measured level of income inequality). In this section, I examine the relationship between the amount of redistribution (R) achieved by the social security and taxation systems and two characteristics of these instruments, namely the progressivity of the instrument (P), and the average incidence of benefits and taxes for the income unit (E). The section also examines the relationship between progressivity, average incidence of benefits and taxes and net redistribution. The variables to be analysed are set out in Table 7.7.

Section 6.1 notes that Kakwani's measure of redistribution (R) is a product of the progressivity of the transfer instrument (P) and the amount of inputs to the instrument (E). Multiple regressions have been carried out to determine how strong this relationship is for each instrument, and also which variable most strongly determines the level of redistribution.

Table 7.7.
Kakwani indices of progressivity, average incidence and redistribution

	P-SS	E-SS	R-SS	P-Tax	E-Tax	R-Tax	R-Net
Australia	0.946	0.099	0.189	0.180	0.216	0.143	0.31
Canada	0.772	0.097	0.161	0.175	0.152	0.090	0.24
France	0.919	0.248	0.270	0.398	0.087	0.109	0.35
Germany	0.919	0.200	0.313	0.148	0.238	0.095	0.38
Netherlands	0.896	0.239	0.296	0.084	0.337	0.107	0.37
Norway	0.906	0.148	0.258	0.160	0.254	0.168	0.39
Sweden	0.813	0.384	0.423	0.139	0.296	0.183	0.53
Switzerland	0.937	0.075	0.137	0.109	0.178	0.050	0.19
UK	0.654	0.203	0.253	0.142	0.169	0.084	0.33
US	0.860	0.084	0.132	0.198	0.210	0.131	0.25

Nearly all of the variation in the redistribution accruing to social security transfers (R_{SS}) can be explained by a linear regression on the progressivity of the social security system (P_{SS}) and the average incidence of social security benefits (E_{SS}). Comparison of the t-statistics suggests that redistribution is mostly attributable to the volume of transfers rather than the progressivity of the transfer instrument as the summary of the regression equation demonstrates:

$$R_{SS} = 0.005 + 0.09\ P_{SS} + 0.90\ E_{SS} \qquad \mathbf{R^2 = 0.91}$$
$$\phantom{R_{SS} = 0.005 + }{\scriptstyle (t=0.8)} \qquad {\scriptstyle (t=8.6)}$$

On the taxation side, the amount of redistribution is less strongly related, in a linear regression, to P and E, In this case however the progressivity of the instrument has a stronger effect on the amount of redistribution achieved, although again not as strong as the effect of the volume of taxes. The resulting regression equation is:

$$R_{tax} = -0.077 + 0.39\ P_{tax} + 0.59\ E_{tax} \qquad \mathbf{R^2 = 0.56}$$
$$\phantom{R_{tax} = -0.077 + }{\scriptstyle (t=2.3)} \qquad {\scriptstyle (t=2.9)}$$

A linear multiple regression explaining net redistribution indicates that it is most strongly influenced by the volume of transfers through the social security system followed by the volume of taxation transfers and, to a lesser extent, the progressivity of the taxation system. The effect of the progressivity of the social security system is virtually negligible and in fact appears weakly negative.

$$R_{net} = 0.066 + 0.65\ E_{SS} + 0.71\ E_{tax} + 0.36\ P_{tax} - 0.071\ P_{SS} \qquad \mathbf{R^2 = 0.881}$$
$$\phantom{R_{net} = 0.066 + }{\scriptstyle (t=2.8)} \qquad {\scriptstyle (t=1.5)} \qquad {\scriptstyle (t=1.0)} \qquad {\scriptstyle (t=0.3)}$$

With so few degrees of freedom (5) and the presence of multi-collinearity between explanatory variables, we cannot place much reliance on the individual coefficient estimates or their t-statistics. The overall regression equation is, however, statistically significant (the overall significance level is given by $p=0.0156$; adjusted $R^2 = 0.786$). In other words, almost all of the variation in net redistribution is explained by the progressivity and volume of taxation and social security. But we cannot identify with any great certainty, the relative importance of these components. There is, however, some indication that it is differences in volume, particularly of social security transfers, which explain the greatest part of the differences which we observe in overall redistribution.

7.5. Summary

The results presented here show that the social security and taxation systems in the LIS countries achieve reductions in inequality without causing systematic adjustments to market incomes. In addition, the level of redistribution achieved appears to be independent of aggregate income in these countries.

The LIS countries diverge substantially in terms of the level of measured inequality at each stage of the income formation process. While there is a general reduction in inequality in each country, the results suggest that there is considerable variation in the extent of policy commitment to inequality reduction - as opposed to poverty reduction - in these countries, as discussed in Chapter 1.

Notes

1 Cf. the discussion of this issue in Chapter 4.
2 Micro-economic analysis might suggest, however, that micro-changes are significant.
3 Source: Summers and Heston, 1988.
4 Appendix E discusses the statistical significance of the inequality measures.

8 Inequality reduction in the LIS countries: efficiency measures

Kakwani's methodology provides us with two direct measures of how efficiently the transfer system reduces income inequality. The primary measure involves the amount of re-ranking which occurs between equivalent income units (H). As noted in Chapter 6, this measure captures the extent to which social security and taxation transfers simply 'shuffle' different income units around, resulting in a loss to the gross income redistribution achieved by each transfer instrument.

A secondary measure is the of the transfer system (P) which is similar to the notion of targeting discussed in Chapter 5. In this context, the progressivity measure gives an indication of the extent to which social security transfers accrue to lower income units and conversely, the extent to which taxes accrue to higher income units. The higher the value of P, the more progressive is the tax or transfer instrument. These measures and their implications are examined in Section 8.1.

Section 8.1 also considers the relationship between these efficiency measures and the volume of transfers as expressed by the average incidence (E). The relationship between these efficiency measures and the volume of transfers is an important consideration for two reasons. Firstly, as a general point the importance attached to the H and P measures will vary directly with the average incidence of the transfers *eg* if transfers, on average, account for only 5 percent of household income then we are unlikely to place any great importance on how progressive a social security or tax system is since it will have very little impact on income redistribution. Such a small level of transfer is also unlikely to result in any significant re-ranking of income units. On the other hand, if transfers comprise 30 to 40 percent of household income, or taxation decreases household income by a similar amount, then these efficiency characteristics may be crucial to the amount of redistribution achieved.

Second, we might expect greater volumes of transfers to be associated with less efficiency *ie* that re-ranking and lower levels of progressivity might be an inevitable consequence of generous and/or universal social security transfers or high levels of taxation.

In Section 8.2, the cost-effectiveness of the transfer system is analysed by comparing the amount of redistribution achieved for each unit of benefits received and taxes paid (*ie* R/E).

8.1. Kakwani's efficiency indicators

Table 8.1 shows the progressivity and re-ranking indices computed for social security and taxation transfers. The table shows that in all countries the progressivity of the social security system is extremely high, around three to four times more progressive than the taxation system. This would be expected since in most of these countries the social security system is focused on lower income earners.

The amount of re-ranking is also higher in the social security system than in the taxation system and again this would be expected because of the combined effects of the volume of transfers and the more targeted (*ie* progressive) nature of the social security system. This aspect is considered later in this section.

The progressivity of the taxation system is similar in most of these countries except for the extremes of France with the highest P index and the Netherlands with the lowest. Although the degree of progressivity varies, the tax systems in these countries are all progressive, *ie* there are no negative indices which would indicate a regressive tax system. The rankings for each of these variables are shown in Tables 8.2 and 8.3.

Table 8.1.
Kakwani's progressivity and re-ranking indices for social security and taxes

	P-SS	H-SS	P-Tax	H-Tax
Australia	0.946	-0.0155	0.180	-0.005
Canada	0.772	-0.0157	0.175	-0.008
France	0.919	-0.118	0.398	-0.002
Germany	0.919	-0.0643	0.148	-0.072
Netherlands	0.896	-0.0739	0.084	-0.023
Norway	0.906	-0.0454	0.160	-0.025
Sweden	0.813	-0.1185	0.139	-0.060
Switzerland	0.937	-0.0211	0.109	-0.017
UK	0.654	-0.0276	0.142	-0.016
US	0.860	-0.0248	0.198	-0.013

Examining the efficiency measures on the social security side, we see that the top six countries have indices of 0.9 or better, with the US slightly behind on 0.85. Countries such as Sweden, Canada and the UK which have a significant amount of transfers accruing across a wide range of income classes, as would be expected, have lower progressivity indices. As the VEE measures discussed in Chapter 5 suggested there is some relationship between countries which target either through income tests or category selection and efficiency measures, this observation is again supported by the progressivity index.[1]

Table 8.2.
Post-social security ranks for progressivity, re-ranking,
average incidence and redistribution indices

	P-SS		H-SS		E-SS		R -SS
Australia	0.946	Australia	-0.015	Sweden	0.384	Sweden	42
Switzerland	0.937	Canada	-0.016	France	0.248	Germany	31
France	0.919	Switzerland	-0.021	Netherlands	0.239	Netherlands	30
Germany	0.919	US	-0.025	UK	0.203	France	27
Norway	0.906	UK	-0.028	Germany	0.200	Norway	26
Netherlands	0.896	Norway	-0.045	Norway	0.148	UK	25
US	0.860	Germany	-0.064	Australia	0.099	Australia	19
Sweden	0.813	Netherlands	-0.074	Canada	0.097	Canada	16
Canada	0.772	France	-0.120	US	0.084	Switzerland	14
UK	0.654	Sweden	-0.120	Switzerland	0.075	US	13

Efficiency losses due to re-ranking vary considerably over the LIS countries. In Table 8.2 we see that, in the top six countries, less than 5 percentage points of the gross redistribution from social security transfers is lost through re-ranking. In France and Sweden however, the efficiency loss decreases redistribution by 12 percentage points. For Sweden, this loss has a smaller impact on the redistributive effect of the social security system because of the volume of social security transfers (on average, 38% of family income is in the form of social security transfers). In the case of France however, this inefficiency strongly affects the redistributive performance of the social security system. Table 8.2 shows that the French social security system is both highly progressive and involves a large volume of transfers, yet its final redistributive impact is ranked 4th, below Germany and the Netherlands. Both these countries have lower progressivity and transfer volumes but, most critically, lower efficiency losses due to re-ranking.

Analysis of the re-ranking measures show that there is virtually no relationship between the degree of progressivity in a system and the amount of re-ranking which takes place ($R^2=0.14$). While Australia figures as the most efficient on both these criteria, it does not follow that high progressivity means less re-ranking. A case in point is the UK where, although progressivity is significantly lower than the other countries, the structure of the transfer instrument appears to ensure that very little re-ranking occurs (less than 3% loss of redistribution).

On the taxation side (Table 8.3), the French taxation system stands out in terms of its high progressivity; as discussed in previous chapters this would be expected because of the structure of taxes which has a minimal impact on lower income earners. Because of the low volume of income which is transferred through the French taxation system, the redistribution accruing to taxes is only 11%. At the other extreme, the progressivity of the Dutch taxation system is nearest to a proportional system (ie when P=0), but because of the large volume of taxes, it achieves the same level of redistribution as the French taxation system.

As noted earlier, efficiency losses through the taxation system are lower than those of the social security system and generally do not affect the rankings expected from the combination of progressivity and volume. The exception to this is Germany where the efficiency loss does have a marked effect on the net redistributive impact of taxes. This can be illustrated by comparing the German outcome with that of Norway. Table 8.3 shows that Norway and Germany are adjacent in ranks on the progressivity and volume measures (separated by just over 1% in absolute terms), on the final redistribution however they are separated by four ranks and a difference of 8% in the amount of redistribution. The source of the disparity in outcomes is the level of re-ranking, where the efficiency loss for Germany is 5% higher than that of Norway.

Table 8.3.
Post-tax ranks for progressivity, re-ranking, average incidence and redistribution indices

P-Tax		H-Tax		E-Tax		R-tax	
France	0.398	France	-0.002	Netherlands	0.337	Sweden	18
US	0.198	Australia	-0.005	Sweden	0.296	Norway	17
Australia	0.180	Canada	-0.008	Norway	0.254	Australia	14
Canada	0.175	US	-0.013	Germany	0.238	US	13
Norway	0.160	UK	-0.016	Australia	0.216	France	11
Germany	0.148	Switzerland	-0.017	US	0.210	Netherlands	11
UK	0.142	Netherlands	-0.023	Switzerland	0.178	Germany	9
Sweden	0.139	Norway	-0.025	UK	0.169	Canada	9
Switzerland	0.109	Sweden	-0.060	Canada	0.152	UK	8
Netherlands	0.084	Germany	-0.072	France	0.087	Switzerland	5

In Chapter 5 I noted that government policy may consciously encourage certain forms of 'inefficiency' in order to achieve desirable outcomes for some groups in the population and that this should be borne in mind in drawing conclusions about efficiency measures generally. This is also true of the progressivity measures described above, but not of the re-ranking measures.

The re-ranking of equivalent income units - which is reflected in the level of H - apart from decreasing the net redistributive effort, has two other undesirable features. First, because transfers are not 'cost-less' the expenditure required to effect redistributions which cause income units to merely exchange places without any addition to welfare represents a dead-weight loss. Second, these inefficiencies engender unequal treatment between equal units, especially on the boundaries of transfer programs (*eg*: where pre-transfer poor families may leap-frog near-poor families who are ineligible for transfers). In the long-run, this may have disincentive effects for families on the boundaries of these systems for example, substituting leisure for labour. A full discussion of this issue is found in Plotnick and Skidmore (1975:154-158). Most governments are aware of the problem of leap-frogging and attempt to structure their transfer instruments to avoid such problems.

Apart from the ability to structure the transfer instruments to avoid leap-frogging, we can observe in the LIS data a strong relationship between the volume of transfers, the progressivity of the instrument and the amount of leap-frogging. On the social security side, the relationship is very strong as the following regression equation demonstrates:

$$H_{ss} = 0.142 - 0.39\,E_{ss} - 0.15\,P_{ss} \qquad R^2 = 0.89$$
$$\quad\quad\quad\;\; (t=7.6) \quad\; (t=2.6)$$

Leap-frogging (H) is measured as a negative number, so we should interpret the negative coefficients to imply that the more progressive is the transfer system, and the greater the volume of transfers, the greater the amount of leap-frogging we can expect to observe. The **volume** of social security transfers appears to be the dominant explanatory variable. On the taxation side this relationship is far weaker ($R^2 = 0.31$).

As noted at the outset to this chapter, the importance attached to the efficiency characteristics of the transfer instruments in the LIS countries should be balanced by the volume of transfers. On the social security side transfers in the top five countries in terms of volume *ie* Sweden, France, the Netherlands, UK and Germany account for 20 to 40 percent of household income, thus the extent of re-ranking and progressivity in these countries may be critical to the eventual amount of redistribution achieved.

On the taxation side six countries (the Netherlands, Sweden, Norway, Germany, Australia and the US) deduct more than 20 percent of household income in the form of taxes. The amount of re-ranking is probably a less important factor than the extent of progressivity in affecting redistribution in these countries. In France the extremely small volume of income taxes indicates that the apparently high progressivity and low re-ranking measures are virtually meaningless in explaining the level of redistribution achieved by the tax system.

8.2. The cost-effectiveness of income transfers

Another way of viewing the impact of transfer efficiency is to examine the cost-effectiveness of social security and taxation transfers. In Table 8.4 cost-effectiveness ratios have been calculated by dividing the net redistribution achieved by each transfer instrument by the average incidence of the transfer. This measure gives an approximation of the percentage reduction in the Gini coefficient achieved by each percentage point of GDP devoted to social security or taxation. We see that in the case of social security transfers, the Australian system is most cost-effective, achieving nearly a 2 percent redistribution for each percent of social security transfers accruing to family income. This is closely followed by Switzerland, Norway, Canada, US and Germany. In the remaining countries the ratio is just over 1:1.

On the taxation side, the ratios are much smaller with most countries achieving less than a 1:1 redistribution. France is the only country where each percentage point of taxation raised results in a 1.2 percent redistribution, however it must be recalled that this is based on a very low level of direct income taxation. In general the taxation systems are not as cost-effective as social security in terms of achieving redistribution, in themselves, *ie* other than as a source of revenue for direct transfers. This finding reflects the lower progressivity of the taxation systems in comparison with the social security systems.

Table 8.4.
Cost-effectiveness ratios for the social security and taxation systems

	R/E-SS		R/E-Tax
Australia	1.9	France	1.2
Switzerland	1.8	Norway	0.7
Norway	1.7	Australia	0.7
Canada	1.7	US	0.6
US	1.6	Sweden	0.6
Germany	1.6	Canada	0.6
UK	1.2	UK	0.5
Netherlands	1.2	Germany	0.4
Sweden	1.1	Netherlands	0.3
France	1.1	Switzerland	0.3

8.3. Summary

The analysis presented in this chapter highlights the diversity of policy approaches adopted in the LIS countries in terms of the volume of transfers and the progressivity of the instruments which distribute these transfers. For example, Sweden and Australia stand out as systems which have radically different approaches to combining these characteristics. On the one hand, the Swedish transfer system combines high volumes of transfers with low progressivity; while on the other, the Australian system combines much lower volumes with much higher progressivity. In Chapter 9, I consider the implications of these very different approaches in the context of the outcomes of the transfer process.

Notes

[1] Chapter 9 directly compares the relationship between the poverty and inequality efficiency measures.

138

9 The outcomes of the redistributive strategies of the LIS countries

This chapter draws together the empirical findings reported in Chapters 4, 5, 7 and 8. The purpose is to place the effectiveness and efficiency measures from the poverty and inequality analyses side by side to determine the relationship between the poverty alleviation and inequality reduction goals and to assess whether, and to what extent, efficiency and effectiveness goals conflict. Section 9.1 summarises and ranks countries on the basis of their effectiveness in alleviating poverty and reducing income inequality. The section also examines whether there is any relationship between the two policy aims as reflected in the outcomes. In other words, is the extent to which poverty is alleviated in these countries related to reductions in income inequality, and vice versa?

Section 9.2 focuses on the efficiency of the transfer systems in aggregate and their social security and taxation components. There are two points of interest here: first, from a methodological perspective a comparison is made between the Beckerman and Kakwani measures in order to establish how closely related the VEE and spillover measures are to the progressivity and leap-frogging measures. Second, the section poses a similar question to that raised above *ie* does efficiency in poverty reduction have any relationship to efficiency in inequality reduction? Related to this last question, is the issue of cost-effectiveness, which is discussed in Section 9.3. Here the poverty reduction efficiency measure (PRE) is compared to the amount of redistribution achieved per unit of transfer to assess whether cost-effectiveness in meeting one aim of policy has any bearing on the other.

Section 9.4 considers whether there is any trade-off between efficiency and effectiveness concerns in the implementation and operation of transfer programs. Here a number of issues are raised, for example does poor targeting, leap-frogging and so on, affect the eventual outcomes as reflected in the effectiveness measures? Or do systems require certain 'inefficiencies' in order to be effective?

9.1. Aggregate effectiveness of income transfers

This section examines whether those countries which are most (least) successful in reducing inequality are also the most (least) successful at reducing poverty. The two objectives are clearly related since a reduction in poverty will almost certainly compress the lower end of the income distribution and hence lead to a reduction in inequality. On the other hand, policies which reduce inequality primarily through transfers within and between the middle and upper ends of the income distribution will not affect poverty. So countries can attach differing weights to the twin objectives of poverty alleviation and inequality reduction. I compare poverty and inequality effectiveness in two ways first, examining the post-transfer outcomes; and second, comparing the proportional reduction of poverty with the proportional reduction in inequality. Table 9.1 summarises the rankings of countries at the 50% poverty interval for each of the outcome measures derived in Chapters 4 and 7: the poverty head-count, the poverty gap and the Gini coefficient.

Table 9.1.
Post-transfer effectiveness rankings, 50% poverty interval OECD scale

Rank	Head-count % families		Poverty gap % GDP		Gini coefficient	
1	Norway	5.3	UK	0.2	Sweden	0.1967
2	Sweden	5.6	Sweden	0.4	Norway	0.2342
3	Germany	6.8	Norway	0.5	Germany	0.2517
4	Netherlands	7.0	Germany	0.6	UK	0.2638
5	France	7.9	Australia	0.9	Australia	0.2872
6	UK	8.2	France	1.0	Canada	0.2931
7	Australia	10.3	Switzerland	1.2	Netherlands	0.2932
8	Switzerland	11.0	Canada	1.3	France	0.3065
9	Canada	12.5	Netherlands	1.4	USA	0.3168
10	USA	17.0	USA	2.3	Switzerland	0.3355

The two notable differences in rankings between the head-count and gap measures are the UK and the Netherlands. The large rank changes in these countries reflect the issue raised by Beckerman (discussed in Chapter 5) concerning the choice in policy approach to poverty alleviation, *ie* whether governments aim to maximise the number of units lifted out of poverty or to minimise the size of the poverty gap. Chapter 4 discussed the disparity between the head-count and poverty gap measures. It was argued that - in the context of cross-national comparisons - the head-count is a less robust measure than the poverty gap and may give a misleading picture of the magnitude of poverty which remains post-transfer. For this reason, the following comparisons between poverty reduction and inequality reduction focus on the relationship between poverty gaps and Gini coefficients.

Moving across the table and comparing the post-transfer poverty gap with the post-transfer Gini coefficient we see some clear policy choices emerging with respect to emphasis on poverty alleviation versus reduction in inequality. Countries where the emphasis in poverty reduction appears to have least effect on the income distribution are the UK, Switzerland and France. On the other hand, while the poverty gap in the Netherlands is the second highest in this group of countries, it moves up several ranks on the inequality measures.

The final outcomes analysed above are, of course, influenced by the pre-transfer distribution. So the emphasis of policy may be best gauged from the rankings of each country in terms of the pre- and post- transfer reductions in the head-count, poverty gap and Gini coefficient (*ie* net redistribution). These are summarised in Table 9.2.

Table 9.2.
Post-transfer percentage reduction and redistribution rankings

Rank	Reduction in head-count	Reduction in poverty gap	Net redistribution
1	Sweden 85	UK 93	Sweden 53
2	Norway 83	Sweden 91	Norway 39
3	Germany 78	Germany 91	Germany 38
4	France 78	Norway 90	Netherlands 37
5	Netherlands 78	France 85	France 35
6	UK 73	Australia 79	UK 33
7	Australia 63	Netherlands 79	Australia 31
8	Switzerland 55	Switzerland 75	USA 25
9	Canada 50	Canada 70	Canada 24
10	USA 37	USA 60	Switzerland 19

From these findings we see a clear dominance of the anti-poverty policy focus in the UK as it drops ranks from 1st to 6th place in terms of the reduction in the poverty gap as opposed to inequality.[1]

Sweden, Norway and Germany, achieve high degrees of effectiveness whether one focuses on poverty or inequality suggesting that both these goals are pursued actively in these countries. In the Netherlands the goal of reducing inequality also appears to be pursued actively, although the size of the reduction in the head-count versus the poverty gap suggests that this may be at the cost of some groups remaining well below the poverty line.[2]

In France both the rankings on poverty alleviation and inequality reduction are similar and suggest that the success in poverty alleviation reduction may be closely linked to redistribution. The main evidence for this is the size of the reduction in the head-count. To a certain extent this is also true of Australia, although it is less effective in reducing both the number of families in poverty and the poverty gap, resulting in a lower reduction in inequality.

In Switzerland, Canada and the US the income transfer systems appear to be moderately effective in reducing poverty and have very little impact on income inequality. This is particularly true of Switzerland whose transfer system has the least impact on income inequality.

How close is the relationship between the poverty and inequality effectiveness measures? Using the poverty gap as the preferred effectiveness measure for the poverty side of the picture, Figures 9.1 and 9.2 plot the aggregate outcome and reduction measures of effectiveness.

In Figure 9.1 the OLS regression of the two outcome measures shows that there is a moderately strong positive relationship between poverty gap and inequality reduction (R^2=0.51). In other words, countries which achieve low inequality, on average, substantially close the poverty gap. We can identify three distinctive groups of countries. First, a group of Northern European countries - Sweden, Norway, Germany and the UK - which achieve both low poverty gaps and low inequality. Second, Canada, the Netherlands, Australia and France achieve moderate levels on both measures. Third, the US and Switzerland which have large post-transfer poverty gaps and/or levels of inequality.

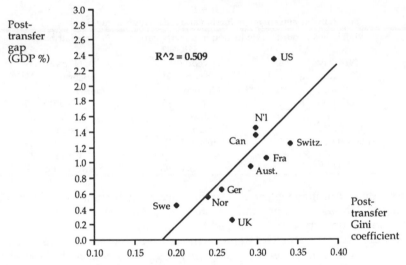

Figure 9.1. Post-transfer poverty and inequality measures (50% interval OECD scale)

There are, however, important differences of emphasis within some of these groups. A country which lies substantially below the regression line in Figure 9.1 can be judged to have relatively greater emphasis on poverty reduction compared with inequality reduction, and vice versa for countries which lie substantially above the line. Within the first group we observe that the UK appears to be relatively more successful in lowering the poverty gap, whereas in Sweden, the emphasis is on lowering inequality. Within the middle group, the variations in emphasis are relatively minor. Within the third group we observe a strong difference in emphasis: the US has a large poverty gap relative to the degree of inequality, whereas Switzerland exhibits the highest level of post-transfer inequality but a lower poverty gap.

The reduction measures - the proportional reduction in poverty and the proportional reduction in the Gini coefficient resulting from the combined effects of social security and taxation - show a similar moderately strong positive relationship (R^2= 0.50). The groupings of countries observed in

Figure 9.2 are similar to those identified in terms of post-transfer outcomes (noting that in this figure it is the countries furthest from the origin which are the most effective). The Northern European group which achieves the lowest poverty rates and the lowest inequality are also the countries which have the greatest proportional reduction in both measures. The relative emphasis on poverty versus inequality reduction also appears to be the same, with the UK system emphasising poverty reduction whilst the Swedish system emphasises inequality reduction.

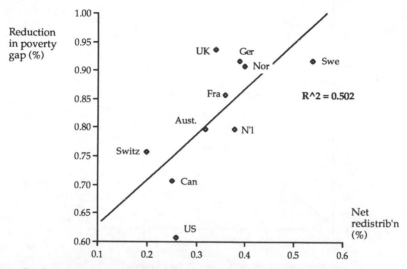

Figure 9.2. Post-transfer reduction measures (50% interval, OECD scale)

France, Australia and the Netherlands are again in the middle group in terms of effectiveness on both measures, although the Netherlands appears to place relatively more emphasis on inequality reduction (net redistribution). Using the proportional reduction measure of effectiveness, Canada now appears to belong to the group of least effective countries. We observe again that the Swiss system emphasises poverty reduction and the US system emphasises inequality reduction.

Taken together, figures 9.1 and 9.2 provide a fairly robust ranking of groups of countries in terms of effectiveness in terms of the twin aims of poverty and inequality reduction. At the same time, we can see that some of these countries place relatively greater emphasis on one objective as opposed to the other.

9.2. Efficiency of income transfers

In examining the efficiency of these systems both the net efficiency and the efficiency of the individual instruments (social security and taxation) are discussed. On the social security side we would expect, theoretically, the vertical expenditure efficiency (VEE) and progressivity measures to be closely related. Both measures attempt to convey a picture of the extent of vertical redistribution. That is, VEE measures the proportion of transfers which accrue to the pre-transfer poor and similarly the progressivity measure reflects the extent to which lower income earners receive a higher proportion of transfers than higher income earners. The OLS regression confirms the theoretical expectation ($R^2=0.89$). Figure 9.3 plots the relationship.

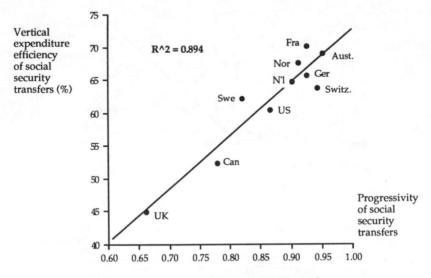

Figure 9.3. Primary efficiency measures (50% interval, OECD scale)

The relationship between the spillover (which is a measure of inefficiency in relation to the objective of poverty alleviation) and losses to redistribution through re-ranking (which captures inefficiencies in relation to the objective of reducing inequality) would be expected, theoretically, to be weaker than that of the vertical efficiency measures. We would expect the relationship to hold along the boundaries of the transfer system where the spillover takes pre-transfer poor families above the poverty line to such an extent that they leap-frog families which may not be eligible for transfers on either an income or category basis. This will result in re-ranking. The re-ranking measure however, will also capture the effects of universal transfers to non-poor families which meet certain categorical criteria irrespective of their income (*eg*: child benefits). These transfers in the Beckerman model are captured by the VEE measure. The OLS regression partially confirms these expectations, the correlation ($R^2=0.79$), is slightly lower than that observed between the primary efficiency measures.

The relationship between the secondary efficiency measures is plotted in Figure 9.4. The two outliers in the figure are France and the Netherlands. In the case of France, the combined measures are suggestive of boundary related inefficiencies *ie* the high levels of spillover for some families cause them to leap-frog non-transfer recipients causing significant re-ranking and a loss to social security redistribution of around 12%. In the case of the Netherlands, the spillover appears to have a moderate re-ranking effect.

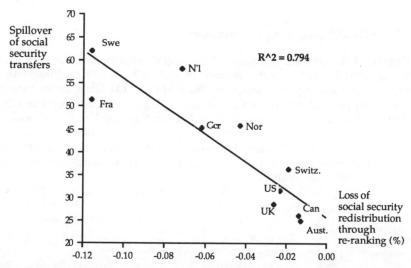

Figure 9.4. Secondary efficiency measures (50% interval, OECD scale)

On the taxation side, the relationship between the post-tax VEE and progressivity of tax measures is fairly weak (R^2=0.31). This would be expected as the post-tax VEE measure incorporates efficiencies already achieved through the social security system. There is a slightly stronger relationship between the size of the clawback of social security transfers through the taxation system and the progressivity of taxes measure (R^2=0.49). Interestingly, this relationship is inverse *ie* the higher the clawback, the less progressive is the taxation system. The size of the post-tax spillover and re-ranking also shows no statistically significant relationship.

Comparing the net efficiency of the income transfer systems in reducing poverty and inequality poses some difficulties for the inequality side. The overall post-transfer PRE measure on the poverty side is the appropriate summary measure, but there is no counterpart summary measure for inequality. As a proxy for this, I have compared the net PRE with the four component efficiency measures *ie* P_{SS}, H_{SS}, P_{tax}, H_{tax} and find that there is a moderately strong relationship (R^2=0.75). The resulting regression equation is:

$$PRE_{net} = 45.4 + 0.20\,P_{SS} + 1.57\,H_{SS} - 0.12\,P_{tax} + 0.83\,H_{tax} \qquad R^2=0.75$$
$$\text{\small(t=0.93)} \qquad \text{\small(t=2.2)} \qquad \text{\small(t=0.36)} \qquad \text{\small(t=0.67)}$$

Although this regression explains three quarters of the variation in poverty reduction efficiency, since there are only ten observations there are only five degrees of freedom. The adjusted R^2 is 0.54 and the probability level for the overall regression is 0.08. In other words, the relationship is not statistically significant at the five percent level. So I conclude that the

145

relationship between efficiency in poverty reduction and efficiency in inequality reduction is not very strong. (See Appendix E for a discussion of the degrees of freedom problem raised here.)

9.3. Cost-effectiveness of the transfer system

In Chapter 8 the cost-effectiveness of the social security and taxation systems was estimated by dividing the amount of redistribution (R) achieved in each system by the average incidence of the transfer (E). Here I compare these indices with the poverty reduction efficiency measures calculated in Chapter 5. Figure 9.5 plots the PRE and R/E index for the social security system. As shown, the relationship between the two measures is moderately strong and positive (R^2=0.73). In other words, those countries which are cost effective in terms of reducing poverty through social security are also cost effective in terms of reducing inequality.

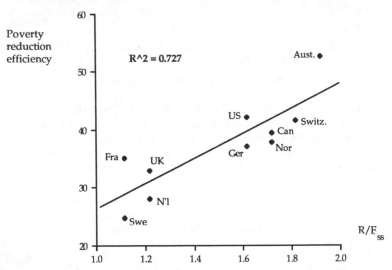

Figure 9.5. Cost-effectiveness of social security in relation to the reduction of poverty and inequality (50% poverty interval , OECD scale)

Inspection of figure 9.5 reveals three distinct groups of countries in terms of their cost effectiveness in reducing both inequality and poverty. Australia stands out as the most cost effective in relation to both objectives. The US, Canada, Germany, Norway and Switzerland are moderately cost effective. France, the UK, the Netherlands and Sweden are unambiguously the least cost-effective.

The relationship on the taxation side between cost effectiveness in poverty reduction and cost effectiveness in inequality reduction, as would be expected shows virtually no relationship since the impact of taxes on poverty alleviation is small and negative. Because of this, the net comparisons have little meaning; the multiple regression of PRE_{net} against R/E_{ss} and R/E_{tax} yields an $R^2=0.61$.

9.4. The relationship between efficiency and effectiveness

Does the efficiency of a transfer system have any bearing on its effectiveness? This is a very important question for policy purposes. On the one hand, for a given level of welfare effort, those countries with a more efficient delivery system (with better targeting and appropriate levels of payment and taxation) will - by definition - be the more effective in reducing poverty or inequality. In this case, where welfare effort is given, we would expect to find a positive relationship between efficiency and effectiveness.

On the other hand, countries may only achieve efficiency by limiting their welfare payments to selected groups and to small amounts - achieving 'efficiency through meanness'. At the same time, countries which wish to be effective in reducing poverty and inequality may find it administratively and politically difficult to achieve these aims without spreading welfare payments more widely and generously. For instance, the middle classes might have to be 'bought off' in order to gain their acceptance for an effective anti-poverty program (Ringen,1987; Esping-Anderson,1990). In this case, we may expect to observe a negative relationship between efficiency and effectiveness.

To investigate these questions I have compared the efficiency and effectiveness measures for the poverty and inequality analyses using simple regressions, the results are reported in Tables 9.3 and 9.4. In terms of the poverty alleviation goal, each of the two measures of effectiveness, the post-transfer poverty gap (as a percentage of GDP) and the reduction in the poverty gap have been compared with the three efficiency measures ie VEE, Spillover and PRE. Note that these measures relate to the combined effects of the social security and taxation systems. The simple correlation coefficients, r, are reported in Table 9.3. (I report r because it shows whether the relationship is positive or negative; the R^2 statistic is the square of r which must be positive).

Table 9.3.
Correlation coefficients between poverty efficiency and effectiveness measures

	Post-transfer gap (r)		Reduction in gap (r)
VEE	-0.069	VEE	0.110
Spillover	-0.224	Spillover	0.470
PRE	0.198	PRE	-0.417

The post transfer gap is not significantly correlated with any of the efficiency measures. On the other hand, the proportional reduction in the poverty gap is weakly correlated with both spillover and poverty reduction efficiency (although the relationships are weak in a statistical sense, significant at only the 80 percent confidence level). Note that the correlation between poverty reduction and spillover is positive, but spillover is a measure of inefficiency, so this implies a negative relationship between efficiency and effectiveness. Multiple regression analysis, not reported here, confirms these findings. This suggests that many of the theoretical arguments concerning the vices and virtues of universal versus income-tested systems in alleviating poverty may have very little basis in practice. It appears that it is possible for a system to be effective either with or without a high degree of efficiency. (This issue will be returned to in Part II which reviews some of the commonly held views about alternative transfer instruments.)

Figure 9.6 illustrates the relationship between the principal measure of effectiveness (the proportional reduction in the poverty gap) and the principal measure of efficiency (poverty reduction efficiency).

Although the linear correlation between the variables is weak, there is some broad evidence for the existence of a trade-off between efficiency and effectiveness in relation to the goal of reducing poverty. The most effective systems, the UK, Sweden, Germany, Norway and France do tend to have lower efficiency than the less effective systems. This implies some weak support for the 'buying off the middle class' hypothesis or the 'efficiency through meanness' hypothesis. The exceptions to this rule, however, are very significant. Those countries lying above the regression line shown in Figure 9.6 are relatively efficient given their level of poverty reduction, whereas those countries lying below the line are relatively inefficient.

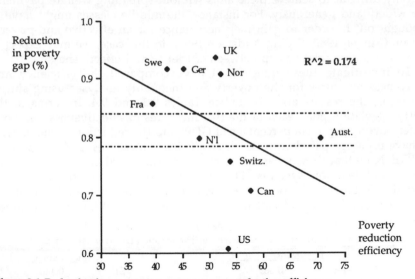

Figure 9.6. Reduction in poverty gap versus poverty reduction efficiency

It is particularly interesting to compare Australia and the Netherlands. These countries both achieve an 80 percent reduction in the poverty gap, about average for the LIS countries, but they are widely differing in their levels of efficiency. Australia is far and away the most efficient whilst the Netherlands is one of the least efficient.

The implication we can draw from this analysis is that there is substantial room for a well-targeted system to combine efficiency with effectiveness. There is no 'iron law' requiring effectiveness to go hand in hand with widespread, 'inefficient' welfare payments.

On the inequality side, the effectiveness measures, the post-transfer Gini coefficient (G^*) and the net redistribution (R_{net}) are compared with the progressivity and re-ranking measures for both the social security and taxation systems. (The efficiency measures in relation to the objective of reducing inequality were computed separately for social security and taxation). Table 9.4 shows the multiple regression statistic (R^2) for these measures. Both regressions indicate that there is a moderately strong relationship between the two sets of measures.

Table 9.4.
Multiple regression analysis of inequality efficiency and effectiveness measures

	Post-transfer Gini (G^*)	Net redistribution (R_{net})
P and H for social security and taxes	0.61	0.75

If we consider the efficiency-effectiveness trade-off for social security alone we find that there is a negative relationship. In other words, the more efficient systems, with less re-ranking and higher progressivity, tend to be those with lower proportional redistribution. The most significant relationship is between re-ranking (H_{SS}) and proportional reduction in the Gini coefficient (R_{SS}). This relationship is illustrated in Figure 9.7.

$$R_{SS} = 0.332 - 0.22\,P_{SS} - 1.92\,H_{SS} \qquad R^2 = 0.75$$
$$\phantom{R_{SS} = 0.332 - }(t=1.09) \quad (t=4.15) \qquad adj.\ R^2 = 0.63,\ p=0.012$$

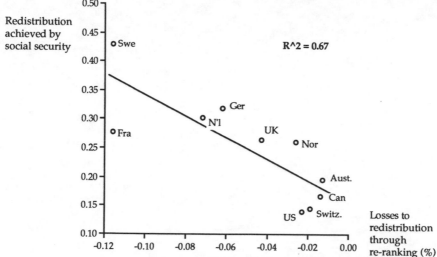

Figure 9.7. Reduction in Gini versus inefficiency due to re-ranking for social security

In the main, we observe a strong efficiency-effectiveness trade-off in relation to inequality reduction through the social security system. This implies that the systems which are most effective in reducing inequality tend

149

to be less progressive (although this tendency is weak) and they achieve their success through a high volume of transfers which have an almost inevitable consequence of a substantial degree of re-ranking. A notable exception is France which has an exceptionally high level of re-ranking but only achieves a moderate reduction in inequality.

On the taxation side, multiple and simple regression analysis reveal no relationship at all between efficiency and effectiveness in relation to inequality reduction. This implies that redistribution through the tax system can be effected either through progressivity and targeting (*ie* efficiency) or through volume, but that there is no systematic relationship between these two approaches.

Notes

1 It should be stressed again that the Gini coefficient may disguise the effectiveness of some systems at the lower end of the redistribution and thus the comments here are intended to be broadly indicative rather than absolute judgements.
2 This result does not take account of the possibility of intra-family transfers to some single adults, as discussed in Chapter 2.

PART II
MICRODATA STUDIES
AND COMPARATIVE
SOCIAL POLICY

10 A new perspective in comparative social policy

The existence of the LIS database presents researchers in the field of comparative social policy with a new perspective on evaluating and comparing income transfer systems. In a paper introducing the LIS database, Smeeding et al (1985a:1) claim that a shift to cross-national studies using microdata will improve social policy analysis:

> Over the past decade the use of household income survey data in policy analysis has increased dramatically. Today the capacity to describe the effects of existing policy and simulate the effects of changes in policy is well-established in most modern nations with elaborate welfare states. However, these analyses tend to be parochial except for the fact that the techniques are similar from country to country. The next step in improving policy analysis can come from moving to a cross-national focus using comparable income surveys in a number of countries. To this end, we have assembled a databank of income surveys that can be used by scholars and policy analysts to study the effects of different kinds of programs on poverty, income adequacy in retirement, and the distribution of economic well-being generally.

This chapter reviews those streams of the comparative social policy literature which are most closely related to the studies generated by the LIS microdata. The purpose of the review is to distinguish the perspective which studies based on microdata bring to the comparative social policy field; how the findings from such studies might influence the related streams of literature; and to assess whether, and in what respects, such studies might 'improve' policy analysis.

The comparison of income transfer systems can be approached in a number of ways, focusing on whole systems, particular programs or groups of beneficiaries. Studies may be concerned with issues as diverse as expenditures on programs, institutional history, characteristics of client groups, delivery mechanisms and so on. In addition to studies specifically concerned with income transfers, studies which are broadly concerned with the welfare state are also an important consideration here for two reasons. First, income transfer expenditures are the dominant component of social welfare expenditures in most OECD countries. In this respect, much which is written about the welfare state is closely associated with income transfer programs. Second, many comparative studies of the welfare state use the characteristics of the transfer system as a way of differentiating between types of welfare states.

Therefore in surveying the literature three streams of studies can be distinguished. These can be divided into those studies which focus on the welfare state in general and those which focus specifically on social security programs (including the interaction between social security and taxation programs). This latter group can be further sub-divided into essentially descriptive comparisons of policies and policy instruments and those which examine the impact of policy. Section 10.1 briefly describes the central concerns and methodologies adopted by each of these streams.

Section 10.2 examines how these streams are related to each other in terms of Hill and Bramley's production of welfare model. The model is used to characterise the concerns of each stream in relation to the transfer process; to locate microdata based studies in relation to the literature; and as a vehicle for examining the limitations of each approach.

Section 10.3 sets out several areas where microdata studies may supplement the knowledge gained from the existing literature and points to a number of issues which may need further consideration by comparative social policy analysts. The section sketches out several questions in these areas which then form the subject matter of Part II of the study.

10.1. Comparing income transfer systems: an overview of the literature

The first stream of literature which deals with welfare state programs in general, includes many studies which emphasise the role of social security programs. Within this stream two approaches are relevant to this discussion.

The first, which compares aggregate welfare expenditures, starts from the observation that there is considerable variation among OECD countries in the size of welfare expenditures, whether measured as a percentage of GDP, government spending or on a per capita basis. Two key questions arise from this observation: what are the determinants of these variations in expenditure? And what are the implications of greater/lesser expenditures for societal living standards, income distribution, equality, economic growth? These studies examine both the broad range of social welfare expenditures - that is social security transfers, social welfare services, education and health - as well as examining each of these sectors individually. Examples of these approaches are: Cutright (1965), Wilensky (1972), Castles (1982).

A second approach is one which develops typologies of welfare states based on the broad characteristics of welfare programs. For example, whether programs are financed from general revenue or social insurance contributions; whether entitlement is universal or selective; whether a system provides a minimal level of benefits or is income replacing. Other studies seek to characterise welfare states based on larger goals of transfer programs for example poverty alleviation versus reducing inequality. Examples of this work are Titmuss (1958;1974;1976), Marshall (1975), Furniss and Tilton (1977), Esping-Andersen (1989;1990).

Social security policy comparisons

The second stream is that concerned specifically with social security policies. Much of this literature focuses on the detailed description of programs on a country-by-country basis, setting out the types of programs available, their operation, coverage, and method of financing. The descriptive material is usually organised around some systematic theme and is frequently accompanied by some historical background on the development of the system, its underlying philosophy, major changes in coverage and trends in recipient numbers and costs. Examples of this approach are Kamerman and Kahn (1978), Flora (1986a,b) and Dixon and Scheurell (1989).

A second group of studies within this stream provide detailed comparisons of a program (or set of programs) directed at a specific group of recipients. These studies compare the level of benefits available under the program in some standardised fashion and draw out implications about the standard of living of recipients relative to the rest of the community. The aim of such approaches (in the absence of incidence data) is to give hypothetical comparisons of the relative generosity of welfare states towards specific demographic groups. This approach is exemplified by Kaim-Caudle (1973), Bradshaw and Piachaud (1980), Kamerman and Kahn (1983) and the OECD (1978) annual studies of the tax-benefit position of a typical worker.[1]

Comparisons of the impact of transfer policies

A third stream of the literature is distinguished by its use of survey data to compare the impact of social security and taxation policies on poverty alleviation and income inequality. Early examples of this work include Cutright (1967), Lydall (1968), Sawyer (1976), and Beckerman (1979a,b). These early studies faced considerable difficulties because of the variation in the definition and measurement of income and taxation variables, or because they used secondary sources.

More recently, a second generation of impact studies based on the LIS data attempts to give a clearer picture of the incidence of transfers using highly comparable data to make direct comparisons of the income levels of various demographic groups at various stages of the transfer process. Like the existing literature, the focus of these studies may be both general and specific. At the general level, the earliest LIS studies provided a descriptive analysis of the impact of income transfer programs on poverty rates and income inequality measures (*eg:* O'Higgins et al,1985; Buhmann et al,1988). At the

155

specific level, a number of studies focused on particular demographic groups such as the aged and families with children, attempting to assess the differential impacts of transfers on these groups in the LIS countries (*eg:* Smeeding et al,1985b,1989,1990; Palme,1989). [2]

10.2. The comparative literature and the 'production' of welfare

From this brief survey it is clear that there are many bases for comparing transfer systems. These involve a range of variables and employ a diverse set of methodologies and comparative criteria. One way of understanding how these streams of the literature are related is presented in Figure 10.1. In this figure I have again used Hill and Bramley's model of the production of welfare which was presented in Chapter 1. Using the same components of the model, we see that the literature divides into discrete areas of concern which parallel the various processes in the production of welfare.

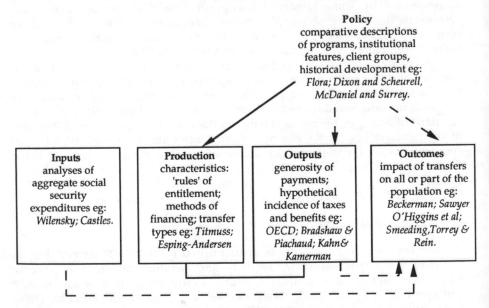

Figure 10.1. Comparing income transfers: a view of the literature

One feature which stands out most strongly in the diagrammatic representation of the literature is the relative isolation of each stream of the literature from the others. This is a distinct difficulty when attempting to comprehend the large scale effects that follow from state intervention in income redistribution processes.[3] It should be stressed that the intensive and detailed description and analyses in each area of the transfer process are a vital part of comprehending and comparing income transfer systems. However, the lack of linkages between each of these streams is also a critical issue. The division of the literature in many ways reflects a lack of data to provide an overview of how the various components of the transfer system work together to produce the desired goals of policy. In the absence of such data, the various streams of the literature have isolated the components of the transfer system in order to draw a fairly detailed picture in each area.

In addition, writers in each stream frequently attempt to generalise from that part of the transfer system with which they are concerned to the whole. In particular they attempt to convey either directly, or by implication, what sorts of outcomes we might expect from given levels of inputs, types of instruments used, the relative generosity of payments.

Using the Hill and Bramley model it is quite clear that the perspective which microdata based studies bring to the comparative field is that of examining the outcomes of transfer policies. In that sense, such studies 'complete' the detailed view of the transfer process which authors in other parts of the process have presented.

Examining this division of the literature in detail I begin with the policy component, here the archetypal studies are descriptive discussions of transfer policies such as Flora's four volume work on the welfare states of Europe. Here also are similar works on taxation such as the OECD and McDaniel and Surrey surveys of taxation expenditures.

On the inputs side is the 'leaders' and 'laggards' literature described above. As noted earlier, the concerns of writers in this stream are largely focused on explanations of why some welfare states spend more on welfare programs than others. However, there is also a normative element in this work which is inferred by the labels 'leaders' and 'laggards'. Part of the implication of this labelling is that 'more is better' *ie* that expenditure levels will influence outcomes. Whether this is so is an issue which will be taken up by this study as it is clearly an area in which the LIS studies may confirm or deny such a relationship.

Studies which focus on the 'production' element are generally concerned with the characteristics of the transfer system and use these to progress a wider argument on types of welfare states. For example, Esping-Andersen (1989,1990) is concerned with the financing and coverage of various types of transfers and the entitlement rules which welfare states employ to achieve their policy goals. This becomes a central means by which welfare states may be differentiated. Esping-Andersen rejects approaches such as the aggregate expenditure measures (which he calls the 'black box of expenditures') as a means of distinguishing welfare states in favour of unpacking more detail about how programs operate. He argues for a:

> ... move away from the black box of expenditures towards the content of welfare states: targeted versus universalistic programs, the conditions of eligibility, the quality of benefits and services and, perhaps most importantly, the extent to which employment and working life are encompassed in the state's extension of citizen rights.[4]

Because of a lack of detailed incidence data other writers have focused on the disaggregated outputs of transfer systems in the form of the level of benefits. For example, studies such as the OECDs tax/benefit position of a typical production worker combines the interaction of market incomes, social security entitlements and tax structures, to give a theoretical outcome in terms of the disposable income of its typical worker.

These analyses compare the relative generosity of transfer payments, hoping as the aggregate studies do, that these will bear some relation to the eventual outcomes. Such studies - like aggregate expenditure analyses - use these as a proxy for outcomes. However, as this study will show, the eventual outcomes are mediated by interaction with other parts of the transfer process for example, taxes and the actual incidence of the transfers.

Moving to outcomes we see that the existence of a data set such as LIS does not automatically mean that these studies should take precedence over other types of studies. Focusing on outcomes in isolation from other parts of the process also has its problems. For example many writers who do report outcomes, do so in a fairly limited fashion. They arrive at a set of observations which compare what has happened in each country's transfer process without making clear **how** it has happened.

The potential for microdata to act as a link between the various stages of the income transfer process is considerable and this has partly been the reason for the approach adopted by this study, which has examined how the inputs are used by different instruments, the incidence of both direct and indirect transfers, and the final outcomes in the form of poverty and income inequality reduction. However it should be stressed that this supplements rather than supplants the other approaches discussed above.

In summary, microdata studies both complement and supplement the analyses of other streams in the literature by supplying a means of comparing the outcomes of transfer policies with the expenditure, instrumental and financing aspects of these policies. These analyses represent a key means of assessing and comparing welfare states. While other streams of the literature provide useful criteria for comparative assessments, outcomes must be considered an important element that has long been missing from the literature. The LIS data has the potential for supplying information which links the findings from other areas together; but this requires some considerable research to develop new theoretical models which comprehend all parts of the transfer process rather than attempting to generalise from the part to the whole which has been the practice in the past.

The review of the literature discussed above has identified some areas in which the analysis of the LIS data may contribute to further developments. The following section examines some of these issues.

10.3. New perspectives on old problems?

There are of course many issues to which the LIS data could potentially bring a useful perspective.The issues outlined here in brief, and studied in detail in the ensuing chapters, have no special claim or priority. The purpose is to demonstrate the spread of possible perspectives which the LIS data can provide.

To begin with some of the earliest literature in the comparative field, I examine the relationship between welfare effort (expenditure) and welfare outcomes. These parts of the income transfer process are the furthest apart, yet there are very strong and obvious theoretical links between the two. That is, we would expect the outcomes of income transfers to be strongly linked to inputs. However, we also know that there are many intervening variables between these parts of the transfer process which may influence the 'straight line' effect of inputs. Part I of this study identified variations in the role of taxation, the distributional and efficiency characteristics of the transfer systems in the LIS countries and how these influence the incidence of transfers. To complete this analysis, we need to link these findings to the larger picture. Thus Chapter 11 addresses the question: are welfare leaders (laggards), in terms of aggregate expenditures, welfare leaders (laggards) in terms of outcomes? Is it possible to use the microdata findings to improve the predictability of these measures in terms of expected outcomes?

In Chapter 12, the broader issue of the welfare state is considered. The chapter focuses on the typologies of welfare states which have been developed to characterise the different approaches to the provision of welfare among the OECD countries. Clearly the welfare state encompasses more than just income transfer programs, so this chapter is limited in the conclusions which can be drawn in relation to the broader welfare state literature. On the other hand, it is important to note that many theorists in this field use the characteristics of direct income transfers as a means of developing these typologies. In this respect, the findings based on the LIS data may have greater significance. There are several questions which Chapter 12 addresses. Are different welfare state types consistently associated with particular types of outcomes? Do these typologies adequately capture critical characteristics (as evidenced by the microdata) of transfer policy and policy instruments? Are these typologies sufficiently tolerant of alternative forms of welfare provision?

Notes

[1] This series reports the theoretical tax/benefit position of wage earners of particular family types assuming they claim all benefits entitled to them and pay scheduled taxes.

[2] At the time of writing most of these studies have been published as working papers by LIS. These have been collected by Smeeding, T et al, 1990.

[3] Although it should be noted that occasionally some authors may venture across several parts of the process.

[4] Esping-Andersen (1989:20).

11 Welfare 'effort' and welfare outcomes

There are several reasons why a 'straight line' relationship between inputs to a transfer system and its outcomes may not hold. In this chapter I examine this relationship and the intervening variables in detail. To begin with, Section 11.1 discusses the problems with the aggregate social expenditures approach (also referred to in the literature as 'welfare effort') identified by other researchers as well as those identified in this study. The section also notes that there are several advantages of these types of measures which may suggest that such measures should be refined rather than rejected in favour of incidence based approaches. In Section 11.2 I construct a conventional welfare effort table for the countries in this study and compare the welfare outcomes against the inputs or 'effort'. Section 11.3 suggests a number of refinements which might improve such aggregate approaches and again tests these against the outcomes in order to draw conclusions about whether the predictive powers of aggregate measures can be improved. The final section of the chapter examines the 'gap' between inputs and outcomes in the LIS countries. Using the findings of Part I, it sets out on a country by country basis some explanation as to why the input measure under- or over- estimates the outcomes evident from the LIS data.

11.1. A critique of conventional welfare effort approaches

Conventional measures of welfare effort have been questioned by a number of writers as an acceptable means of comparing welfare states on two main grounds. In the first instance, Esping-Andersen (1989:19) rejects the welfare

161

effort approach entirely and argues that the measurement of social expenditure is irrelevant and/or misleading:

> By scoring welfare states on spending we assume that all spending counts equally. But, some welfare states, the Austrian for example, spend a large share on benefits to privileged civil servants... Some nations spend enormous sums on fiscal welfare in the form of tax privileges... that mainly benefit the middle classes. In Britain, total social expenditure has grown during the Thatcher period; yet, this is almost exclusively a function of very high unemployment. Low expenditures on some programs may signify a welfare state more seriously committed to full employment.

In rejecting this approach Esping-Andersen goes on to argue in favour of a more 'qualitative' approach to distinguishing welfare states via the comparison of program characteristics, eligibility conditions, quality of services. This approach is considered in Chapter 12.

Other writers such as Gilbert and Moon (1988) do not reject the welfare effort approach in its entirety, but argue that considerable care should be exercised in using such a measure. Their first point, which is similar to Esping-Andersen's, is that there is an implicit judgement built-in to this approach ie that 'more is better' and that welfare effort measures do not distinguish how funds are expended nor whom they benefit. More importantly, they argue that it should be recognised that the theoretical equation of effort with outcomes may not hold empirically (1988:339):

> The measure of welfare effort should not be confused with that of welfare outcome. Theoretically we would expect higher welfare efforts ... to result in higher welfare outcome (e.g., reduction of poverty and improvement of other social conditions.) But that remains an empirical question, which among other things depends upon the actual distribution of welfare benefits, how efficiently they are delivered, and their unanticipated consequences for the well being of recipients.

Having established grounds for caution, Gilbert and Moon go on to suggest a number of ways in which the welfare effort approach can be improved - by taking account of taxation expenditures, constructing indices of 'need' which can be compared with the level of welfare expenditures and so on.

These writers raise several questions which the LIS data may help to answer. First, should the aggregate expenditures approach be rejected? While both Esping-Andersen's and Gilbert and Moon's comments on the inherent weaknesses of expenditures as a means of comparing welfare states provide strong *a priori* reasons for doing so, it may be that such measures remain a useful proxy for outcomes. As I have suggested above, one test of this would be to compare welfare effort with the outcomes observed in the LIS data. If there is no strong relationship between these measures we could reasonably conclude that expenditure is not a good indicator of the level of 'welfare' which is generated by the transfer systems in the LIS countries and, by extension, welfare states generally.

Alternatively, we could take Gilbert and Moon's approach and attempt to improve the welfare effort measure. However, even if such improvements could be made are there grounds for attempting such a task? Heidenheimer et al (1990:18) suggest one reason which is particularly important in regard to income transfer programs:

> For a variety of reasons ... income maintenance and taxation policies are subject to more direct and exclusive government control than any of the other three policies ..

They argue that unlike other welfare state programs such as education, housing and health, income maintenance programs may be more sensitive to short term policy shifts, for example, in respect of taxation schedules, eligibility criteria and generosity of benefits. It is therefore possible that the incidence of taxes and transfers evident in the microdata in any given year may shift substantially over a two to three year period, whereas aggregate expenditure itself may remain fairly constant. This observation is an important one when considering the weight which should be attached to findings and conclusions based on microdata estimates.

An additional point in favour of aggregate data is that it is more readily available than microdata, covers more countries on a comparable basis and is collected more frequently. So even though analysis of welfare outcomes using microdata may be the preferred option, data availability may restrict us to using aggregate data for some countries in some years. If so, we may wish to know how good a prediction of outcomes the aggregate data can be expected to give.

If we accept that there remains a place in the literature for aggregate expenditure analyses, how might we attempt to improve such measures? Is it possible to combine the findings from microdata studies with aggregate measures to give a more accurate estimate of the level of welfare outcomes?

11.2. Should we reject the welfare effort approach?

The conventional measure of welfare effort expresses direct government outlays for social programs as a percentage of a country's gross domestic product. Direct welfare expenditures for each country are compiled by the OECD (1985) and comprise expenditures on: health, education, income transfers and social services.

On the basis of this measure, countries such as Sweden and the Netherlands are said to be 'leaders' in social welfare effort while the US, Australia and Japan are considered as 'laggards.'[1]

In this section I confine the welfare effort measure to social security outlays as this is the closest measure of welfare 'inputs' against which to compare the outcomes observed in the LIS data. Social security is a dominant element of welfare expenditures, Castles and Dowrick (1990) report that social security expenditures comprised, on average, 53% of welfare spending amongst these countries in 1980. In Table 11.1 'social security effort' is shown in two ways, as a percentage of GDP and on a per capita basis. The data has been drawn from an OECD series prepared by Varley (1986) and reflects only direct outlays on pensions and benefits, ie it does not include administrative or program delivery costs. Appendix D shows the full derivation of these estimates. The year chosen for comparison is 1980, which represents the

163

approximate mid-point for the period over which the data was collected for the LIS countries in the first wave. The table also shows the percentage of total welfare outlays which is expended on social security.

Table 11.1.
Social security effort in the LIS countries, 1980

	Social Security/ GDP@ %	Social Security per capita 1980 $US #	Social security expenditure as a percentage of total welfare expenditure, 1980*
Australia	6.9	624	43.5
Canada	7.4	838	45.3
France	16.8	1597	58.0
Germany	16.4	1638	62.2
Netherlands	19.0	1836	61.5
Norway	11.0	1136	53.1
Sweden	16.2	1926	52.8
Switzerland	9.0	984	45.5
UK	9.3	771	50.9
USA	8.1	906	53.6

@ Source: Varley (1986)
# Converted to $US using purchasing power parities
* Source: Castles and Dowrick (1990)

Table 11.2 shows the rankings of the countries based on the two alternative measures of 'social security effort'. We see that although the rankings change between each measure, these changes are 'within group' changes, that is those in the top/bottom half of the table on the SS/GDP measure are re-ranked but remain in the top/bottom half of the table on the SS/per capita measure.

Table 11.2.
Ranking of countries by social security effort, 1980

Country rank on SS/GDP	Country rank on SS/per capita
Netherlands 1	Sweden 1
France 2	Netherlands 2
Germany 3 > 10%	Germany 3 >$US1000
Sweden 4	France 4
Norway 5	Norway 5
UK 6	Switzerland 6
Switzerland 7	US 7
US 8 < 10%	Canada 8 <$US1000
Canada 9	UK 9
Australia 10	Australia 10

Comparing the rankings of the countries with several of the outcomes measures derived in Part I, Table 11.3 shows that apart from Sweden, Germany and to a lesser extent Canada, using aggregate per capita expenditures to predict outcomes would be highly misleading. Several countries - the UK, Norway and Australia - do considerably better than their aggregate expenditures would predict; while France, the Netherlands,

Switzerland and the US all have a lower level of outcome than countries with lower expenditures.

A fuller analysis of these relationships is presented in Table 11.4 which reports the simple regression results for the various effort and outcomes measures. In each case, the R^2 statistic between the effort measure and the outcome measure is reported. The statistical significance of this summary measure is discussed in Appendix G. In the simple regressions reported here, with ten observations and one explanatory variable, the value of R^2 must be greater than 0.4 for the linear relationship between the two variables to be significant at the 5% level (in other words, to be 95% confident that the relationship is not spurious). The value of R^2 must lie between zero and one. It can be interpreted loosely as a measure of how well the explanatory variable (welfare effort) explains or predicts the dependent variable (welfare outcome).

Table 11.3.
Comparison of social security effort and outcome measures by rank, 1980

Rank	Social security/ GDP	Post-transfer head-count#	Post-transfer poverty gap#	Post-transfer Gini coefficient
1	Netherlands	4	9	7
2	France	5	6	8
3	Germany	3	4	3
4	Sweden	2	2	1
5	Norway	1	3	2
6	UK	6	1	4
7	Switzerland	8	7	10
8	USA	10	10	9
9	Canada	9	8	6
10	Australia	7	5	5

50% poverty interval using OECD equivalence scale.

Table 11.4.
Simple regressions between social security effort and outcomes measures

Outcome measure	SS/GDP	SS/per capita
Post-transfer head-count	0.43 (-)	0.37 (-)
Reduction in head-count	0.51	0.43
Post-transfer poverty gap	0.05 (-)	0.03 (-)
Reduction in poverty gap	0.22	0.16
Post-transfer Gini coefficient	0.11 (-)	0.18 (-)
Net redistribution	0.44	0.51

Figures with a minus sign in brackets indicate an inverse relationship.

The regression analysis tends to confirm the poor to moderate correspondence in rankings observed in Table 11.3. The signs of the relationships between effort and outcomes are as we might expect. Negative relationships between effort and post-transfer poverty or post-transfer inequality imply that, on average, the high spending countries tend to achieve lower poverty and inequality rates. Positive relationships between effort and the reduction measures imply that, on average, high spending does lead to greater reduction in poverty and inequality. But these relationships are generally fairly weak with the exception of the reduction in the head-count and SS/GDP (R^2=0.51, p=0.02); and net redistribution and SS/per capita

($R^2=0.51$, $p=0.02$). Note that while an R^2 of 0.51 indicates a statistically significant relationship, it also implies that 49 percent of the cross-country variation in welfare outcomes is still unexplained.

Part of the explanation for the absence of a particularly strong correlation between expenditures and outcomes may be attributed to the role of taxation. As the analysis in Chapter 7 showed, Norway and Australia achieve substantial redistribution through their taxation systems, while France and the Netherlands achieve less redistribution via this instrument. We see from Table 11.3 that welfare outcomes for Norway, the UK and Australia are indeed better than their social security expenditures would imply and also that France, Switzerland and the Netherlands under-achieve in relation their expenditures.

As the Hill and Bramley model indicates, the combination of the incidence of transfers, taxation and efficiency may supply a fuller picture of the inputs-outcomes relationship. This issue has also been picked up by Gilbert and Moon (1988) whose work attempts to capture similar considerations. In the following section I examine ways in which these might be added to the welfare effort measure to improve its predictions of welfare outcomes.

11.3. Improving the income transfer component of welfare effort measures

Gilbert and Moon (1988) have suggested a number of ways in which welfare effort measures can be improved. While their work refers to the larger question of total welfare expenditures (*ie* including education, health and social services expenditure), this section adapts some of their suggestions to the income transfer context. Gilbert and Moon nominate four factors which should be taken into consideration when assessing the relationship between expenditures and outcomes. These are taxes, the distribution (or incidence) of benefits, the efficiency of expenditure and the level of pre-transfer 'need'. Improvements to effort measures based on these factors are considered below separately, and together, in order to establish how the social security component of welfare effort measures may be improved.

Why might we want to use the microdata in this way? Comparable microdata from LIS is only available for roughly one year in five, whereas aggregate data is available for most years. Would it be possible to factor in some of the observations from the LIS data (*eg:* clawback, efficiency, distributional measures) in order to adjust the aggregate expenditures to give a more reliable picture of these countries in between the survey years? If so, which of these adjustments would best improve the correlation between social security effort and the outcomes of the transfer process?

Accounting for taxes

The social security and taxation systems of the LIS countries interact and overlap in a number of important ways - social security payments may be subject to taxation; tax reliefs can be used to implement government policies and may often be substitutes for direct social security expenditures; and revenue which is foregone in the taxation system may affect the amount of funds available to governments and ultimately social security spending. To account for the role of taxation two approaches may be taken. The first, suggested by Gilbert and Moon, is to estimate the level of tax expenditures in each country and add these to welfare expenditure to give a compound expenditure estimate.

Tax expenditures are so-called since they represent the taxation revenue foregone by governments through the operation of deductions, concessions and rebates and are thus retained in household disposable income in much the same way as a direct benefit. The rationale for including tax expenditures is as follows: two countries may make allowance for the cost of raising children, in country A such allowances may be paid in the form of a direct child benefit; in country B a tax deduction/concession/rebate may serve exactly the same purpose. Thus, to exclude these tax expenditures is to underestimate the true level of support country B gives to the raising of children.

There are two sources of this data, the primary source is an OECD (1984) document which was prepared using data from a survey in which member countries were asked to provide estimates of tax expenditures following a set of consistent definitions and guidelines. Not all countries responded to the OECD request and a second source, McDaniel and Surrey (1985), has been used to supplement the OECD data. The McDaniel and Surrey survey employed similar guidelines to those of the OECD. Two of the countries in this analysis, Norway and Switzerland were in neither survey.

A major problem with this approach, identified by a number of member countries in response to the OECD request was the difficulty in distinguishing between expenditures which are a part of the normal structure of the tax system and those which are additional expenditures to serve certain purposes.

To illustrate this point consider the following difference between the Australian and UK responses. The UK included as an 'expenditure' the Married Man's, Single Person's and Working Wives' Allowances. In effect the majority of these allowances are akin to the tax exempt area of income which operates in the Australian system, ie the first $5,000 before tax begins to be deducted.[2] On the other hand, Australia reported only the Dependent Spouse and allied rebates, which are **in addition to** the tax exempt area. Notionally, part of the Married Man's Tax Allowance ie the difference between the single and married allowances is similar to the Dependent Spouse Rebate.

There is no clear cut way of adjusting for these differences; one could take the view that tax exempt areas in all countries are a form of tax expenditure and should be counted as such.[3] Alternatively, they could be counted as part of the normal structure and not sufficiently explicit enough as a welfare policy, and therefore not included. The question becomes more difficult when comparing countries which do not have a tax exempt area but low marginal rates at low income levels.

For the purposes of this discussion I have taken the approach of not counting tax exempt areas as an explicit anti-poverty device, and included those expenditures (or part expenditures) which were defined by the OECD survey as reflecting some welfare or equity aim.

These expenditures have been added to the direct transfer expenditures shown above in Table 11.1. The resulting compound transfer expenditure (CTE) is calculated by CTE = SS + TE. The compound estimates are shown in Table 11.5 where they are again expressed both as a percentage of GDP and on a per capita basis. Where the tax expenditure data was not collected for 1980 the figures have been adjusted using the CPI estimates reported by the OECD (1989).

A second way of accounting for taxation is to use the estimates of the clawback of social security transfers calculated in Chapter 5. Recalling the discussion of Chapter 5, the clawback represents the portion of direct transfers which is reclaimed by the government through the taxation system. It is important to note that many of the large-spending welfare states reclaim a considerable proportion of their expenditures through the tax system. Conversely, some - but not all - of the smaller spenders reclaim proportionately smaller amounts of expenditure this way.

Since the clawback has the effect of reducing the amount of social security which finally accrues to the population, the most appropriate way of adjusting for this is to reduce the aggregate expenditure by the size of the clawback to give a net expenditure (NE) estimate. Thus, NE = SS - (SS x Clawback). These estimates are also shown in Table 11.5.[4]

The comparison of these adjustments (reported only for the proportion of GDP measures) with the outcome measures are shown in Tables 11.6 and 11.7. We see that there is not much improvement in the correspondence between the expenditure and outcome measures. The R^2 statistics shown in Table 11.8 for the relationship between welfare effort, measured by CTE/GDP, and welfare outcomes can be compared with the statistics shown in Table 11.4 where the welfare effort measure (SS/GDP) did not include tax expenditures. In general, the addition of tax expenditures produces only marginal improvement in the prediction of outcomes in terms of either poverty head-counts or of income inequality.

Table 11.5.
Estimating social security effort after taxes, 1980

	CTE/GDP %	CTE/per capita 1980 $US	NE/GDP %	NE/per capita 1980 $US
Australia	8.5	765	5.1	458
Canada	9.6	1087	4.9	559
France	17.1	1625	14.8	1410
Germany	16.8	1684	13.2	1322
Netherlands	23.1	2226	10.8	1041
Norway	*	*	7.9	812
Sweden	20.6	2443	9.3	1100
Switzerland	*	*	6.8	742
UK	10.3	897	5.9	486
USA	10.2	1140	6.3	703

* Tax expenditure data not available.

168

Table 11.6.
Comparison of CTE/GDP and outcome measures by rank, 1980*

CTE/GDP	Post-transfer head-count#	Post-transfer poverty gap#	Post-transfer Gini coefficient
1 Netherlands	3	6	7
2 Sweden	1	2	1
3 France	4	5	8
4 Germany	2	3	2
5 UK	5	1	3
6 USA	8	8	6
7 Canada	7	7	5
8 Australia	6	4	4

* Tax expenditure data not available for Norway and Switzerland.
\# 50% poverty interval using OECD equivalence scale.

Table 11.7.
Comparison of NE/GDP and outcome measures by rank, 1980

Net expenditure/ GDP	Post-transfer head-count#	Post-transfer poverty gap#	Post-transfer Gini coefficient
1 France	5	6	8
2 Germany	3	4	3
3 Netherlands	4	9	7
4 Sweden	2	2	1
5 Norway	1	3	2
6 Switzerland	8	7	10
7 USA	10	10	9
8 UK	6	1	4
9 Australia	7	5	5
10 Canada	9	8	6

\# 50% poverty interval using OECD equivalence scale.

Table 11.8.
Simple regression results - CTE/GDP, NE/GDP and outcome measures

Outcome measure	CTE/GDP	NE/GDP
Post-transfer head-count	0.48 (-)	0.27 (-)
Reduction in head-count	0.52*	0.35
Post-transfer poverty gap	0.03 (-)	0.03 (-)
Reduction in poverty gap	0.16	0.18
Post-transfer Gini coefficient	0.15 (-)	0.02 (-)
Net redistribution	0.55 *	0.22

There is no significant relationship between effort and poverty gap outcomes. The net expenditure adjustment is not as good as the CTE adjustment for the purpose of predicting outcomes. To conclude, adjusting for taxes only slightly improves the relationship between aggregate expenditure and outcomes.

In Chapter 9 I noted that many tax reliefs are regressive and therefore may provide less financial assistance to the poor than to other income groups. This is partly supported by the regression results - for example, the relationship between CTE and the poverty gap measure is weaker. On the other hand, the relationship between the Gini measures and welfare effort is strengthened by the addition of tax expenditures. The explanation for this may lie with the fact that the Gini is biased towards the median income ranges and therefore 'middle class' tax reliefs such as superannuation deductions will show up here as an improvement to the income distribution.

Accounting for the distribution of transfers

A second factor which Gilbert and Moon identify in the translation of effort to outcomes is the distribution of benefits. In Part I two measures were used to reflect the distributional aspects of income transfers. The first is the vertical expenditure efficiency (VEE) measure discussed in Chapter 5. This measure estimates the proportion of direct transfers which accrue to the pre-transfer poor population. While this measure does not give a full picture of the distribution of transfers, it is closely related to the outcomes, especially in respect of the low income population, in which we are interested.

A second measure is the progressivity index of benefits which was discussed in Chapter 8. This index reflects the distribution of benefits across the total population, in particular the extent to which the poorest income units receive a proportionally greater percentage of benefits and conversely, the richest receive lesser proportions. Ideally, the latter measure would be best used to adjust the aggregate expenditure measure, however it is not clear how this summary index could be used. Although it is worth noting that there is a strong relationship between the progressivity of social security transfers and VEE ($R^2=0.89$) as discussed in Chapter 9.

The VEE measure on the other hand, has a more obvious usage which is similar to the use of the clawback. That is, aggregate expenditures could be reduced to only that proportion which accrues to the poor and which may be said to be 'effective' expenditure. In Table 11.9 Effective social security expenditures (ESS) have been calculated by: ESS = (SS x VEE).

In addition this measure could be further refined by taking account of the clawback of aggregate expenditures (NE) and then adjusting for the amount of the net expenditure which accrues to the pre-transfer poor. These effective net expenditures are also shown in Table 11.9 and have been calculated by: ENE = (NE x VEE).

Table 11.9.
Accounting for incidence of social security expenditures among the poor population, 1980

	Effective SS/GDP %	Effective SS/per capita 1980 $US	Effective NE/GDP %	Effective NE/per capita 1980 $US
Australia	4.7	427	4.6	414
Canada	3.8	433	3.7	417
France	11.6	1108	11.2	1066
Germany	10.7	1067	10.4	1043
Netherlands	12.2	1175	9.3	899
Norway	7.4	761	6.8	703
Sweden	10.0	1184	7.8	926
Switzerland	5.7	622	5.2	568
UK	4.1	341	4.0	329
USA	4.9	542	4.7	528

Tables 11.10 and 11.11 compare the rankings of these two measures with the outcome measures. Again there is a poor correspondence between the ranks and this is confirmed by the regression measures shown in Table 11.12. The evidence from the regression results indicate that these adjusted measures of social security effort are less closely related to outcomes than the unadjusted measures.

Table 11.10.
Comparison of effective SS/GDP and outcome measures by rank, 1980

Effective social security expenditure/ GDP	Post-transfer head-count#	Post-transfer poverty gap#	Post-transfer Gini coefficient
1 Netherlands	4	9	7
2 France	5	6	8
3 Germany	3	4	3
4 Sweden	2	2	1
5 Norway	1	3	2
6 Switzerland	8	7	10
7 USA	10	10	9
8 Australia	7	5	5
9 UK	6	1	4
10 Canada	9	8	6

50% poverty interval using OECD equivalence scale.

Table 11.11.
Comparison of effective NE/GDP and outcome measures by rank, 1980

Effective net expenditure /GDP	Post-transfer head-count#	Post-transfer poverty gap#	Post-transfer Gini coefficient
1 France	5	6	8
2 Germany	3	4	3
3 Netherlands	4	9	7
4 Sweden	2	2	1
5 Norway	1	3	2
6 Switzerland	8	7	10
7 USA	10	10	9
8 Australia	7	5	5
9 UK	6	1	4
10 Canada	9	8	6

50% poverty interval using OECD equivalence scale.

Table 11.12.
Simple regression results: R^2 between effective SS/GDP or NE/GDP and outcome measures

Outcome measure	Effective SS/GDP	Effective NE/GDP
Post-transfer head-count	0.39 (-)	0.34 (-)
Reduction in head-count	0. 47	0.43
Post-transfer poverty gap	0.02 (-)	0.03 (-)
Reduction in poverty gap	0.17	0.19
Post-transfer Gini coefficient	0.07 (-)	0.04 (-)
Net redistribution	0.39	0.29

Figures with a minus sign in brackets indicate an inverse relationship.

Accounting for the efficiency of transfers

The efficiency of transfers was measured in two ways in Part I. First in relation to the proportion of transfers which reduces the poverty gap, poverty reduction efficiency (PRE), and second in the loss to redistribution through re-ranking (H). Like the progressivity index the re-ranking index is difficult to use in adjusting expenditures to reflect this aspect of efficiency. Therefore I use the PRE measure to adjust aggregate expenditures to reflect only that proportion which closes the poverty gap. Thus "efficient" social security expenditure is calculated by: Eff SS = (SS x PRE). These estimates are shown in Table 11.13.

In addition, I have also included taxation expenditures and estimated the efficiency of compound transfer expenditure (CTE), by adjusting CTE by the net PRE (*ie* post-tax). These estimates are also shown in Table 11.13.

Table 11.13.
Accounting for the efficiency of social security expenditures, 1980

	Efficient SS/GDP %	Efficient SS/per capita 1980 $US	Efficient CTE/GDP %	Efficient CTE/per capita 1980 $US
Australia	3.6	323	5.9	534
Canada	2.9	324	5.5	620
France	5.7	548	6.6	629
Germany	5.9	593	7.5	749
Netherlands	5.2	501	10.9	1055
Norway	4.1	420	*	*
Sweden	3.9	460	8.5	1011
Switzerland	3.7	402	*	*
UK	3.0	247	5.6	452
USA	3.4	375	5.4	600

* Tax expenditure data not available for Norway and Switzerland.

Table 11.14.
Comparison of efficient SS/GDP and outcome measures by rank, 1980

Efficient social security expenditure/ GDP	Post-transfer head-count#	Post-transfer poverty gap#	Post-transfer Gini coefficient
1 Germany	3	4	3
2 France	5	6	8
3 Netherlands	4	9	7
4 Norway	1	3	2
5 Sweden	2	2	1
6 Switzerland	8	7	10
7 Australia	7	5	5
8 USA	10	10	9
9 UK	6	1	4
10 Canada	9	8	6

50% poverty interval using OECD equivalence scale.

Table 11.15.
Comparison of efficient CTE/GDP and outcome measures by rank, 1980

Efficient CTE/ GDP	Post-transfer head-count#	Post-transfer poverty gap#	Post-transfer Gini coefficient
1 Netherlands	3	6	7
2 Sweden	1	2	1
3 Germany	2	3	2
4 France	4	5	8
5 Australia	6	4	4
6 UK	5	1	3
7 Canada	7	7	5
8 USA	8	8	6

50% poverty interval using OECD equivalence scale.

Table 11.16.
Simple regression results efficient SS and CTE/GDP and outcome measures

Outcome measure	Efficient SS/GDP	Efficient CTE/GDP
Post-transfer head-count	0.25 (-)	0.39 (-)
Reduction in head-count	0.31	0.39
Post-transfer poverty gap	0.01 (-)	0.01 (-)
Reduction in poverty gap	0.13	0.09
Post-transfer Gini coefficient	0.01 (-)	0.10 (-)
Net redistribution	0.14	0.39

The comparison of these measures and the outcomes are shown in Tables 11.14 and 11.15. Again there is not any strong correspondence between the effort and outcome measures. However, it is worth noting that when efficiency is taken into consideration, the inter-country differences in expenditure are considerably compressed. For example in Table 11.1 the range for the unadjusted SS/per capita expenditure between Sweden and Australia is US $1302; adjusting for efficiency (ie the level of transfers accruing to the pre-transfer poor) the range between Germany and the UK in Table 11.13 is US $346.

The regression results shown in Table 11.16 indicate that the relationship between the efficiency adjusted expenditures and outcomes is weaker than that obtained with the original unadjusted expenditure measures. This evidence appears to suggest, rather surprisingly, that adjustment for efficiency criteria does not improve the predictability of welfare outcomes; but we shall see later that this apparent anomaly can be explained once we also take account of welfare need.

Aggregate expenditure and the level of pre-transfer 'need'

A further refinement to the welfare effort measure suggested by Gilbert and Moon is one which takes into account the level of 'need' to which the social welfare expenditure by governments is responding. They argue that current welfare effort measures may be misleading for a number of reasons - for example, they exclude demographic differences and wages and labour market policies which may act as alternatives to welfare policies. They cite the following example (Gilbert and Moon,1988:327):

173

Should a country with a relatively small elderly population be regarded as making an inferior welfare effort if they spend a lower proportion of their GDP on social security pensions than a country with substantially more elderly persons? What if the first country spent less as an overall percent of their GDP, but more per capita on the elderly?

In addition they argue that to compare expenditures without some adjustment for need assumes that the level of need is either equal among the countries being compared or irrelevant (Gilbert and Moon,1988:331):

> ... a meaningful analysis of differential welfare effort requires some fundamental estimate of need against which levels of expenditure can be assessed. To the extent that welfare effort implies an attempt to meet human needs through social provisions allocated outside of the market economy, a country with greater need would have to allocate a larger proportion of its resources to achieve a level of welfare equivalent to a country with a lesser magnitude of need. If welfare efforts are made to achieve a desirable social condition, then to compare these efforts without reference to needs would convey the impression that needs are either equal among countries under comparison or are irrelevant to the social condition being sought.

The major difficulty for Gilbert and Moon is locating a variable which captures need for comparative purposes. Their preferred measure is pre-transfer poverty rates, however, at the time of publication such measures were not available on a cross-national basis and they use instead a composite index of the demographic groups they considered most likely to be in need *ie* the aged, sole parents, number of dependent children.

In this section I adapt Gilbert and Moon's approach to the social security effort measures, using the pre-transfer head-count, poverty gap and Gini coefficient as proxies for the level of need being addressed by transfer expenditure. There is no immediately apparent way of adjusting expenditure for these measures of need. I have therefore used multiple regression to analyse whether there is any relationship between aggregate expenditure and need on the one hand, and outcomes on the other. Later in the section I also incorporate some of the incidence and efficiency measures into the regressions.

Table 11.17.
Simple regressions (R^2) for expenditure and need, 1980

Need measure	SS/GDP	SS/per capita
Pre-transfer head-count	0.66	0.62
Pre-transfer gap	0.40	0.30
Pre-transfer Gini coefficient	0.41	0.31

The simple regression shows that there is a positive relationship between the degree of pre-transfer need and levels of expenditure. This is most strongly evident in the relationship between the pre-transfer head-count and the level of expenditure.

If we incorporate the level of pre-transfer need into the relationship between expenditure and outcomes does a stronger picture emerge? Table 11.18 reports the R^2 statistics from multiple regressions where the dependent variable, an outcome measure, is regressed on social security expenditures plus the appropriate pre-transfer need measure (*ie* pre-transfer head-count, poverty gap and Gini coefficient).

The explanatory power of each regression is much improved by the addition of pre-transfer indicators of the level of need. Most of the regressions with SS/GDP and pre-transfer need as explanatory variables are now statistically significant (with two explanatory variables and ten observations, the value of R^2 must be at least 0.57 for the overall regression to be considered statistically significant at the 5% level - see appendix E). Comparing Table 11.18 with Table 11.4 we can see that the addition of measures of need increases the explanatory power of the regressions by anywhere between ten percentage points, in the case of the head-count measures, and 50 percentage points in the regressions explaining post-transfer poverty gaps and post-transfer Gini coefficients.

Table 11.18.
Multiple regression of welfare outcomes on pre-transfer need and expenditure.

Post-transfer outcome measure	SS/per capita, need (R^2)	SS/GDP, need (R^2)
Head-count	0.48	0.50
Head-count reduction	0.64	0.64
Poverty gap	0.41	0.57
Reduction in gap	0.37	0.57
Gini coefficient	0.67	0.67
Net redistribution	0.62	0.60

This evidence certainly supports the Gilbert and Moon argument that it is important to adjust welfare effort for the level of need. The regressions still leave unexplained, however, at least one third of the variation in the poverty and inequality related outcomes. These "unexplained" variations are, by definition, related to the relative efficiency of the various transfer systems. Roughly speaking, one can conclude from this analysis that efficiency considerations account for around 40% of the variation in welfare outcomes in the LIS countries; cross-country differences in welfare expenditures account for most of the remaining variation in the numbers of families in poverty and cross-country differences in pre-transfer inequality account for most of the variation in post-transfer inequality.

The contribution of efficiency considerations can be illustrated most clearly in the case of the poverty gap. We have seen from Table 11.18 that in a multiple regression social security expenditure and pre-transfer poverty together explain 57% of the post-transfer gap and also 57% of the reduction in the gap. Table 11.19 gives the full regression results when social security expenditures are adjusted for poverty reduction efficiency (to give efficient social security expenditure).

These regression results demonstrate that the efficiency adjustment to social security expenditures does indeed explain almost all of the residual variation in poverty gap reduction and outcomes. Whilst not claiming that efficiency measures are necessarily the most important in explaining welfare outcomes, this evidence certainly suggests that efficiency considerations are at least as important as either welfare expenditure or pre-transfer need.

Table 11.19.
Multiple regression of post-transfer poverty gap /gap reduction
on the pre-transfer gap and efficient social security expenditure

Gap = -0.09 + 1.02 Pre-trans Gap - 0.99 Eff.SS/GDP	R^2=0.984
$(t=20.3)$ $(t=18.5)$	adjR^2=0.979 p<0.0001
Reduction = 87.3 - 16.5 Pre-trans Gap + 18.8 Eff.SS/GDP	R^2=0.964
$(t=12.8)$ $(t=13.6)$	adjR^2=0.954 p<0.0001

A similarly high level of explanatory power in relation to inequality outcomes can be obtained by adding to the multiple regressions additional explanatory variables capturing the size of tax effort, the progressivity of social security and taxation respectively, and the degree of inefficient re-ranking. These results are not reported here because the loss of degrees of freedom in such a small sample and the presence of collinearity between the explanatory variables obscures analysis of the detailed regression results. The same general point does, however, remain. Efficiency considerations are very important in explaining the inequality outcomes.

In conclusion, in addition to the theoretical objections raised by several writers, there appears to be only qualified empirical support for the use of aggregate expenditure approaches as an indicator of the welfare levels which transfer systems produce. There seems little doubt that in the LIS sample of countries welfare effort is not correlated very strongly with welfare outcome. Adjusting expenditures for either tax expenditures, tax clawback or targeting efficiency makes the income transfer effort of the LIS countries much more homogeneous, but on their own, none of these adjustments is sufficient to significantly improve the ability to predict welfare outcomes.[5] On the other hand, adjusting for pre-transfer need (poverty or inequality) does improve the predictive power of these measures. But even effort adjusted for need leaves unexplained around 40 percent of the variation amongst LIS countries in post-transfer poverty rates and inequality.

I noted at the outset that one reason why we might seek to improve these measures is that the availability of aggregate data, particularly on a cross-national basis and in time series, is much greater than that of microdata. I have shown that adjusting social security effort by any one of the taxation, incidence or efficiency measures does very little to improve the correlations with transfer outcomes. It appears that the best approach to predicting the outcomes of expenditure would be to adjust for need. In general, this requires microdata however Gilbert and Moon (1988:331) suggest as a proxy, a composite index of unemployment levels, dependency ratios (ie the number of children and aged persons as a percentage of the workforce) and the percentage of sole parents as a means of reflecting the level of need in each country. The advantage of such an index is that the data can be obtained from a number of OECD publications and is available for most years.

The analysis presented here strongly supports the principles of Gilbert and Moon's work from the perspective of social security expenditure but it also indicates that even these 'need adjusted' measures of welfare effort are likely to be only moderately good predictors of welfare outcomes. In order to gain a complete picture of the production of welfare outcomes, we do need to analyse the efficiency with which transfer instruments translate welfare inputs into outputs.

In the following section I present summary case studies to illustrate the importance of combining analysis of efficiency considerations with analysis of both welfare expenditures and need in order to understand the welfare outcomes in the LIS countries.

11.4. Using the microdata to explain the gap between inputs and outcomes

Of the countries examined here, only Sweden, Germany and Canada appear to have outcomes commensurate with their levels of expenditure. Below I examine some of the reasons why aggregate expenditures are poor predictors of the outcomes in the remaining countries.

Countries where expenditures under-estimate outcomes

Australia spends the least of this group of countries, either in GDP or per capita terms, on social security. The level of pre-transfer need being addressed by this expenditure is close to, or slightly less than, some of the bigger spenders. Australia is ranked fourth lowest in terms of the pre-transfer head-count and gap and fifth in terms of pre-transfer inequality. While this level of expenditure is not commensurate with need, Australia's very high levels of transfer efficiency mean that it has an outcome some where in the middle to lower middle ranks. Target efficiency is the strongest explanation for its better than expected outcome. Australia is ranked the highest in terms of its poverty reduction efficiency (Chapter 5) and in terms of the progressivity of its social security system; it has the least loss to redistribution through re-ranking in social security transfers; and is ranked second to France in terms of progressivity of taxes and re-ranking losses through taxes.

The United Kingdom, like Australia, is at the bottom of this group in terms of expenditure (at least in per capita terms). Again, the UK has a much better than expected outcome. Here there are two explanations. First it is important to note that the UK starts from a much lower level of need than many countries. In terms of the pre-transfer Gini, the UK is ranked third lowest; it has the fourth lowest poverty head-count and the lowest aggregate poverty gap. Thus the initial level of need which its transfer expenditure must address is much lower than many other countries. In addition, the UK is in the middle of this group in terms of efficiency. Together, these factors produce the following outcomes - the UK is ranked sixth in terms of the head-count, first or second in terms of the poverty gap and fourth in terms of income inequality. Overall, it is the UKs starting position of a relatively more equal income distribution and low relative poverty which appears the most influential factor.

Norway is probably the country which aggregate expenditures most under-estimate in terms of outcomes. It is ranked fifth in terms of expenditure, but the level of need which this expenditure addresses is much lower than many of the larger welfare states. It is has the lowest level of pre-transfer inequality, it is fifth in terms of its pre-transfer poverty gap, and fifth in terms of the head-count. Overall it has a level of expenditure commensurate with its level of need. However, its final outcomes (usually in the top two on most measures) are strongly influenced by its comparative efficiency for the level of expenditure, and the high degree of progressivity in its tax and social security systems both of which result in very little re-ranking. The other important point to note about Norway is that it achieves considerable amount of redistribution through its tax system.

Countries where expenditures over-estimate outcomes

While France is one of the highest spenders in this group, its level of need is the greatest among all these countries. On all pre-transfer measures, France is at the bottom of the table. Its level of expenditure in GDP terms appears appropriate (ranked second) to the size of the need being addressed; however converting to a per capita basis, France falls to fourth and this is clearly one factor in explaining its poor performance in comparison with lower spending countries. On an outcomes basis France ranks fifth in terms of the head-count, sixth in terms of the gap and eighth in terms of inequality. In addition to the inappropriate level of expenditure in relation to the size of need, there are other factors which worsen France's performance. I noted in Chapter 8 that there is considerable inefficiency in the French social security system with a large loss to potential redistribution occurring through re-ranking (12%). This is particularly critical in the case of France (as opposed to Sweden for example) because it relies on the social security system to achieve 80% of its redistribution. The poor efficiency of the French system is also reflected in its overall poverty reduction efficiency which is the lowest of all these countries. The combination of the low starting point and poor efficiency of expenditure, means that France's apparently high level of welfare effort grossly over-estimates its outcomes.

The Netherlands, like France, starts from a position of great need, ranking ninth on all pre-transfer measures. Unlike France its expenditures are commensurate with this level of need, ranking first in SS/GDP terms and second in per capita terms. In outcome terms the Netherlands does well in terms of the head-count, but poorly in terms of the gap and inequality measures. A first point to note is that there are a significant number of persons reporting zero disposable incomes in this data. There may be some concern whether under-reporting of incomes may have biased the results for the Netherlands however, even if these persons are excluded from the head-count it does not change the rankings significantly. How do we explain the Netherlands position? While the Netherlands is a big spender it is also a big taxer. Of all the LIS countries, the Netherlands claws-back the highest amount of social security expenditure from recipients (43%) thus the size of the welfare effort being made which is apparent in the aggregate measures is considerably reduced once taxes are taken into account. A critical point to remember is that this is for a country which starts with a high level of need. This is also not helped by poor efficiency, the Netherlands is ranked 7th in terms of poverty reduction efficiency and loses the third highest amount of redistribution accruing to social security to re-ranking effects. The most important factor in explaining the disparity between expenditure and outcomes for the Netherlands appears to be the size of the tax clawback.

The level of need which Swiss income transfers address is about commensurate with its effort. It is ranked 6th or 7th in terms of effort and while it starts with the lowest pre-transfer head-count, it is ranked, respectively, 6th and 5th on the gap and Gini. In outcome terms Switzerland is in 8th place on the head-count; 7th on the gap and last on the Gini. The explanation for the low welfare outcome appears to be a combination of poor targeting, where expenditures are concentrated on the aged to the detriment of other pre-transfer poor groups; and a high concentration of transfers to the non-poor. Switzerland has the second highest level of spillover of social security transfers (85% of transfers which spillover do so at a level greater than 30% above the poverty line). In addition as Figure 5.5 illustrated, around 30% of all transfers accrue to just 10% of the pre-transfer non-poor population. In many countries, these inefficient transfers are partially corrected by sizeable tax clawbacks, but this is not the case for Switzerland which has the third lowest clawback rate.

The United States has an expenditure level which is commensurate with its level of pre-transfer need. With Switzerland, it ranks 6th or 7th in expenditure terms and in terms of need, it is 3rd on the head-count, 7th on the gap and 8th on the Gini. However, its outcomes are consistently the lowest of this group, ranking 10th on the head-count and gap and 9th on income inequality. The explanation for this is fairly similar to that of Switzerland. Poor efficiency of expenditures is indicated by high levels of spillover; even after tax clawback, 60% of pre-transfer poor recipients whose expenditures spillover are more than 30% above the poverty line - a level greater than that estimated for Sweden. Similar to Switzerland there is also a high degree of concentration of transfers to the non-poor. Third, the net redistribution achieved by transfers is evenly split between the social security and taxation systems. As noted earlier, transfers through the taxation system generally favour middle income earners, and this is possibly more true in the US than in any other country; for example, 80% of taxation expenditures in the US are superannuation related expenditures.[6] Overall, the US appears to devote a level of expenditure to social security which is appropriate to its needs, however a great deal of this expenditure is poorly targeted and, in the case of taxation transfers, probably regressive.

These country-specific analyses indicate that in order to understand the generation of welfare outcomes we really do need to examine the full picture: pre-transfer need, social security effort, the target efficiency and progressivity of that effort and the level and progressivity of taxation. Any one part of the transfer process will not necessarily bear a consistent relationship to outcomes. Nevertheless, I have shown that if one is limited by data availability to using aggregate data which does not contain estimates of efficiency measures, a reasonably consistent proxy for outcomes would appear to be a measure of welfare effort adjusted for pre-transfer need.

Notes

1 The terms 'leaders' and 'laggards' were first coined by Harold Wilensky (1972) and continues to be used by writers in comparative studies of welfare states.

2 In 1989-90 tax year.

3 These exemptions tend to be an important part of the tax structure in English speaking countries.

4 Appendix D shows the calculations of these estimates.

5 With the exception of tax expenditures which does improve the prediction of the net redistributive effects of transfers.

6 See Table D1, Appendix D.

12 Welfare states and welfare outcomes

In this chapter I examine the contribution which microdata based studies may potentially make to our understanding of the welfare state. It is important to again stress that in using the empirical findings set out in Part I, this chapter refers to only one component of the welfare state, *ie* the income transfer system. The comments deal with the nature of the instruments which 'produce' welfare. Section 12.1 takes this characterisation further and discusses how this literature relates to the Hill and Bramley model.

In Section 12.2 several models of the welfare state are considered in terms of their usage of the characteristics of the production instruments to distinguish different welfare state types. These models are critically assessed and a preferred typology is selected for analysis using the results of Part I. Using the preferred typology, Section 12.3 compares the outcomes of the income transfer process with the types of welfare states which have been distinguished in order to assess whether various welfare state types are associated with particular outcomes. The section also considers why we might be interested in observing the relationship between outcomes and welfare state types.

In Section 12.4 I consider the drawbacks of relying entirely on outcomes without tempering such judgements by the means by which these are achieved. Section 12.5 considers how microdata based studies may 'inform' welfare state typologies and sets out several critical aspects of transfer systems which current models may need to take into consideration in formulating such typologies. These particular aspects include: the role of taxation, which goes virtually unheeded in the analysis of welfare state types; the extent to which the characteristics of various instruments should be relied upon as a means of distinguishing different welfare state types; the extent to which the needs of different groups are met by various welfare state types; and finally efficiency issues.

12.1 The division of welfare states based on production characteristics

In my division of the literature in Chapter 10, I argued that a number of writers have focused on the characteristics of the instruments which produce welfare - or in this study, which transfer income - as a means of distinguishing different welfare state types. The welfare state typology approach differs substantially from that of writers who focus on inputs or aggregate expenditures. The limitations of the inputs based approaches were highlighted in Chapter 11. A further set of constraints on this type of approach - particularly when we come to consider generalisations about the welfare state from this one part of the process - are the limited connection between inputs and other parts of the welfare producing process. Most obviously, inputs are closely linked with policy decisions relating to how much is to be expended and on which sectors of the welfare state. This has an indirect connection with 'need'. Apart from these links, aggregate expenditures reflect nothing of how the expenditures are to be utilised and very little of what the outputs or outcomes will be.

In contrast to this are approaches to the welfare state which take their cues from the instruments of welfare production. By the 'instruments of production' I mean both the type and quality of welfare services provided by the state. For example, 'types of services' refers to the education and health systems or the means by which income is transferred (*eg*: through social security or taxation). These instruments also have qualitative characteristics: whether they are universal or selective; the nature of the 'rules' which govern access, entry and exit to programs, services or benefits; whether they act to integrate, or isolate, users/recipients from non- users/recipients. We see that the instruments of production have a very strong connection with the goals of policy. Thus the rules of access spell out quite clearly who the government intends should benefit from its welfare programs, while the level of taxes, service fees or means tests determine the extent to which different groups are subsidised.

Another aspect of 'production' characteristics is the attention it pays to how programs are financed. In this way the question of how the welfare state operates is expanded to include 'who pays?' as well as the traditional 'who benefits?' It is these qualitative connections with policy which may provide a stronger basis for production-based studies of welfare states as compared with those based solely on expenditure.

12.2 Three welfare state typologies compared

From the brief description in the previous section it will be clear that there are numerous production characteristics which could potentially be used to compare welfare states. For example, the rules of access to welfare services or benefits; the means by which these services and benefits are financed; the balance of choice between types of instruments which can achieve similar ends - such as direct transfers through the social security system versus indirect transfer through the taxation system; whether responsibility for income maintenance rests predominantly with the market, state or family. I examine below three welfare state typologies which use differing characteristics to distinguish various welfare state types.

Institutional, industrial achievement and residual welfare states

One of the earliest typologies of the welfare state was that developed by Titmuss (1974:30-31). While not referring directly to his models as those of welfare states - he used instead the term 'model of social policy' - Titmuss made a division between three models based essentially on the extent to which welfare policy is distanced from the market.

In the residual model, needs are met either through the market or the family. Only when these break down should the social security net come into play and then, most crucially for this model, only temporarily.

His second model is the industrial achievement-performance model where there is a significant role for social security as an adjunct to economic requirements. In this model social needs are met on the basis of merit, work performance and productivity. Titmuss noted that an important product of this model was 'the formation of class and group loyalties.'

The third model is the institutional redistributive model in which Titmuss (1974:31) describes social welfare policy as:

> ... a major integrated institution in society, providing universalistic services operating outside the market system on the principle of need... It is basically a model incorporating systems of redistribution in command-over-resources through time.

In discussing these models, Titmuss (1974) assigns the US to the residual model, appears to argue that the UK is a combination of the residual and industrial achievement models, and implies that the Scandinavian countries are examples of the institutional model.[1]

Social welfare, social security and positive states

Furniss and Tilton (1977) identify three types of welfare states. They argue that while most modern democratic states do address difficulties arising from the operation of the market, the extent of intervention varies significantly:

> ... the major issue is not that all states have a policy of intervention, but that different states employ different policies for different purposes. Abstracting from the historical record, we can aggregate these different forms of intervention in three 'models': the *positive state*, the *social security state*, and the *social welfare state*.[2]

In their typology the positive state is identified by the limitation of government intervention to what is necessary to enhance economic efficiency - for example, the maintenance of employment levels which ensure

183

a high level of consumption - and to protect property holders both from the difficulties arising from unregulated markets and from potential redistributive demands. In the field of welfare, there is a disinclination to do anything which is inconsistent with such efficiency concerns. So we find welfare states whose programs are strongly shaped by concerns with disincentive effects and where the emphasis is on social insurance programs, whether privately or publicly funded. This model partly corresponds to Titmuss' residual welfare model in terms of its 'safety net' attributes, but differs in respect of the location of social insurance schemes.

The social security state has similar characteristics as the positive state but makes sharper distinctions between economic and social policy concerns, for example, social policy is not entirely conditional on efficiency concerns. Most importantly, Furniss and Tilton argue, it is the adoption of a **guaranteed** national minimum - whether in terms of income, access to educational or health services - which distinguishes these two types of states.

Social welfare states present a radical alternative to the former approaches by placing social goals before economic goals. Such a state, they argue, uses its power in more radical ways to ensure equality. Here economic and wages policies are employed in concert with social policy to achieve this end; and public services remove important sectors of social life from the influence of market forces.

Social democratic, corporativist and liberal welfare states

Esping-Andersen (1989,1990) describes three clusters of welfare 'regime-types' which he distinguishes by their different arrangements between the state, the market and the family. In the first cluster, he defines the liberal welfare state:

> ... in which means-tested assistance, modest universal transfers, or modest social insurance plans predominate. These cater mainly to a clientele of low income, usually working class, state dependents.[3]

Like the residual and positive categories described above, Esping-Andersen notes the strong policy concerns of liberal states with disincentive effects and its encouragement of private insurance. The second regime-type he identifies as corporativist states where:

> ... the liberal obsession with market efficiency and commodification was never pre-eminent and, as such, the granting of social rights was hardly ever a seriously contested issue. What predominated was the preservation of status differentials; rights, therefore, were attached to class and status.[4]

In addition these regimes have a strong commitment to maintaining traditional family patterns. This aspect, which Esping-Andersen considers as a strong characteristic of these welfare states, Titmuss treats as marginal and a characteristic of the residual model, and Furniss and Tilton ignore. Esping-Andersen (1989:25) notes two examples where family patterns play a role in the shape of such welfare states. The first is connected with patterns of assumed female dependency and traditional roles hence 'day care and similar family services remain conspicuously underdeveloped.' The second is the case of German unemployment assistance, in which, once entitlements to normal insurance benefits are exhausted, continued eligibility depends on the resources of the immediate family, irrespective of age or residency.

Social democratic regimes are identified by the 'emancipation' of policy from both the market and the family. So that on the one hand, the individual has to rely on neither the market nor the family for income support; while on the other, the state ensures that the individual has the guarantee of employment, thereby obviating the need for such support:

> Perhaps the most salient characteristic of the social democratic regime is its fusion of welfare and work. It is...a welfare state genuinely committed to a full employment guarantee... and entirely dependent on its attainment. On the one side, it is a model in which the right to work has equal status to the right of income protection. On the other side, the enormous costs of maintaining ...[the] welfare system means that it must minimize social problems and and maximize revenue income. This is obviously best done with most people working, and the fewest possible living off social transfers.[5]

The correspondence between typologies

In Table 12.1, I use the central characteristics of the welfare state types distinguished by these authors, to nominate the group to which each of the LIS countries belongs. In the case of Esping-Andersen this classification is based on the assignment of countries reported by him in his recent work (1990:52). In the other two cases the assignment is approximate, based on the key characteristics of the systems described by the authors combined with any published assignment of countries. In the case of Furniss and Tilton, their work identified only Sweden, the UK and the US as archetypal examples of respectively social welfare, social security and positive states.

Table 12.1.
The classification of the LIS countries according to the three typologies

Titmuss		Furniss and Tilton		Esping-Andersen	
	Sweden	*Social*	Sweden	*Social*	Sweden
Institutional	Norway	*welfare*	Norway	*democratic*	Norway
	Netherlands		Netherlands		Netherlands
	Germany		Germany		Switzerland
Industrial	France	*Social*	France	*Corporativist*	Germany
achievement	Switzerland	*security*	Switzerland		France
?	UK		UK		UK
?	Australia		Australia		Australia
Residual	Canada	*Positive*	Canada	*Liberal*	Canada
	USA		USA		USA

Comparing these typologies we see that, at the extremes, these authors are in agreement with respect to Sweden, Norway and the Netherlands as countries in which the welfare state is entrenched and pursuing policy goals with a strong egalitarian emphasis. At the other extreme the US and Canada are considered by the authors as having minimalist welfare states, where programs have a precarious existence, fill the gaps left by the market, and are

185

strongly oriented towards individual rather than collective responsibility for welfare.

In between these extremes, the picture is not so clear. Partly this may reflect incorrect assignment of the countries int his work, but it may also reflect some fundamental difficulties in operationalising these concepts. For example Ringen (1987:13) questions whether the degree of institutionalism present in welfare states can be demonstrated:

> The degree of institutionalism in welfare states needs to be demonstrated empirically but has hitherto for the most part been postulated as a property of particular welfare states. Such empirical inquiries as have been made suggest that the distinction in the use of means between marginal and institutional types may not be tenable.[6]

Looking at some cases where typologies are unclear we see that Switzerland and the UK pose great difficulties for these authors. In the case of the UK it is clear that Furniss and Tilton and to some extent Titmuss would not consider it a positive or residual state in the same way as the US. Like the institutional states, there is a safety net of programs available to all, irrespective of past contributions. Unlike the institutional states, benefit levels are not generous and programs aim for a minimum guarantee rather than income replacement, and using this characteristic, Esping-Andersen does group the UK with the US.

In the case of Switzerland a great deal of ambiguity is also present. This may be best illustrated by Esping-Andersen's development of his typology. Writing in 1989 (p.25), he argued that Switzerland approximates the liberal model. In 1990 (p.52) using his de-commodification scale, Switzerland is placed clearly in the corporativist model.[7]

For both Titmuss and Esping-Andersen, Australia is identified along with Canada and the US as a residual or liberal welfare state type. On the other hand, Furniss and Tilton's classification would place Australia more closely to the UK and its flat-rate, means-tested transfer system part of the social security model, by virtue of its guaranteed minimum.

The purpose in comparing the differences between these typologies is not to demonstrate any fundamental confusion in the literature. Rather that, depending on the characteristics of production in which one is most interested, one can be lead to quite different groupings of countries.

There is one critical difference between the authors discussed above. That is that the first two, Titmuss and Furniss and Tilton, are largely ahistorical in their approach to welfare state types. Their division of welfare states into different types depends on a 'snapshot' of the welfare state instruments in place at a particular point in time as a basis on which to assign countries to different models. By contrast, Esping-Andersen brings not only an historical understanding of the development of these systems to his classification but also the political and social contexts which maintain their character. This is a strength of the Esping-Andersen model to which I will return later in this chapter. For the present I have chosen the Esping-Andersen model to consider whether there is a relationship between welfare state types and outcomes.

This choice has been made for two reasons: first, the assignment of the LIS countries to Esping-Andersen's regime-types is unambiguous, based on his assignment through the de-commodification index (1990:52); second, the historical perspective which Esping-Andersen brings to his typology increases the explanatory power of his typology since it describes not only what different states 'look like' in the present, but how they got there.

Before moving on to the question of the relationship between welfare state types and outcomes, I flag here several issues arising from the foregoing discussion for later consideration. If the validity of these typologies rests on the characteristics of the instruments of production, are the selected characteristics the most appropriate? Are there key characteristics missing from these typologies? More fundamentally, are typologies which are based on the characteristics of the production instruments empirically sustainable?

12.3. Comparing Esping-Andersen's typology with outcomes

Are different welfare state types consistently associated with particular outcomes? At first sight this question may appear as a somewhat mechanistic, or even tangential, concern to the higher aim of sketching out more qualitative aspects of the welfare state. In defence, I would argue that there is a tendency in the comparative literature to divorce the outcomes of different welfare states from their production characteristics and use the latter to make judgements about what a 'good' welfare state does and how it operates as opposed to a 'bad' welfare state. Such judgements may only be justified to a large extent on the basis of what outcomes these good and bad states produce. As Ringen (1987:26) notes that 'the welfare state can be said to work if the strategy of redistribution is successful.'

While this study would not claim that outcomes are the entire basis for making judgement about different welfare states - and in the following sections I examine some other aspects - they should count for a substantial part of such judgements. To this end, Table 12.2 shows the characterisation of countries in this study based on Esping-Andersen's typology and his rankings based on his de-commodification scores.[8] The table also shows country ranks for the outcome measures derived in Part I.

Table 12.2.
A comparison of Esping-Andersen's regime-types with post-transfer outcomes

| | Esping-Andersen typology | | Outcomes rankings post-transfer | | | | | |
	Welfare state type	Rank	Head-count	Red'n in count	Poverty gap	Red'n in gap	Gini coeff.	Net Redist.
Sweden		1	2	1	2	2	1	1
Norway	*Social*	2	1	2	3	4	2	2
N'lands	*democratic*	3	4	5	9	7	7	4
Switzerland		4	8	8	7	8	10	10
Germany	*Corporat-*	5	3	3	4	3	3	3
France	*ivist*	6	5	4	6	5	8	5
UK		7	6	6	1	1	4	6
Canada		8	9	9	8	9	6	8
USA	*Liberal*	9	10	10	10	10	9	9
Australia		10	7	7	5	6	5	7

An important point to make at the outset is that the outcomes observed here relate to the transfer systems in place in the early 1980s, fortunately this is also the period for which Esping-Andersen has constructed his de-commodification index. Thus the two frameworks of analysis coincide quite closely, with the exception of the Netherlands. For the reasons discussed in Chapter 2 - concerning the macro-economic business cycle - this difference in timing for the Netherlands may be of critical importance. Therefore I exclude the Netherlands from the ensuing analysis, noting only that it appears to be one of the cases in which Esping-Andersen's typology does not coincide with the pattern of outcomes.

Examining Table 12.2 we see that in general there is a reasonable degree of clustering of outcomes which sits well with Esping-Andersen's typology. However, there are three countries which consistently have de-commodification scores that are not closely linked with outcomes, suggesting that they may well be miscast and that there may be some fundamental problems with the de-commodification index. I will discuss these weaknesses in the latter part of this section.

To begin with, the Swiss welfare state clearly does not produce outcomes commensurate with the other corporativist states in this study. Indeed the outcomes would clearly indicate that Switzerland might be more appropriately grouped with Canada and the US. Recalling the discussion of Chapter 11, I noted that the distribution of transfers in Switzerland is highly skewed, concentrated on some groups, particularly the aged, to the exclusion of others. This is one aspect of the operation of the welfare state which typologies based on legalistic rules of entitlement cannot capture. In addition, as the spillover estimates for Switzerland show, the Swiss pension system is indeed generous, thus scoring highly on Esping-Andersen's index. But in outcome terms this generosity may well be to the detriment of others who are in need. It would seem that Esping-Andersen's first approximation of Switzerland as belonging to the liberal group of countries (1989:25) was more appropriate than that suggested by the de-commodification index.

The next country which appears to be seriously miscast by this index is the UK. In terms of the poverty gap and the level of income inequality, the outcomes of the UK system are closer to the corporativist group of countries. In a similar vein, but to a lesser extent, this is also true of of Australia. This is not to suggest that these countries in any way resemble the corporativist countries in terms of the institutional features of their welfare states, but rather, via other routes, these countries have achieved a level of outcome similar to the corporativist states.

A key aspect of these 'other routes' - and one which deeply influences the outcomes in these countries - is the extensive use of means-tested, flat-rate benefits which effectively fill the gaps left after the operation of the market. One could argue that this appears **on paper** not to be so very different from the situation obtaining in say the US and Canada.[9] However, there are some quite important distinctions to be made here. First, there is no time limit on these benefits (especially unemployment benefits) in Australia and the UK; nor are there rules which disqualify the unemployed from benefit receipt because of the circumstances under which employment was lost.

Sinfield (1978:132) also draws these distinctions when comparing unemployment benefits in the UK and US.

Second, the Esping-Andersen de-commodification index includes a score for the contribution period required to qualify for a pension (Esping-Andersen, 1990:54). However, such a weighting is not possible for Australia as all pensions and benefits are financed from general revenue.[10] Esping-Andersen's solution is to give a score of zero for means-tested payments, yet this seems contradictory in terms of de-commodification. The very fact that pensions and benefits are not premised on labour force attachment suggests that these might be given the top score. This observation is supported historically by the fact that that the British Fabians and the social reformers in Australia at the turn of the century held the view that means-testing was an evident principle of social justice (Castles,1985:15,102). In Australia this was partly held to be so because general revenue financing -ie through progressive taxation - implied a cross-subsidisation from the better-off to the less well-off over the life-cycle (Castles,1985:22).

Together these characteristics would suggest that these guaranteed minimum benefits in Australia and the UK are more highly de-commodified than the Esping-Andersen index would lead us to believe.

One last aspect of this index, which is also a general point about what should be measured, concerns the generosity of benefits. Low replacement rates, particularly for age pensions, in the Anglo-Saxon countries should be offset by other considerations. For example, the LIS data shows (circa 1980) that in Australia around 80% of aged families owned - or were buying - their own home. Conversely, in Sweden home ownership amongst the aged was around 20%. The income needs of the aged in these two countries are therefore likely to be very different.[11] Thus for a large percentage of the aged population the need for more generous pensions to cover housing costs may not be as imperative in Australia (and other welfare states where home ownership is the norm amongst the aged population) as in other welfare states. One could argue that the two systems simply provide alternative means for financing housing costs for the aged - Australia through private saving and investment, Sweden through state saving and provision. For this reason replacement rates should be carefully considered against other aspects of social policy.

To return to Esping-Andersen's model, Castles and Mitchell (1990) propose that a fourth type of welfare state can be identified by separating from Esping-Andersen's 'liberal' category those countries with a labourite tradition. Countries in this category would include the UK, Australia, New Zealand and Ireland. While labour party power in these countries has been weaker than in the Scandinavian countries it is important to note that many of the reforms which have shaped present day transfer policies have been either initiated by, or enacted with, labour party support.[12]

Apart from historical and political arguments which can be mustered from the literature, there is strong support for this fourth grouping from the empirical evidence presented in Part I. If we examine Figures 4.5, 4.10 and 7.3 which map out, respectively, the reduction in the poverty head-count against the post-transfer head-count; the reduction in the poverty gap against the post-transfer gap; and the net redistribution against the post-transfer Gini index of inequality; we see that the UK and Australia are quite distinctly separated from Canada and the US.

If this fourth category is added to the Esping-Andersen model, it does indeed provide a very persuasive view of the variations in the welfare state across OECD countries. In addition to its clear distinctions based on institutional and historical features, such a model clearly associates particular welfare state types with particular outcomes.

12.4. Vices and virtues: alternative approaches to income transfer systems

In the previous section I stressed that outcomes from welfare producing processes - and in this instance from income transfers - should be a major concern of welfare state analysts, particularly if they wish to move from simple type-casting exercises to normative and prescriptive judgements.

In emphasising the outcomes of these processes in terms of the distribution of disposable incomes, the aim is not to exclude qualitative considerations concerning the 'means' of welfare production. Quite clearly, as many writers have insisted, welfare state instruments which stigmatise recipients, confer unequal status or are otherwise socially divisive must be questioned as to their appropriateness as a welfare producing instrument, independently of these outcomes. Unfortunately the tendency of the welfare state literature has been to **assert** that certain types of instruments are associated with social division and stigma, and these writers can do little else since very few empirical studies have been conducted to discover the exact extent of such divisiveness. In reality we have very little comparative evidence about whether recipients feel more or less stigmatised by different transfer regimes; whether this has prevented them from taking up benefits to which they are entitled; or whether society wants changes in the form or structure of its transfer systems.

Taking the case of Australia as an example of what many writers consider as a highly stigmatised system by virtue of its extensive income-testing arrangements, what evidence is there for the existence of dissatisfaction with its welfare system?

One recent study in Australia has attempted to gauge the satisfaction of the population toward the current **form** of provision (*ie* the characteristics of the pension system rather than payment levels) of age pensions and private superannuation. The study showed that 90% of respondents felt that it was 'very' or 'fairly' important that the present provisions continue in their current form (Papadakis,1990).

But mostly the evidence we do have is largely indirect. For example, the Australian Department of Social Security (1989:25) has estimated that take-up rates for most basic pension and benefit programs is in excess of 95% of the eligible population. This is confirmed in the LIS data in two ways: the number of families reporting zero disposable income is extremely low (Table 2.6), as is the percentage of pre-transfer poor families who do not receive any form of social security transfer (Table 5.9). Admittedly this evidence is lacking in respect of families who do not take up assistance which is supplemental to market incomes.

While this evidence is unavoidably scant, it does suggest that commonly held beliefs regarding different transfer instruments may be out-dated and empirically dubious.[13] We need substantially more empirical research, along the lines suggested earlier, before making judgements in favour of or against different transfer instruments or, by extension, ascribing deleterious effects to the operation of particular instruments. At the very least these problems should be considered on a country by country basis. For example, the experience of means testing in the UK may be very different from income testing in Australia and New Zealand.

12.5. Using microdata studies to 'inform' welfare state typologies

In Chapter 10 I argued that, at a superficial level, microdata based studies 'complete' the picture of the outcomes of welfare production processes. I also noted that microdata has potentially a much more powerful role in linking together the various stages of this production process. Using the example of income transfers, we see from the empirical analysis in Part I that microdata has much to say about questions of efficiency, distribution and incidence of income transfers.

Utilising these findings it may be possible to clear up some of the differences in the categorisation of welfare state types evident in the literature. This argument may be pursued in two ways. First, there is a vast difference between the stated intentions of various programs and their actual operation. As Section 12.3 noted, in theory the rules of entitlement and eligibility of various transfer systems may convey a quite different picture to that which is presented by the actual incidence of transfers within the population. If microdata are used to the fullest extent it may be possible to overcome, for example, some of the blurred distinction between residual or positive states and institutional or social security states.

A second way of using microdata may be to introduce into welfare state analyses a greater tolerance of alternative policies or instruments and the way welfare states are viewed and categorised.[14] There is no doubt that the welfare literature is permeated by normative judgements concerning 'good' and 'bad' welfare producing processes. Consider the following examples. In discussing the Australian welfare state Heidenheimer et al (1990:241) note:

The results were those typical of all means-tested public assistance programs. The examination of personal financial resources required by such state charity continued to arouse resentment and shame.

Or Esping-Andersen's assertion (1990:48):

One type of system, historically most pronounced in the Anglo-Saxon nations, builds entitlement around demonstrable and abject need.

191

Such characterisations may lead to unwarranted judgements about what type of programs qualify as 'legitimate' welfare state instruments. Nowhere is this more clear than Esping-Andersen's recent observation (1989:19):

> Others spend disproportionately on means-tested social assistance. Few contemporary analysts would agree that a reformed poor relief tradition qualifies as a welfare state commitment.

How can the use of microdata help to assess the validity of such assertions? While it is difficult to counter the views expressed above without the evidence from the type of surveys discussed in the previous section, the LIS data for example, shows that income-tested systems in Australia and the UK, *circa* 1980, had a significant impact on poverty and inequality.

Set in a broader context, there are two ways in which microdata may assist in determining the importance of alternative policy instruments. The first is highlighted by Heidenheimer et al (1990: 11):

> Similar outcomes may be achieved through a range of policy instruments, while ostensibly similar policies may well be associated with quite different outcomes.

Here Heidenheimer is re-focusing arguments about different policy instruments and approaches by emphasising that outcomes may be independent of the policy instrument. This implies that there may be some doubt whether production characteristics are an accurate guide to distinguishing welfare states.

Secondly, at a more fundamental level Ringen (1987:12) questions whether the conventional characterisation of different policy approaches is tenable:

> ... truly universal programs are, in fact, very rare. Even large welfare states commonly have a number of income-tested benefits, such as social assistance, housing support and family support for child care.

> ... A search for selectivity in the Swedish welfare state, presumably the model institutional type, has revealed that, although selectivity by income is not widespread, the system is thoroughly selective by occupational experience so that clients with different careers in gainful employment have different rights to benefits.

Ringen therefore introduces another element into this debate: are we sure that the conventional labels which are attached to different policy instruments, and the assumptions we make about the usage of such instruments in different countries, appropriate or accurate? This study cannot, of course, give detailed answers to such intriguing questions. However, I feel that the evidence presented in Part I suggests that there may be room for doubting these 'conventional wisdoms' of the literature.

In the following discussion I use the microdata to comment on which policy instruments, and which characteristics of these instruments, appear to be the most critical in determining how the LIS countries depart from existing typologies.

Which characteristics are important?

Using the evidence from Part I it is reasonable to conclude that one of the weakest aspects of the current comparative welfare state literature is its lack of attention to the operation and characteristics of taxation instruments. This seems a curious omission from present-day analysis, since Titmuss (1974) and subsequent writers, stressed the importance of fiscal welfare and its growth alongside of the more apparent manifestations of the welfare state.

There are four issues which I wish to consider here: the fundamental influence which taxation has on outcomes; the differential use of the taxation system for redistribution in different welfare states; the seemingly contradictory stance taken in the literature on state intrusiveness in administering means-tests with respect to welfare benefits in comparison with the administration and enforcement of taxation; and the absence of any characterisation of the taxation system as part of the general characterisation of welfare state types.

The influence of taxation on transfer outcomes has been demonstrated at several levels in this study. First, at the aggregate level, Table 5.11 shows that in some countries there is an extremely large gap between social security expenditure and the amount of that expenditure which is actually retained in family disposable income. My estimates of the proportion of clawback through the tax system range from 43% in the Netherlands to 11% in France.

Secondly, disaggregating the clawback by family type, Table 5.14 shows that the taxation systems in the social democratic countries achieve precisely the same effect as income-tests in some of the 'liberal' states: that is they do distinguish on the basis of income the level of income transfers which should be retained in household disposable income. Consider this description by Heidenheimer et al (1990:246):

> Sweden's approach is dominated by a strategy of common entitlement whereby all citizens participate in the same programs (while benefit taxation, income-related fees, contributions and so on vary the extent to which people are subsidized.)

A counter point to this which is frequently made in the literature (see Heidenheimer et al, 1990:241) is that the disadvantage of income-testing benefits at point of receipt is the intrusiveness of the state in its 'examination of personal financial resources'. Yet in the same volume, the intrusiveness of the state in collecting taxes, passes without comment on what would appear to be a similar level of scrutiny. For example:

> In Sweden inspectors can refer cases for scrutiny by local tax boards - one for each area of 2,000 inhabitants - whose members will be knowledgeable about their neighbors' lifestyles.[15]

> Among small business people in Germany the more frequent confrontation with tax officials have fed an undercurrent of hostility, with the officials themselves complaining about the difficulty of enforcing overly detailed regulations ... Moreover, prosecutions there are relentless.[16]

These examples expose a good deal of uncertainty on the part of comparative theorists in approaching the taxation side of the transfer process. There appears to be a reluctance to apply the same analytical frameworks to indirect transfers (*ie* taxes) as those applied to direct transfers. In part, this may be due to the traditional separation of taxation from welfare concerns on the grounds that taxation does have other functions, and revenues are raised from sources other than income-earners.

Counter to this, is Titmuss' (1974) observations concerning the role of fiscal welfare and the more obvious fact that taxation cannot be passed off as being unrelated to the operation of the welfare state, if for no other reason than the intimate connection between taxation and the levels of funds available for social welfare expenditure (Sinfield;1978:152). Moreover, there is little room for doubt that taxation systems are designed to interact with social security systems in quite specific ways. We have only to look at the evidence (presented in Chapter 5) on the clawback of benefits to infer intentionality in all systems to clawback transfers from the non-poor and most strikingly in the social democratic states to clawback the generous payments which spillover the poverty line.

Additionally, this study has shown that the taxation system plays a vital role by virtue of the extent of its progressivity in achieving not just redistribution between the economically active and passive population but also amongst the economically active population itself. Evidence for this can be found in Table 7.6 which shows the percentage of net redistribution which accrues to social security and to taxation. If the redistribution of the tax system was limited only to that from the economically active to the economically passive population, then the social security system would account for 100% of net redistribution. In fact, the level of redistribution accruing to social security is at a maximum of 80% in Sweden and is as low as 50% in the US. This suggests that taxation is itself a transfer instrument whose characteristics should be considered in any typology of the welfare state. Whether taxation is an **effective** instrument, and who benefits from its transfers, is a matter of considerable import for all these welfare states.

How might we take account of the characteristics of the taxation instrument in distinguishing different welfare state types? This study offers some initial possibilities: the degree of progressivity; the level of reliance on taxation to redistribute income; and the size of the clawback. Other writers such as Heidenheimer et al (1990:200-216) distinguish more qualitative aspects such as degrees of self-assessment in taxation returns, the growth of tax expenditures, and the level of detail in taxation codes.

The incidence of transfers

It is in the area of incidence of transfers which microdata studies have potentially the most to offer to the study of the welfare state. While questions of incidence have been an underlying theme of much of this chapter, this issue requires some separate treatment. A first consideration is one on which I touched earlier with regard to the gap between the statements of legal rules of entitlement, instrument characteristics and so on and how these are played out in terms of actual incidence and final outcomes. I have indicated that there are a number of intervening factors which can be concretely established from the microdata (*eg:* taxation, efficiency and distributional intentions) which affect the incidence of transfers. However, there are also less tangible blocks to the translation of instrument characteristics into outcomes. Thus for example, administrative tactics may be employed to discourage, deny or delay benefit entitlement.

Secondly, Part I of this study examined the impact of transfers, not from a beneficiary type perspective but using broader family type characteristics. A distinct advantage of this approach is that we are not confined to examining those groups which are expected to benefit from income transfers but rather we can examine the level of need from an income perspective, regardless of status. To spell this out more clearly, consider the example of Esping-Andersen's de-commodification index which is based on a series of judgements comparing three types of benefits: age pensions, unemployment and sickness benefits. I noted earlier that there was a considerable gap between Switzerland's de-commodification score (and ranking) and the outcomes of the transfer process evident in the LIS data. One possible explanation for this is that much of the Swiss welfare state is concerned with provision for the aged, and less with other needy groups such as lone parents and working families with children. The Swiss welfare state, like Australia, the US and to a lesser extent Germany, is quite 'unbalanced' in its poverty alleviation efforts. This may indicate that another characteristic which typologies of welfare state types should take into consideration is the extent to which different systems address a range of needs rather than confining analysis to a few selected benefit types.

A last issue concerns the extent to which income transfers accrue to the non-poor while at the same time considerable numbers of families remain poor, and sizeable poverty gaps exist, post-transfer. There seems little point in proclaiming any type of welfare state regime 'successful' or 'more successful' when, after sizeable amounts of expenditure have been pushed through the transfer system, between 4 and 16 percent of families in this sample of countries remain poor.

This point is even more telling when we consider that all of the LIS countries devote a level of resources to income transfers (measured in GDP terms) which is more than sufficient to close the pre-transfer poverty gap in each country.[17] Here I suggest that efficiency issues must receive more than a cursory glance in welfare state typologies and that such issues should not be necessarily considered in a negative fashion (see for example Heidenheimer et al, 1990: 250). As Chapter 11 demonstrated, efficiency is a central element in explaining the outcomes observed in the LIS countries.

Notes

[1] The assignment of these countries is scattered throughout the essays in the volume.

[2] Furniss and Tilton (1977:15), original emphasis.

195

3   Esping-Andersen (1989:25), this framework is maintained in his latter publication.

4 Ibid.

5 Ibid,26.

6   Ringen (1987:13). Unfortunately, Ringen does not reference these 'empirical inquiries'.

7   See the description of the de-commodification index in the following footnote.

8   Esping-Andersen (1990: 49-54). In his work de-commodification for age pensions is measured by an additive index based on: the minimum replacement rates of pensions; standard pension rates; the contribution period required to qualify for a standard pension; and the share of financing by the individual. For sickness and unemployment benefits de-commodification is measured in terms of: replacement rates; contribution period to qualify; number of waiting days before benefits are paid; number of weeks for which a benefit is maintained.

9 The UK system of benefits to the unemployed is somewhat complicated and potentially misleading in that there is a contribution-based and time-limited 'unemployment benefit'; but this defaults to the generic social security benefit when entitlement runs out, or if there is no entitlement, and for most beneficiaries there is little or no difference in the level of payments - indeed 'unemployment benefits' are often topped-up by social security payments.

10   In the case of the UK the mix of general revenue financing and social insurance contributions varies with pension and benefit type. The critical point (see previous footnote) is that when benefits based on contributions run out or is insufficient, payments either default to, or are supplemented by, payments from general revenue .

11   In Australia, policy analysts use an estimate of 25% of gross income to reflect housing costs.

12   Castles, 1985: Chapter 2 *passim*.

13   Theoretically, it is also possible to counter some of these assertions - at least from the Australian perspective - by observing that the Australian system since 1986 is totally income-tested and therefore no distinction is made between beneficiary categories. If one source of stigma lies in the realm of perceptions of differences in treatment between ostensibly identical claimants, then it is the status-preserving systems which may be more likely to engender stigmatisation.

14   A useful analogy here may be Esping-Andersen's comments on the Swedocentrism which the class-mobilisation thesis reflects (1990:17). In the same way that this thesis is informed by the Swedish experience, so too taking Swedish income transfer systems as a norm may divert us from a more informed view of the alternative routes to successful redistributive strategies.

15   Heidenheimer et al (1990:201).

16 Ibid.

17 Compare Tables 4.6 to 4.8 (aggregate pre-transfer poverty gap as a percentage of GDP) with 11.1. (social security expenditure as a percentage of GDP).

PART III
APPENDICES

Appendix A
Luxembourg Income Study database description

Table A.1.
Data sets in the first wave of LIS

Country	Year	Survey source	Sample
*Australia	1981-82	Income and Housing Survey	15985
*Canada	1981	Survey of Consumer Finances	15136
*France	1979	Survey of Individual Income Tax Returns	11044
France	1981	INED-CERC Survey of Women & Children	3639
*Germany	1981	1981 German Transfer Survey	2727
Israel	1979	Family Expenditure Survey	2271
*Netherlands	1983	Survey of Income and Program Users	4833
*Norway	1979	Survey of Norwegian Tax Files	10414
*Sweden	1981	Swedish Income Distribution Survey	9625
*Switzerland	1982	Swiss Income and Wealth Survey	7036
*United Kingdom	1979	Family Expenditure Survey	6888
*United States	1979	March Current Population Survey	15225

* Indicates the data sets used in this study.

Table A.2.
Data sets in the second wave of LIS

Country	Year	Survey source	Country	Year	Survey source
Australia	1985	Income and Housing Survey	Lux'bourg	1985	Household Panel Study
Belgium	1985		N'lands	1987	Income and Program Users
Canada	1987	Survey of Consumer Finances	Poland	1986	Household Budget Survey
Germany	1984	German Panel Survey	Sweden	1987	Income Distribution Survey
Hungary	1987		UK	1986	Family Expenditure Survey
Israel	1986	Family Expenditure Survey	USA	1985	Current Population Survey
Italy	1986	Bank of Italy Income Survey			

Table A.3.
Income Variables

Variable	Variable description	Variable	Variable description
V1	Wage and Salary Income (Gross)	V22	Maternity Allowances
V2	Mandatory Employer Contributions	V23	Military/Veterans' Benefits
V3	Nonmandatory Employer Contrib's	V24	Other Social Insurance
V4	Farm Self-Employment Income	V25	Means-Tested Cash Benefits
V5	Nonfarm Self-Employment Income	V26	Near Cash Benefits
V6	In-Kind Earnings	V27	Food Benefits
V7	Mand. Contrib'ns: Self-Employed	V28	Housing Benefits
V8	Income from Property	V29	Medical Benefits
V9	Noncash Property Income	V30	Heating Allowances
V10	Market Value of Residence	V31	Education Benefits
V11	Income Tax	V32	Private Pensions
V12	Property or Wealth Taxes	V33	Public Sector Pensions
V13	Mandatory Employee Contributions	V34	Alimony/Child Support
V14	Other Direct Taxes	V35	Other Regular Private Income
V15	Indirect Taxes	V36	Other Cash Income
V16	Sick Pay	V37	Realized Lump Sum Payments
V17	Accident Pay	V38	Total (or Net) Income
V18	Disability Pay	V39	Head — Net Wage/Salary
V19	Social Retirement Benefits	V40	Head — Hourly Wage Rate
V20	Child or Family Allowance	V41	Spouse — Net Wage/Salary
V21	Unemployment Pay	V42	Spouse — Hourly Wage Rate

Table A.4.
Derived Variables (available for all countries)

SELFI=	Income from Self Employment	= V4 + V5
EARNING=	Earnings	= V1 + V4 + V5
PENSIOI=	Pension Income	= V32 + V33
MEANSI=	Means-tested Income	= V25 + V26
OTHSOCI=	Other Social Security	= V16 + V17 + V18 + V22 +V23 + V24
SOCI=	Total Social Security	= V19 + V20 + V21 + OTHSOCI
SOCTRANS=	Social Transfers Total	= MEANSI + SOCI
PRIVATI=	Private Income	= V34 + V35
PAYROLL=	Payroll Taxes	= V7 + V13
FI=	Factor Income	= EARNINGS + V8
TRANSI=	Transfer Income	= SOCI + MEANSI + PRIVATI
MI=	Market Income	= FI + PENSIOI
GI=	Gross Income	= MI + TRANSI + V36
DPI=	Disposable Income	= GI-V11-PAYROLL
PI=	Per Capita Income	= DPI/D4

Table A.5.
Demographic Variables

Var	Variable description	Var	Variable description
D1	Age-Head	D17	Spouse — Industry Classification
D2	Age-Spouse	D18	Head — Type of Worker Group
D3	Sex-Head	D19	Spouse — Type of Worker Group
D4	Persons in Family (Unit)	D20	Location Indicator — Rural/Urban
D5	Family Structure	D21	Marital Status of Head
D6	Number Earners	D22	Housing Tenure
D7	Location farm, non farm	D23	Head — Full-Time, Part-Time
D8	Ethnicity -Head	D24	Spouse — Full-Time, Part-Time
D9	Head — Race	D25	Head — Disability Status
D10	Head — Level of Education	D26	Spouse — Disability Status
D11	Spouse — Level of Education	D27	Number of Children Under 18
D12	Head — Occupational Training	D28	Age Youngest Child
D13	Spouse — Occupational Training	LFSHD	Head — Labour Force Status
D14	Head — Occupation	LFSSP	Spouse — Labour Force Status
D15	Spouse — Occupation	HRSHD	Head — Hours Worked Per Week
D16	Head — Industry Classification	HRSSP	Spouse — Hours Worked Per Week

The unit of analysis variable

The following discussion is drawn from notes prepared by the LIS Technical Director, John Coder. The LIS variable D5 *'Family Structure'* assists researchers to identify the type of unit for which the data was originally collected. In Chapter 1 I set out the problems associated with comparing data from different types of units. Here I describe the types of units for which data was collected in each country.

Australia, Germany, UK, US: These countries' databases allow the choice between household and family units. The variable D5 has the following values:

    1= Single family household

    2= Multi-family household

    3= Separate family from a multi-family household

    Selecting cases where D5= 1 or 2, yields household units for analysis; selecting 1 or 3 yields family units.

Switzerland: only family records are available. D5=1.

Canada: the unit of observation in Canada is the 'economic unit'. Coder notes that the definition is based on household relationships and is virtually identical to the family definition used in the US. D5=4.

Netherlands: the data from The Netherlands is for households only, D5=5.

Norway and Sweden: these units are coded D5=6 to indicate that they are based on taxation or administrative units. Coder notes that in the past these have been loosely termed as families. As noted in Chapter 1 however, in Sweden unmarried persons over the age of 18 years are considered as separate units and not as 'family' members if they reside with their parents.

France: The only unit of analysis available in the French taxation data is that of the household. The household is constituted by combining the tax returns of all members: D5=8.

Appendix B
Poverty head-counts and gaps: additional tables

Table B.1.

Composition of poverty population by family type before social security transfers at 40,50 and 60% poverty intervals adjusted using OECD equivalence scale, circa 1980

[a] 40% poverty interval

	Aged (S)	Aged (C)	Single (NC)	Couple (NC)	Lone Parent	Couple (CH)	Other	Total
Australia	23.9	21.4	19.8	8.4	11.4	11.9	3.3	100
Canada	25.1	18.1	19.5	5.9	11.9	15.1	4.4	100
France	33.3	26.4	7.1	10.3	2.9	15.9	4.0	100
Germany	44.8	26.2	14.9	6.6	2.0	2.6	2.8	100
Netherlands	21.9	18.8	17.7	14.6	7.9	14.5	4.6	100
Norway	47.1	20.7	15.7	2.9	9.6	4.0	*	100
Sweden	43.0	21.8	25.6	3.4	3.5	2.8	*	100
Switzerland	45.3	19.1	27.0	3.1	3.6	1.8	*	100
UK	38.4	26.6	11.3	3.9	7.8	6.5	5.3	100
USA	27.3	18.5	17.0	5.0	17.0	9.6	5.6	100

[b] 50% poverty interval

	Aged (S)	Aged (C)	Single (NC)	Couple (NC)	Lone Parent	Couple (CH)	Other	Total
Australia	22.7	20.3	19.5	8.7	11.2	14.3	3.3	100
Canada	22.5	17.6	19.1	6.5	11.4	18.5	4.5	100
France	29.4	24.1	6.9	10.6	3.1	21.6	4.3	100
Germany	43.3	25.8	14.6	7.1	2.1	4.3	2.7	100
Netherlands	22.2	19.0	17.2	14.3	7.6	15.0	4.7	100
Norway	45.3	21.1	15.7	2.8	9.9	5.2	*	100
Sweden	41.1	20.9	26.5	3.9	4.0	3.6	*	100
Switzerland	42.6	19.9	27.3	3.3	3.9	3.0	*	100
UK	35.9	26.1	10.9	4.3	7.8	9.6	5.4	100
USA	24.8	18.3	16.9	5.5	16.3	12.5	5.7	100

[c] 60% poverty interval

	Aged (S)	Aged (C)	Single (NC)	Couple (NC)	Lone Parent	Couple (CH)	Other	Total
Australia	21.2	19.3	19.1	8.8	11.0	17.2	3.5	100
Canada	20.4	17.0	18.5	7.2	10.4	21.8	4.7	100
France	26.4	22.3	6.5	11.5	3.2	25.8	4.4	100
Germany	40.9	25.0	14.5	7.6	2.5	6.4	3.1	100
Netherlands	21.7	19.2	16.7	14.5	7.5	15.5	4.8	100
Norway	43.3	20.9	15.6	3.0	10.2	7.0	*	100
Sweden	38.7	20.3	27.0	4.3	4.5	5.2	*	100
Switzerland	39.8	19.5	27.0	3.4	3.7	6.5	*	100
UK	32.9	24.8	10.7	4.5	7.7	14.0	5.4	100
USA	23.0	17.4	17.3	5.8	15.9	15.1	5.4	100

Table B.2.
Composition of poverty population by family type after social security transfers at
40,50 and 60% poverty intervals adjusted using OECD equivalence scale, circa 1980

[a] 40% poverty interval

	Aged (S)	Aged (C)	Single (NC)	Couple (NC)	Lone Parent	Couple (CH)	Other	Total
Australia	2.2	5.1	33.0	9.3	18.7	30.2	1.6	100
Canada	5.3	3.1	31.7	8.6	21.4	25.5	4.2	100
France	1.3	3.6	18.6	24.7	7.7	36.7	7.4	100
Germany	27.2	17.1	29.7	6.5	4.0	5.2	10.3	100
Netherlands	8.5	2.9	33.2	18.5	1.7	30.8	4.1	100
Norway	29.4	3.5	37.3	6.3	9.8	13.7	*	100
Sweden	0.0	0.0	84.0	4.2	5.9	5.9	*	100
Switzerland	19.2	3.2	64.1	2.2	7.8	3.6	*	100
UK	6.1	1.0	30.3	5.1	15.2	38.4	4.0	100
USA	14.6	7.7	24.7	5.5	26.2	15.9	5.5	100

[b] 50% poverty interval

	Aged (S)	Aged (C)	Single (NC)	Couple (NC)	Lone Parent	Couple (CH)	Other	Total
Australia	3.1	5.6	29.6	8.0	19.9	31.9	1.8	100.0
Canada	7.5	5.8	29.2	8.6	18.1	26.4	4.3	100.0
France	2.0	4.7	14.8	20.2	7.1	43.7	7.4	100.0
Germany	30.7	18.1	26.4	6.2	3.4	7.7	7.4	100.0
Netherlands	8.3	3.2	29.5	20.1	1.5	32.2	5.3	100.0
Norway	25.3	5.3	32.0	5.3	14.7	17.3	*	100.0
Sweden	0.0	0.0	80.5	3.8	6.9	8.8	*	100.0
Switzerland	26.7	7.8	50.5	2.5	6.4	6.0	*	100.0
UK	25.5	26.0	13.5	6.1	11.0	15.3	2.6	100.0
USA	18.5	8.9	21.4	5.8	22.9	17.6	5.0	100.0

[c] 60% poverty interval

	Aged (S)	Aged (C)	Single (NC)	Couple (NC)	Lone Parent	Couple (CH)	Other	Total
Australia	14.6	13.1	23.2	8.5	15.6	23.5	1.4	100.0
Canada	15.5	8.9	23.9	7.7	13.9	25.5	4.4	100.0
France	15.5	6.3	9.7	15.9	5.2	42.0	5.4	100.0
Germany	32.4	20.6	21.7	4.8	2.8	11.9	5.7	100.0
Netherlands	7.2	5.4	26.1	20.2	2.0	32.0	7.2	100.0
Norway	19.8	9.9	25.2	5.4	20.7	18.9	*	100.0
Sweden	16.5	0.8	62.4	4.6	6.8	8.9	*	100.0
Switzerland	30.1	12.7	38.6	2.5	4.9	11.2	*	100.0
UK	31.6	27.7	11.6	4.4	8.1	12.4	4.2	100.0
USA	19.3	9.8	20.8	5.7	20.4	19.2	4.7	100.0

Table B.3.
Composition of poverty population by family type before social security transfers at 40,50 and 60% poverty intervals adjusted using Whiteford equivalence scale, circa 1980

[a] 40% poverty interval

	Aged (S)	Aged (C)	Single (NC)	Couple (NC)	Lone Parent	Couple (CH)	Other	Total
Australia	24.2	21.3	20.4	8.5	11.3	11.0	3.3	100
Canada	25.4	18.3	21.0	6.2	11.4	13.2	4.5	100
France	34.4	27.2	7.9	10.8	2.4	13.2	4.1	100
Germany	45.0	26.6	15.0	6.6	2.0	2.0	2.8	100
Netherlands	22.5	18.8	17.9	14.4	7.7	14.0	4.6	100
Norway	47.5	20.8	16.2	2.9	9.2	3.4	*	100
Sweden	42.9	21.7	26.7	3.4	3.1	2.2	*	100
Switzerland	45.8	18.7	28.1	3.1	3.3	1.0	*	100
UK	38.9	26.9	11.6	4.0	7.6	5.6	5.3	100
USA	27.8	18.6	18.3	5.0	16.2	8.3	5.7	100

[b] 50% poverty interval

	Aged (S)	Aged (C)	Single (NC)	Couple (NC)	Lone Parent	Couple (CH)	Other	Total
Australia	22.9	20.4	20.4	8.8	11.1	13.0	3.4	100
Canada	23.2	17.8	20.7	6.7	11.0	15.7	4.7	100
France	30.6	24.9	7.4	11.1	3.0	18.4	4.5	100
Germany	43.7	25.7	15.6	7.2	2.1	3.1	2.7	100
Netherlands	22.5	19.1	17.3	14.4	7.5	14.5	4.7	100
Norway	45.6	21.1	16.2	2.9	9.6	4.5	*	100
Sweden	41.3	20.8	27.8	3.9	3.4	2.8	*	100
Switzerland	43.0	19.6	28.8	3.2	3.6	1.8	*	100
UK	36.5	26.6	11.7	4.3	7.7	7.7	5.4	100
USA	25.6	18.7	18.1	5.6	15.7	10.4	5.8	100

[c] 60% poverty interval

	Aged (S)	Aged (C)	Single (NC)	Couple (NC)	Lone Parent	Couple (CH)	Other	Total
Australia	21.6	19.4	20.2	9.1	10.9	15.2	3.5	100
Canada	21.0	17.0	20.2	7.4	10.4	18.7	4.8	100
France	27.3	22.8	7.1	12.0	3.1	23.1	4.6	100
Germany	41.9	25.3	15.0	10.5	2.1	4.9	3.2	100
Netherlands	22.4	19.3	16.7	14.5	7.4	14.8	4.8	100
Norway	44.0	21.2	16.4	3.1	9.6	5.7	*	100
Sweden	39.4	20.5	28.1	4.3	4.0	3.8	*	100
Switzerland	41.6	19.5	28.7	3.4	3.6	3.1	*	100
UK	33.9	25.6	11.3	4.7	7.6	11.4	5.5	100
USA	23.7	17.7	18.5	6.2	15.4	13.0	5.6	100

Table B.4.
Composition of poverty population by family type after social security transfers at 40,50 and 60% poverty intervals adjusted using Whiteford equivalence scale, circa 1980

[a] 40% poverty interval

	Aged (S)	Aged (C)	Single (NC)	Couple (NC)	Lone Parent	Couple (CH)	Other	Total
Australia	3.8	5.1	41.2	9.5	15.7	22.6	2.0	100
Canada	7.2	3.3	39.6	8.9	17.3	19.2	4.5	100
France	1.5	3.9	23.5	26.6	6.5	29.9	8.0	100
Germany	32.7	13.6	33.0	5.1	3.2	4.2	8.2	100
Netherlands	9.7	3.0	34.7	18.4	1.0	29.2	4.2	100
Norway	31.6	2.8	38.6	6.4	8.8	10.5	*	100
Sweden	0.0	0.0	85.6	4.2	5.1	5.1	*	100
Switzerland	24.9	2.6	62.4	2.1	5.8	2.1	*	100
UK	34.3	9.0	28.9	4.8	5.4	14.5	3.0	100
USA	21.5	7.5	27.3	5.3	21.2	11.9	5.2	100

[b] 50% poverty interval

	Aged (S)	Aged (C)	Single (NC)	Couple (NC)	Lone Parent	Couple (CH)	Other	Total
Australia	7.4	5.9	33.2	7.9	17.5	25.8	1.9	100
Canada	16.1	6.0	30.8	8.0	15.2	19.5	4.4	100
France	20.6	4.4	15.2	18.5	5.6	28.0	7.3	100
Germany	38.5	15.8	27.0	5.5	2.7	3.3	7.2	100
Netherlands	8.4	3.3	30.3	19.8	1.5	31.5	5.1	100
Norway	26.6	6.3	34.2	6.4	12.7	13.9	*	100
Sweden	0.0	0.0	86.3	3.8	5.0	5.0	*	100
Switzerland	33.0	6.5	50.5	2.3	4.9	2.9	*	100
UK	39.1	23.9	15.6	5.0	5.9	8.1	2.5	100
USA	22.0	9.1	23.9	5.9	20.5	13.7	4.9	100

[c] 60% poverty interval

	Aged (S)	Aged (C)	Single (NC)	Couple (NC)	Lone Parent	Couple (CH)	Other	Total
Australia	21.9	13.9	24.6	8.1	12.6	17.2	1.5	100
Canada	20.7	9.7	25.1	7.5	12.4	20.3	4.2	100
France	21.9	10.7	12.1	15.5	4.8	29.8	5.3	100
Germany	38.8	19.0	24.6	4.1	2.2	5.0	5.3	100
Netherlands	7.4	5.5	27.7	20.4	1.8	29.8	7.4	100
Norway	46.3	9.1	25.0	3.0	8.8	7.9	*	100
Sweden	24.1	0.8	60.5	4.1	5.3	5.3	*	100
Switzerland	36.7	11.5	40.7	2.3	4.2	4.6	*	100
UK	40.9	25.4	12.2	4.0	6.3	7.4	3.8	100
USA	22.2	10.0	22.7	5.9	18.8	15.8	4.7	100

Table B.5.
Poverty gaps as a percentage of poverty line, by family type, Australia OECD equivalence scale

Pre-transfer poverty gaps as a percentage of poverty line

Poverty interval	Aged (S)	Aged (C)	Single (NC)	Couple (NC)	Lone Parent	Couple (CH)	Other
40	87	80	79	76	87	67	70
50	87	81	78	73	85	58	69
60	87	81	76	71	82	51	66

Post social security poverty gaps as a percentage of poverty line

Poverty interval	Aged (S)	Aged (C)	Single (NC)	Couple (NC)	Lone Parent	Couple (CH)	Other
40	42	32	61	47	36	43	26
50	27	28	48	42	32	34	26
60	8	13	41	29	33	35	30

Post tax poverty gaps as a percentage of poverty line

Poverty interval	Aged (S)	Aged (C)	Single (NC)	Couple (NC)	Lone Parent	Couple (CH)	Other
40	42	32	61	46	36	41	23
50	27	28	48	41	30	32	26
60	8	13	41	29	33	30	30

Table B.6.
Poverty gaps as a percentage of poverty line, by family type, Australia Whiteford scale

Pre-transfer poverty gaps as a percentage of poverty line

Poverty interval	Aged (S)	Aged (C)	Single (NC)	Couple (NC)	Lone Parent	Couple (CH)	Other
40	86	80	78	75	87	69	69
50	87	82	78	73	85	61	69
60	88	82	76	70	82	55	67

Post social security poverty gaps as a percentage of poverty line

Poverty interval	Aged (S)	Aged (C)	Single (NC)	Couple (NC)	Lone Parent	Couple (CH)	Other
40	28	33	50	46	37	49	24
50	17	28	46	42	30	34	29
60	14	14	40	29	31	35	27

Post tax poverty gaps as a percentage of poverty line

Poverty interval	Aged (S)	Aged (C)	Single (NC)	Couple (NC)	Lone Parent	Couple (CH)	Other
40	28	33	50	46	37	48	22
50	17	28	46	41	28	33	28
60	14	14	39	29	31	31	28

Table B.7.
Poverty gaps as a percentage of poverty line, by family type, Canada OECD equivalence scale

Pre-transfer poverty gaps as a percentage of poverty line

Poverty interval	Aged (S)	Aged (C)	Single (NC)	Couple (NC)	Lone Parent	Couple (CH)	Other
40	79	67	74	59	76	46	68
50	79	65	70	55	73	42	64
60	79	65	68	50	74	40	59

Post social security poverty gaps as a percentage of poverty line

Poverty interval	Aged (S)	Aged (C)	Single (NC)	Couple (NC)	Lone Parent	Couple (CH)	Other
40	23	25	48	39	34	31	31
50	21	20	43	36	37	31	31
60	16	18	44	36	42	31	31

Post tax poverty gaps as a percentage of poverty line

Poverty interval	Aged (S)	Aged (C)	Single (NC)	Couple (NC)	Lone Parent	Couple (CH)	Other
40	23	25	48	39	33	30	30
50	21	20	43	36	37	29	29
60	16	18	44	34	41	28	29

Table B.8.
Poverty gaps as a percentage of poverty line, by family type, Canada Whiteford scale

Pre-transfer poverty gaps as a percentage of poverty line

Poverty interval	Aged (S)	Aged (C)	Single (NC)	Couple (NC)	Lone Parent	Couple (CH)	Other
40	80	67	71	57	77	48	67
50	79	65	68	53	74	44	62
60	80	65	67	50	74	42	59

Post social security poverty gaps as a percentage of poverty line

Poverty interval	Aged (S)	Aged (C)	Single (NC)	Couple (NC)	Lone Parent	Couple (CH)	Other
40	23	23	42	37	35	32	29
50	16	19	44	36	36	31	29
60	20	17	45	36	40	30	32

Post tax poverty gaps as a percentage of poverty line

Poverty interval	Aged (S)	Aged (C)	Single (NC)	Couple (NC)	Lone Parent	Couple (CH)	Other
40	23	22	42	37	35	31	29
50	16	19	44	35	36	29	29
60	20	17	43	33	39	28	31

Table B.9.
Poverty gaps as a percentage of poverty line, by family type, France OECD equivalence scale

Pre-transfer poverty gaps as a percentage of poverty line

Poverty interval	Aged (S)	Aged (C)	Single (NC)	Couple (NC)	Lone Parent	Couple (CH)	Other
40	90	83	78	71	61	39	70
50	91	82	75	66	56	36	64
60	91	82	75	60	57	36	61

Post social security poverty gaps as a percentage of poverty line

Poverty interval	Aged (S)	Aged (C)	Single (NC)	Couple (NC)	Lone Parent	Couple (CH)	Other
40	75	33	48	38	40	31	38
50	33	27	48	41	39	27	35
60	9	19	47	36	38	25	35

Post tax poverty gaps as a percentage of poverty line

Poverty interval	Aged (S)	Aged (C)	Single (NC)	Couple (NC)	Lone Parent	Couple (CH)	Other
40	70	37	48	38	40	31	38
50	33	29	48	41	38	27	35
60	10	19	47	36	38	25	35

Table B.10.
Poverty gaps as a percentage of poverty line, by family type, France Whiteford scale

Pre-transfer poverty gaps as a percentage of poverty line

Poverty interval	Aged (S)	Aged (C)	Single (NC)	Couple (NC)	Lone Parent	Couple (CH)	Other
40	90	83	75	70	69	40	70
50	91	83	75	66	56	36	63
60	91	82	72	59	55	35	60

Post social security poverty gaps as a percentage of poverty line

Poverty interval	Aged (S)	Aged (C)	Single (NC)	Couple (NC)	Lone Parent	Couple (CH)	Other
40	73	33	48	40	47	35	38
50	6	25	47	39	39	30	32
60	15	12	41	37	34	26	35

Post tax poverty gaps as a percentage of poverty line

Poverty interval	Aged (S)	Aged (C)	Single (NC)	Couple (NC)	Lone Parent	Couple (CH)	Other
40	70	37	47	40	45	35	39
50	6	27	47	39	39	30	32
60	15	12	41	36	34	25	35

Table B.11.
Poverty gaps as a percentage of poverty line, by family type, Germany OECD equivalence scale

Pre-transfer poverty gaps as a percentage of poverty line

Poverty interval	Aged (S)	Aged (C)	Single (NC)	Couple (NC)	Lone Parent	Couple (CH)	Other
40	95	91	89	82	69	53	82
50	94	90	89	77	69	39	85
60	93	87	85	71	60	33	72

Post social security poverty gaps as a percentage of poverty line

Poverty interval	Aged (S)	Aged (C)	Single (NC)	Couple (NC)	Lone Parent	Couple (CH)	Other
40	36	25	47	47	46	53	26
50	26	23	35	32	35	26	31
60	25	21	35	35	35	18	35

Post tax poverty gaps as a percentage of poverty line

Poverty interval	Aged (S)	Aged (C)	Single (NC)	Couple (NC)	Lone Parent	Couple (CH)	Other
40	36	23	43	43	46	27	27
50	26	23	36	34	25	19	30
60	25	21	35	38	24	16	34

Table B.12.
Poverty gaps as a percentage of poverty line, by family type, Germany Whiteford scale

Pre-transfer poverty gaps as a percentage of poverty line							
Poverty interval	Aged (S)	Aged (C)	Single (NC)	Couple (NC)	Lone Parent	Couple (CH)	Other
40	95	90	90	82	66	65	82
50	94	90	84	77	67	46	86
60	93	88	85	72	67	36	70

Post social security poverty gaps as a percentage of poverty line							
Poverty interval	Aged (S)	Aged (C)	Single (NC)	Couple (NC)	Lone Parent	Couple (CH)	Other
40	30	25	39	48	44	49	27
50	24	24	36	33	35	41	29
60	25	22	33	30	36	26	34

Post tax poverty gaps as a percentage of poverty line							
Poverty interval	Aged (S)	Aged (C)	Single (NC)	Couple (NC)	Lone Parent	Couple (CH)	Other
40	30	24	38	47	44	29	28
50	24	23	35	37	30	27	28
60	25	21	31	34	30	17	34

Table B.13.
Poverty gaps as a percentage of poverty line, by family type, Netherlands OECD scale

Pre-transfer poverty gaps as a percentage of poverty line							
Poverty interval	Aged (S)	Aged (C)	Single (NC)	Couple (NC)	Lone Parent	Couple (CH)	Other
40	77	78	98	91	93	86	89
50	78	78	97	90	93	83	86
60	80	78	96	87	92	80	84

Post social security poverty gaps as a percentage of poverty line							
Poverty interval	Aged (S)	Aged (C)	Single (NC)	Couple (NC)	Lone Parent	Couple (CH)	Other
40	36	34	93	80	55	79	75
50	46	40	92	70	54	71	56
60	55	29	91	66	40	67	44

Post tax poverty gaps as a percentage of poverty line							
Poverty interval	Aged (S)	Aged (C)	Single (NC)	Couple (NC)	Lone Parent	Couple (CH)	Other
40	49	36	94	73	46	73	65
50	59	31	91	65	28	59	51
60	66	26	89	53	17	39	34

Table B.14.
Poverty gaps as a percentage of poverty line, by family type, Netherlands Whiteford scale

Pre-transfer poverty gaps as a percentage of poverty line

Poverty interval	Aged (S)	Aged (C)	Single (NC)	Couple (NC)	Lone Parent	Couple (CH)	Other
40	77	78	97	92	95	88	89
50	79	78	97	91	94	84	87
60	79	78	96	88	93	82	83

Post social security poverty gaps as a percentage of poverty line

Poverty interval	Aged (S)	Aged (C)	Single (NC)	Couple (NC)	Lone Parent	Couple (CH)	Other
40	39	35	92	83	72	85	75
50	51	40	93	71	51	71	60
60	59	29	91	66	41	71	43

Post tax poverty gaps as a percentage of poverty line

Poverty interval	Aged (S)	Aged (C)	Single (NC)	Couple (NC)	Lone Parent	Couple (CH)	Other
40	54	36	94	75	55	76	64
50	63	31	88	64	30	66	51
60	63	27	84	52	24	52	35

Table B.15.
Poverty gaps as a percentage of poverty line, by family type, Norway OECD equivalence scale

Pre-transfer poverty gaps as a percentage of poverty line

Poverty interval	Aged (S)	Aged (C)	Single (NC)	Couple (NC)	Lone Parent	Couple (CH)	Other
40	81	72	82	70	71	45	*
50	83	72	81	74	71	43	*
60	84	72	79	70	69	39	*

Post social security poverty gaps as a percentage of poverty line

Poverty interval	Aged (S)	Aged (C)	Single (NC)	Couple (NC)	Lone Parent	Couple (CH)	Other
40	48	26	53	43	45	38	*
50	49	24	51	42	31	33	*
60	51	18	51	38	25	31	*

Post tax poverty gaps as a percentage of poverty line

Poverty interval	Aged (S)	Aged (C)	Single (NC)	Couple (NC)	Lone Parent	Couple (CH)	Other
40	49	33	52	41	44	33	*
50	49	28	49	42	28	29	*
60	48	16	48	40	24	24	*

Table B.16.
Poverty gaps as a percentage of poverty line, by family type, Norway Whiteford scale

Pre-transfer poverty gaps as a percentage of poverty line

Poverty interval	Aged (S)	Aged (C)	Single (NC)	Couple (NC)	Lone Parent	Couple (CH)	Other
40	82	73	81	70	71	50	*
50	83	72	79	73	70	45	*
60	84	73	78	71	71	41	*

Post social security poverty gaps as a percentage of poverty line

Poverty interval	Aged (S)	Aged (C)	Single (NC)	Couple (NC)	Lone Parent	Couple (CH)	Other
40	48	32	51	41	45	39	*
50	51	19	52	41	33	33	*
60	16	11	33	42	26	31	*

Post tax poverty gaps as a percentage of poverty line

Poverty interval	Aged (S)	Aged (C)	Single (NC)	Couple (NC)	Lone Parent	Couple (CH)	Other
40	48	30	48	40	44	41	*
50	49	21	47	39	32	31	*
60	16	12	33	37	24	24	*

Table B.17.
Poverty gaps as a percentage of poverty line, by family type, Sweden OECD equivalence scale

Pre-transfer poverty gaps as a percentage of poverty line

Poverty interval	Aged (S)	Aged (C)	Single (NC)	Couple (NC)	Lone Parent	Couple (CH)	Other
40	78	73	65	62	66	44	*
50	80	76	66	57	59	42	*
60	82	76	65	56	56	35	*

Post social security poverty gaps as a percentage of poverty line

Poverty interval	Aged (S)	Aged (C)	Single (NC)	Couple (NC)	Lone Parent	Couple (CH)	Other
40	0	0	44	44	48	43	*
50	0	15	44	45	39	32	*
60	4	11	48	34	37	31	*

Post tax poverty gaps as a percentage of poverty line

Poverty interval	Aged (S)	Aged (C)	Single (NC)	Couple (NC)	Lone Parent	Couple (CH)	Other
40	0	0	42	40	45	26	*
50	0	15	42	33	35	27	*
60	5	10	43	31	30	24	*

Table B.18.
Poverty gaps as a percentage of poverty line, by family type, Sweden Whiteford scale

Pre-transfer poverty gaps as a percentage of poverty line

Poverty interval	Aged (S)	Aged (C)	Single (NC)	Couple (NC)	Lone Parent	Couple (CH)	Other
40	79	76	64	62	68	45	*
50	80	75	64	57	65	44	*
60	83	77	66	56	58	39	*

Post social security poverty gaps as a percentage of poverty line

Poverty interval	Aged (S)	Aged (C)	Single (NC)	Couple (NC)	Lone Parent	Couple (CH)	Other
40	0	0	48	45	52	41	*
50	0	0	45	47	49	42	*
60	8	9	47	34	35	33	*

Post tax poverty gaps as a percentage of poverty line

Poverty interval	Aged (S)	Aged (C)	Single (NC)	Couple (NC)	Lone Parent	Couple (CH)	Other
40	0	0	40	39	45	29	*
50	3	34	44	33	44	26	*
60	8	9	43	31	31	27	*

Table B.19.
Poverty gaps as a percentage of poverty line, by family type, Switzerland OECD scale

Pre-transfer poverty gaps as a percentage of poverty line

Poverty interval	Aged (S)	Aged (C)	Single (NC)	Couple (NC)	Lone Parent	Couple (CH)	Other
40	67	56	67	70	62	34	*
50	68	56	65	65	58	29	*
60	69	56	63	61	60	20	*

Post social security poverty gaps as a percentage of poverty line

Poverty interval	Aged (S)	Aged (C)	Single (NC)	Couple (NC)	Lone Parent	Couple (CH)	Other
40	18	21	59	43	40	25	*
50	20	15	53	35	40	20	*
60	22	16	51	32	42	16	*

Post tax poverty gaps as a percentage of poverty line

Poverty interval	Aged (S)	Aged (C)	Single (NC)	Couple (NC)	Lone Parent	Couple (CH)	Other
40	18	24	56	35	38	23	*
50	20	16	50	30	37	16	*
60	22	18	50	31	39	16	*

Table B.20.
Poverty gaps as a percentage of poverty line, by family type, Switzerland Whiteford scale

Pre-transfer poverty gaps as a percentage of poverty line

Poverty interval	Aged (S)	Aged (C)	Single (NC)	Couple (NC)	Lone Parent	Couple (CH)	Other
40	68	56	67	70	64	43	*
50	69	55	63	65	58	32	*
60	69	57	63	60	59	27	*

Post social security poverty gaps as a percentage of poverty line

Poverty interval	Aged (S)	Aged (C)	Single (NC)	Couple (NC)	Lone Parent	Couple (CH)	Other
40	17	22	56	42	39	30	*
50	20	16	51	35	40	22	*
60	22	16	49	32	41	19	*

Post tax poverty gaps as a percentage of poverty line

Poverty interval	Aged (S)	Aged (C)	Single (NC)	Couple (NC)	Lone Parent	Couple (CH)	Other
40	18	25	54	40	37	45	*
50	21	17	51	31	36	20	*
60	22	17	49	31	37	16	*

Table B.21.
Poverty gaps as a percentage of poverty line, by family type, UK OECD equivalence scale

Pre-transfer poverty gaps as a percentage of poverty line

Poverty interval	Aged (S)	Aged (C)	Single (NC)	Couple (NC)	Lone Parent	Couple (CH)	Other
40	83	72	84	69	81	54	76
50	84	73	83	65	78	42	73
60	84	73	78	61	74	34	70

Post social security poverty gaps as a percentage of poverty line

Poverty interval	Aged (S)	Aged (C)	Single (NC)	Couple (NC)	Lone Parent	Couple (CH)	Other
40	25	7	38	21	15	22	16
50	9	8	27	15	15	23	14
60	13	15	24	21	21	23	14

Post tax poverty gaps as a percentage of poverty line

Poverty interval	Aged (S)	Aged (C)	Single (NC)	Couple (NC)	Lone Parent	Couple (CH)	Other
40	31	7	40	36	15	22	13
50	9	8	27	20	15	20	17
60	14	15	25	22	21	20	14

Table B.22.

Poverty gaps as a percentage of poverty line, by family type, UK Whiteford equivalence scale

Pre-transfer poverty gaps as a percentage of poverty line						
Poverty interval	Aged (S)	Aged (C)	Single (NC)	Couple (NC)	Lone Parent	Couple (CH)	Other
40	83	72	83	69	82	58	77
50	84	72	79	65	78	46	74
60	85	73	78	61	75	37	71

Post social security poverty gaps as a percentage of poverty line						
Poverty interval	Aged (S)	Aged (C)	Single (NC)	Couple (NC)	Lone Parent	Couple (CH)	Other
40	6	2	30	16	18	24	15
50	12	10	24	16	13	22	12
60	18	17	28	22	18	24	16

Post tax poverty gaps as a percentage of poverty line						
Poverty interval	Aged (S)	Aged (C)	Single (NC)	Couple (NC)	Lone Parent	Couple (CH)	Other
40	8	21	33	30	18	24	13
50	13	10	25	20	13	20	13
60	18	17	28	23	18	20	16

Table B.23.

Poverty gaps as a percentage of poverty line, by family type, USA OECD equivalence scale

Pre-transfer poverty gaps as a percentage of poverty line						
Poverty interval	Aged (S)	Aged (C)	Single (NC)	Couple (NC)	Lone Parent	Couple (CH)	Other
40	80	64	74	60	75	48	66
50	80	63	70	55	73	42	64
60	80	65	65	53	70	39	65

Post social security poverty gaps as a percentage of poverty line						
Poverty interval	Aged (S)	Aged (C)	Single (NC)	Couple (NC)	Lone Parent	Couple (CH)	Other
40	28	27	57	41	40	36	43
50	27	28	52	36	41	33	42
60	31	30	49	37	45	33	43

Post tax poverty gaps as a percentage of poverty line						
Poverty interval	Aged (S)	Aged (C)	Single (NC)	Couple (NC)	Lone Parent	Couple (CH)	Other
40	28	27	57	42	40	33	41
50	27	28	50	37	41	30	43
60	31	30	48	37	43	29	42

Table B.24.
Poverty gaps as a percentage of poverty line, by family type, USA Whiteford equivalence scale

Pre-transfer poverty gaps as a percentage of poverty line

Poverty interval	Aged (S)	Aged (C)	Single (NC)	Couple (NC)	Lone Parent	Couple (CH)	Other
40	80	64	71	60	76	49	65
50	80	63	68	54	73	44	64
60	80	65	65	52	71	40	64

Post social security poverty gaps as a percentage of poverty line

Poverty interval	Aged (S)	Aged (C)	Single (NC)	Couple (NC)	Lone Parent	Couple (CH)	Other
40	24	28	53	40	40	38	42
50	30	28	51	36	40	33	42
60	33	30	49	37	43	32	43

Post tax poverty gaps as a percentage of poverty line

Poverty interval	Aged (S)	Aged (C)	Single (NC)	Couple (NC)	Lone Parent	Couple (CH)	Other
40	24	28	52	39	40	37	39
50	30	28	49	37	39	31	43
60	33	30	47	36	42	30	42

Appendix C
Inequality measures:
additional tables

Table C.1.
Income inequality measures after social security OECD equivalence

	G	G*	P	R	H	V	E	C	CD
Australia	0.4143	0.3359	0.9456	0.1892	-0.0155	0.2047	0.0985	-0.5313	0.3295
Canada	0.3865	0.3245	0.7717	0.1605	-0.0157	0.1762	0.0968	-0.3852	0.3184
France	0.4707	0.3435	0.9190	0.2703	-0.1180	0.3883	0.2483	-0.4482	0.2879
Germany	0.4066	0.2796	0.9188	0.3125	-0.0643	0.3767	0.2001	-0.5122	0.2534
Netherlands	0.4672	0.3291	0.8963	0.2957	-0.0739	0.3696	0.2387	-0.4291	0.2945
Norway	0.3848	0.2854	0.9059	0.2583	-0.0454	0.3037	0.1481	-0.5211	0.2679
Sweden	0.4168	0.2407	0.8127	0.4225	-0.1185	0.5409	0.3840	-0.3959	0.1913
Switzerland	0.4142	0.3574	0.9374	0.1373	-0.0211	0.1584	0.0753	-0.5232	0.3486
UK	0.3928	0.2933	0.6541	0.2532	-0.0276	0.2809	0.2029	-0.2613	0.2825
US	0.4252	0.3690	0.8596	0.1322	-0.0248	0.1570	0.0842	-0.4344	0.3585

Notes to tables:

G = pre-transfer Gini coefficient
G*= post-transfer Gini coefficient
P = progressivity index of the benefit or tax
R = net redistribution achieved by the social security or tax system
H = re-ranking index
V = vertical (or gross) redistribution
E = average incidence of benefits and taxes for the income unit
C = index of benefits received by the unit ranked by pre-transfer position
CD= concentration index of post-transfer income

Table C.2.

Income inequality measures after social security Whiteford equivalence

	G	G*	P	R	H	V	E	C	CD
Australia	0.4024	0.3264	0.9238	0.1888	-0.0120	0.2009	0.0959	-0.5214	0.3216
Canada	0.3758	0.3146	0.7612	0.1627	-0.0131	0.1758	0.0950	-0.3855	0.3097
France	0.4628	0.3350	0.8936	0.2761	-0.0974	0.3735	0.2398	-0.4308	0.2900
Germany	0.3958	0.2733	0.8853	0.3096	-0.0488	0.3583	0.1908	-0.4895	0.2540
Netherlands	0.4575	0.3204	0.8572	0.2998	-0.0520	0.3517	0.2311	-0.3997	0.2966
Norway	0.3733	0.2776	0.8894	0.2562	-0.0357	0.2919	0.1396	-0.5162	0.2643
Sweden	0.4103	0.2362	0.7971	0.4242	-0.1007	0.5249	0.3702	-0.3868	0.1949
Switzerland	0.4056	0.3500	0.9505	0.1371	-0.0168	0.1539	0.0703	-0.5449	0.3432
UK	0.3826	0.2866	0.6386	0.2509	-0.0268	0.2777	0.1996	-0.2560	0.2763
US	0.4152	0.3591	0.8634	0.1352	-0.0215	0.1566	0.0815	-0.4482	0.3502

Table C.3.

Income inequality measures after taxes OECD equivalence

	G	G*	P	R	H	V	E	C	CD
Australia	0.3349	0.2872	0.1802	0.1426	-0.0053	0.1479	0.2156	0.5151	0.2854
Canada	0.3220	0.2931	0.1747	0.0899	-0.0075	0.0974	0.1522	0.4967	0.2906
France	0.3438	0.3065	0.3984	0.1085	-0.0023	0.1108	0.0873	0.7422	0.3057
Germany	0.2780	0.2517	0.1480	0.0946	-0.0719	0.1665	0.2383	0.4259	0.2317
Netherlands	0.3284	0.2932	0.0843	0.1074	-0.0233	0.1307	0.3373	0.4128	0.2855
Norway	0.2816	0.2342	0.1595	0.1682	-0.0248	0.1930	0.2541	0.4411	0.2273
Sweden	0.2408	0.1967	0.1388	0.1829	-0.0598	0.2427	0.2963	0.3795	0.1823
Switzerland	0.3533	0.3355	0.1089	0.0504	-0.0165	0.0668	0.1781	0.4622	0.3297
UK	0.2880	0.2638	0.1417	0.0841	-0.0158	0.0999	0.1687	0.4297	0.2592
US	0.3645	0.3168	0.1981	0.1307	-0.0133	0.1440	0.2095	0.5625	0.3120

Table C.4.

Income inequality measures after taxes Whiteford equivalence

	G	G*	P	R	H	V	E	C	CD
Australia	0.3255	0.2760	0.1845	0.1519	-0.0043	0.1562	0.2161	0.5100	0.2746
Canada	0.3120	0.2820	0.1801	0.0963	-0.0075	0.1038	0.1524	0.4921	0.2797
France	0.3354	0.2980	0.4034	0.1114	-0.0023	0.1137	0.0864	0.7388	0.2973
Germany	0.2718	0.2425	0.1550	0.1078	-0.0727	0.1806	0.2405	0.4269	0.2227
Netherlands	0.3197	0.2814	0.0890	0.1199	-0.0224	0.1423	0.3382	0.4088	0.2742
Norway	0.2736	0.2251	0.1609	0.1773	-0.0236	0.2009	0.2547	0.4345	0.2187
Sweden	0.2363	0.1929	0.1374	0.1835	-0.0615	0.2450	0.2964	0.3737	0.1784
Switzerland	0.3457	0.3274	0.1108	0.0531	-0.0165	0.0697	0.1785	0.4565	0.3217
UK	0.2813	0.2578	0.1381	0.0833	-0.0164	0.0997	0.1687	0.4194	0.2532
US	0.3545	0.3051	0.2041	0.1394	-0.0131	0.1525	0.2095	0.5586	0.3005

Appendix D
Welfare effort calculations

Table D.1.
Social Security and related tax expenditures, 1980

	Social security expenditure	Tax expenditure non-super	Tax expenditure super	CTE
Australia	9478	926	1226	11630
Canada	22727	3626	3140	29493
France	470580	7198	1240	479018
Germany	242210	2720	3996	248926
Netherlands	64050	3914	9717	77681
Norway	31334	*	*	31334
Sweden	85090	11037	11832	107959
Switzerland	15260	*	*	15260
UK	21361	2623	1644	25628
USA	218796	19869	36745	275410

	Social Security/GDP %	Social Security per capita $US #	CTE/GDP %	CTE per capita $US #
Australia	6.9	624	8.5	765
Canada	7.4	838	9.6	1087
France	16.8	1597	17.1	1625
Germany	16.4	1638	16.8	1684
Netherlands	19.0	1836	23.1	2226
Norway	11.0	1136	*	*
Sweden	16.2	1926	20.6	2443
Switzerland	9.0	984	*	*
UK	9.3	771	10.3	897
USA	8.1	906	10.2	1140

Notes to table D.1.
 * Data not available
Converted to $US using purchasing power parities
Social security transfers: millions of currency unit
Tax expenditures non-super: millions of currency unit
Tax expenditures super: millions of currency unit
Net transfer expenditure: millions of currency unit
Social security transfers as a percentage of GDP
Social security transfers per capita in $US
Net transfer expenditure as a percentage of GDP
Net transfer expenditure per capita in $US

Sources: Social security transfers- Varley, R (1986)
Tax expenditures- OECD (1984); McDaniel,P and Surrey,S (1985)
GDP- OECD National Accounts (1986)
Purchasing Power Parities- OECD National Accounts (1986)

Table D.2.
Accounting for taxes in social security effort measures

	Clawback	CTE/GDP	CTE/per capita#	NE/GDP	NE/per capita#
Australia	26.5	8.5	765	5.1	458
Canada	33.3	9.6	1087	4.9	559
France	11.7	17.1	1625	14.8	1410
Germany	19.3	16.8	1684	13.2	1322
Netherlands	43.3	23.1	2226	10.8	1041
Norway	28.5	*	*	7.9	812
Sweden	42.9	20.6	2443	9.3	1100
Switzerland	24.6	*	*	6.8	742
UK	36.9	10.3	897	5.9	486
USA	22.4	10.2	1140	6.3	703

Notes to table as above.

Table D.3.
Accounting for incidence of social security expenditures on poor population, 1980

	Vertical expenditure efficiency %	VEE Post-tax %	Effective SS/GDP %	Effective SS/per cap 1980 $US	Effective NE/GDP %	Effective NE/p c 1980 $US
Australia	68.4	90.3	4.7	427	4.6	414
Canada	51.7	74.6	3.8	433	3.7	417
France	69.4	75.6	11.6	1108	11.2	1066
Germany	65.1	78.9	10.7	1067	10.4	1043
Netherlands	64	86.4	12.2	1175	9.3	899
Norway	67	86.6	7.4	761	6.8	703
Sweden	61.5	84.2	10.0	1184	7.8	926
Switzerland	63.2	76.6	5.7	622	5.2	568
UK	44.3	67.6	4.1	341	4.0	329
USA	59.8	75.1	4.9	542	4.7	528

Table D.4.
Efficiency of social expenditures

	Poverty reduction efficiency %	Efficient SS/GDP %	Efficient SS/per capita 1980 $US	Efficient CTE/GDP %	Efficient CTE/per capita 1980 $US
Australia	51.8	3.6	323	5.9	534
Canada	38.7	2.9	324	5.5	620
France	34.3	5.7	548	6.6	629
Germany	36.2	5.9	593	7.5	749
Netherlands	27.3	5.2	501	10.9	1055
Norway	37.0	4.1	420	*	*
Sweden	23.9	3.9	460	8.5	1011
Switzerland	40.9	3.7	402	*	*
UK	32.1	3.0	247	5.6	452
USA	41.4	3.4	375	5.4	600

Appendix E
Sampling error and statistical significance

This appendix discusses the reliability of the statistics quoted in this study and the inferences which are drawn from them. The discussion relates only to random sampling error, that is to say the probability that the value of a sample statistic will differ to some extent from the true population value because a random sample will never be truly representative. Other sorts of possible error, such as non-random sampling and problems in defining and measuring variables, are discussed in the text where appropriate.

There are three levels at which data are analysed and compared in this study: aggregate country statistics; disaggregated country statistics; and inter-country comparisons of statistics. Each of these is discussed in turn.

Aggregate country statistics

Typical statistics which are reported in this study are the percentage of a country's LIS sample which is in poverty, or the Gini coefficient measuring the inequality of the income distribution. These reported statistics are based on samples of at least several thousand observations. The sample sizes reported in Appendix A are listed below in Table E.1.

Because the samples are fairly large, the sample statistics should provide reliable estimates of the population statistics, but there is likely to be at least some small element of random sampling error.

For example, if the sample size for a country is n=10,000 and the proportion of the sample in poverty is p=0.250, the sample standard error s is

$$\sqrt{p(1-p)/n} \quad s = \sqrt{0.25 \times 0.75 / 10000} = 0.0043.$$

Table E.1. Size of LIS samples

Country	Sample size
Australia	15985
Canada	15136
France	11044
Germany	2727
Netherlands	4833
Norway	10414
Sweden	9625
Switzerland	7036
UK	6888
USA	15225

The 95% confidence interval for the estimate of the proportion of the population in poverty is p +/- 2s = [0.2414, 0.2586]. More simply, we can be reasonably sure that the true poverty rate lies between 24.5% and 25.5%, and very sure that it lies between 24% and 26%.

The standard errors of the sample estimates for the countries with larger samples are, of course, even lower. For the smallest sample, Germany, however, the standard error of the estimate would be, in this example, $s = \sqrt{0.25 \times 0.75/2727} = 0.0083$.

When countries are ranked in terms of the sample poverty rates we are interested in the confidence interval for the *difference* between two estimated population proportions. The standard error of the estimated difference is given by $s = \sqrt{p_1(1-p_1)/n_1 + p_2(1-p_2)/n_2}$.

Take, for example, the post-transfer poverty rates reported in Table 4.3 for France (0.152) and Germany (0.127). With what degree of confidence can we assert that poverty in Germany is lower than poverty in France? The sample difference is 0.025. The sampling standard error is:

$s = \sqrt{0.152 \times 0.848/11044 + 0.127 \times 0.873/2727} = 0.0072$.

The 95 percent confidence interval for the difference between the German and French poverty rates is [0.011, 0.039]. In other words the ranking which places France with a higher poverty rate than Germany is very robust.

The standard errors of the estimated Gini coefficients are more complex to determine. Bishop et al (1989b, Table 3) report standard errors for their LIS sample Gini coefficients which are generally less than one percentage point. Their estimate of the German Gini coefficient, however, has a standard error of five percentage points.

Disaggregated country statistics

Some of the aggregate statistics are broken down by family type. The disaggregated sample statistics are necessarily based on smaller samples and will have correspondingly greater standard errors.

For example, Table 4.24 reports that the average post-transfer gap for lone parents in Australia was 0.333 of the poverty line. In this case, there were 163 observations of lone parent families in poverty and the sample standard deviation was 0.233. The standard error of the sample mean is:

$s/\sqrt{n} = 0.233/\sqrt{163} = 0.018$. The 95% confidence interval for the sole parent poverty gap is therefore [29.7%, 36.9%]. This example indicates that the disaggregated sample statistics must be treated with caution when cell sizes become small.

Inter-country comparisons

The study compares sets of aggregate statistics across the sample of ten LIS countries. Diagram 4.6, for example, compares poverty reduction with post-transfer poverty rates. The illustrated linear regression line (based on Ordinary Least Squares regression) indicates the nature of the relationship between these variables; in this case a downward-sloping line indicates that, on average, higher levels of poverty reduction are associated with lower levels of post-transfer poverty.

The extent of the scatter of observations away from this regression line indicates the strength of this linear relationship. The diagram displays the summary R^2 statistic which measures (inversely) the extent of the scatter. Values close to zero indicate that there is no linear relationship, whereas values close to unity indicate a strong linear relationship.

With ten observations and one explanatory variable there are eight degrees of freedom. The F-test for statistical significance is $F_{1,8} = 8R^2/(1-R^2)$. The critical values at the 10%, 5% and 1% significance levels are, respectively, 3.46, 5.32 and 11.26. The corresponding "critical values" of R^2 are 0.302, 0.399 and 0.585.

Put simply, if the reported R^2 is greater than 0.3, we can infer that there is less than a ten percent probability that the estimated linear relationship is spurious. If the R^2 is greater than 0.4 (0.6), the probability of a spurious relationship is less than five percent (one percent).

In the case of multiple regressions, where there are two or more explanatory variables in the regression equation, the degrees of freedom are lower and the critical values of R^2 are higher. With n observations and (k-1) explanatory variables, the F statistic is $F_{k-1,n-k} = \dfrac{n-k}{k-1} \times \dfrac{R^2}{1-R^2}$. (See for example, Koutsoyiannis, 1977).

The corresponding critical values of R^2, for significance at the five percent level, are 0.575 with two explanatory variables, 0.704 with three explanatory variables and 0.806 with four explanatory variables.

In the text, I generally refer to relationships which are significant at the 5% level as *moderately strong* or *significant* and to those which are significant at the 1% level as *strong* or *very significant*. Relationships which are not significant at the 5% level are generally referred to as *weak* or *insignificant*.

Notes

Koutsoyiannis, A. 1977. <u>Theory of Econometrics</u>, 2nd edition. London: Macmillan.

References

Aguilar, R. and B. Gustaffson. 1987. <u>Public Sector Transfers and Income Taxes</u>. Luxembourg Income Study Working Paper No: 10. Luxembourg: LIS-CEPS Institute.

Atkinson, A. 1970. "On the measurement of inequality." <u>Journal of Economic Theory</u>, 2 : 244-263.

Atkinson, A. 1983. <u>Social Justice and Public Policy</u>. London: Wheatsheaf.

Atkinson, A. 1983. <u>The Economics of Inequality</u>. 2nd Ed Oxford: Clarendon Press.

Atkinson, A. 1985. <u>Income Maintenance and Social Insurance: A Survey</u>. London School of Economics, Welfare State Programme, Discussion Paper No. 5. London: London School of Economics.

Atkinson, A. 1986. <u>Social Insurance and Income Maintenance</u>. London School of Economics, Welfare State Programme, Discussion Paper No. 11. London: London School of Economics.

Atkinson, A. 1987. "On the Measurement of Poverty." <u>Econometrica</u>. 55 (4) : 749-763.

Atkinson, A. 1989a. <u>Measuring Inequality and Differing Social Judgments</u>. Luxembourg Income Study Working Paper No:27. Luxembourg: LIS-CEPS Institute.

Atkinson, A. 1989b. <u>Poverty and Social Security</u>. London: Harvester Wheatsheaf.

Atkinson, A. et al. 1986. <u>The Welfare State in Britain 1970-1985: Extent and Effectiveness</u>. London School of Economics, Welfare State Programme, Discussion Paper No. 9. London: London School of Economics.

Beckerman W. and S. Clark. 1982. Poverty and Social Security in Britain since 1961. London: Oxford University Press.

Beckerman, W. 1979a. Poverty and the Impact of Income Maintenance Programmes in Four Developed Countries. Geneva: International Labour Office.

Beckerman, W. 1979b. "The Impact of Income Maintenance Payments on Poverty in Britain 1975", Economic Journal. June: 261-279.

Bishop, J. et al. 1989a. International Comparison of the Redistributive Effects of Taxes and Transfers: Australia, Canada, Sweden and the US. University of Alabama. Unpublished mimeo.

Bishop, J.et al. 1989b. International Comparisons of Income Inequality: Tests for Lorenz Dominance Across Nine Countries. Luxembourg Income Study Working Paper No:26. Luxembourg: LIS-CEPS Institute.

Blank, R. 1989. "Disaggregating the Effect of the Business Cycle on the Distribution of Income". Economica. 56: 141-163.

Bolderson, H. 1986. "Comparing Social Policies: Some Problems of Method and the Case of Social Security Benefits in Australia, Britain and the USA", Journal of Social Policy. 17 (3): 267-288.

Bradshaw, J and D. Piachaud. 1980. Child Support in the European Community. London: Bedford Square Press.

Bradshaw, J et al. 1987. "Evaluating Adequacy: the Potential of Budget Standards", Journal of Social Policy. 16(2): 165-81.

Buhmann, B. et al. 1987. Improving the Luxembourg Income Study Income Measure. Luxembourg Income Study Working Paper No:13. Luxembourg: LIS-CEPS Institute.

Buhmann, B. et al. 1988. "Equivalence Scales, Well-Being, Inequality and Poverty: Sensitivity Estimates Across Ten Countries Using the Luxembourg Income Study Database." International Review of Income and Wealth (34) : 115-142.

Castles, F. 1982. The Impact of Parties: Politics and Policies in Democratic Capitalist States. London: Sage.

Castles, F. 1985. The Working Class and Welfare. Sydney: Allen and Unwin.

Castles, F. 1987. "Trapped in an Historical Cul-de-sac: The Prospects for Welfare Reform in Australia." In Social Welfare in the Late 1980s: Reform, Progress or Retreat? eds P. Saunders, and A. Jamrozik. Social Welfare Research Centre, University of New South Wales.

Castles, F. 1989. Welfare and Equality in Capitalist Societies: How and Why Australia was Different. In Australian Welfare: Historical Sociology. ed. R. Kennedy. Melbourne: Macmillan.

Castles, F and S. Dowrick. 1990. "The Impact of Government Spending Levels on Medium-Term Economic Growth in the OECD, 1960-85." Journal of Theoretical Politics, 2(2): 173-204.

Castles, F. and D. Mitchell. 1990. Three Worlds of Welfare Capitalism or Four? Public Policy Discussion Paper No:21. Canberra: Australian National University.

Champernowne, D. 1974. "A Comparison of Measures of Inequality of Income Distribution." Economic Journal 84: 787-816.

Chichilnisky, G. 1982. Basic Needs and the North/South Debate. World Order Model Project, Working Paper No:21.

Coder, J. 1990. "Technical Notes on LIS Variable D5." LIS Newsletter 2(1): 5-7.

Cowell, F. 1977. Measuring Inequality. Deddington: Phillip Allen.

Cutright, P. 1967. "Income Re-distribution: A Cross-national Analysis", Social Forces, 46: 180-90.

Danziger, S. and M. Taussig 1979. "The Income Unit and the Anatomy of Income Distribution." Review of Income and Wealth. 25: 365-375.

Department of Social Security. 1989. Social Security Portfolio. Budget Related Paper No 8.14, Explanatory Notes 1989-90. Canberra: Australian Government Publishing Service.

Dixon, J and P. Scheurell. eds. 1989. Social Welfare in Developed Market Countries. London: Routledge.

Edwards, M. 1981. "Financial Arrangements within Families." Social Security Journal, December: 1-16. Canberra: Australian Government Publishing Service.

Esping-Andersen, G. 1989. "The Three Political Economies of the Welfare State." Canadian Review of Sociology and Anthropology. 26(1): 10-36.

Esping-Andersen, G. 1990. The Three Worlds of Welfare Capitalism. Cambridge: Polity Press.

Flora, P. ed .1986a Growth to Limits: The Western European Welfare States since World War II. Volume 1. Berlin: de Gruyter.

Flora, P. ed. 1986b. Growth to Limits: The Western European Welfare States since World War II. Volume 2. Berlin: de Gruyter.

Foster, J. 1984. "On Economic Poverty: a Survey of Aggregate Measures." Advances in Econometrics, 3: 215-251.

Fuchs, V. 1965. Toward a Theory of Poverty. in The Concept of Poverty. Task Force on Economic Growth and Opportunity, Washington: Chamber of Commerce of the United States.

Fuchs, V. 1969. "Measuring the Size of the Low Income Population: a comment on the paper by L. Epstein" in L.Soltow ed Six Papers on the Size Distribution of Wealth and Income. New York: National Bureau of Economic Research, Columbia University Press.

Furniss, N. and T. Tilton. 1977. The Case for the Welfare State. Bloomington: University Press.

Gilbert, N. and A. Moon. 1988. "Analyzing Welfare Effort: An Appraisal of Comparative Methods." Journal of Policy Analysis and Management. 7(2) : 328-332.

Goedhart, T et al. 1977. "The Poverty Line: Concept and measurement", Journal of Human Resources, 12: 503-520.

Golladay, F and R. Haveman. 1977. The Economic Effects of Tax-Transfer Policy. New York: Academic Press.

Goodin, R. and Le Grand, J. 1987. Not Only the Poor. London: Allen & Unwin.

Hagenaars, A. 1985. The Perception of Poverty. Amsterdam: North-Holland.

Hagenaars, A. 1987. "A Class of Poverty Indices." International Economic Review, 28 (3) : 583-607.

Hagenaars, A. 1989. Poverty Research Using LIS Datasets. Preliminary Report to Eurostat. Eurostat Contract No: OS D/00009756.

Haveman,R. 1987. Poverty Policy and Poverty Research. Madison: University of Wisconsin Press.

Heidenheimer, A et al. 1990. Comparative Public Policy. 3rd Ed. New York: St Martin's Press.

Hill, M and G. Bramley. 1986. Analysing Social Policy. Oxford: Basil Blackwell.

International Labour Office. 1967;1975;1978;1981. The Cost of Social Security. Geneva: ILO.

Kaim-Caudle, P. 1973. Comparative Social Policy and Social Security: A Ten Country Study. London: Robertson.

Kakwani, N. 1980. "On a Class of Poverty Measures." Econometrica, 48 (2) : 437-446.

Kakwani, N. 1986. Analysing Redistribution Policies. Cambridge: Cambridge University Press.

Kamerman, S and A. Kahn. 1978. Family Policy: Government and Families in Fourteen Countries. New York: Columbia University Press.

Lydall, H. 1968. The Structure of Earnings. Oxford: Oxford University Press.

McDaniel, P. and S. Surrey. 1985. International Aspects of Tax Expenditures: A Comparative Study. Netherlands: Kluwer.

Mitchell, D. 1985. Constructing a Poverty Line for the UK: an Exploration of the Budget Standard Approach. MA dissertation. York: University of York.

Mitchell, D. 1990a. "Targeting Efficiency of Social Security Programs." Australian Journal of Public Administration, 49 (1) : 12-16.

Mitchell, D. 1990b. Comparative Measures of Welfare Effort. Public Policy Program Discussion Paper No:16. Canberra: Australian National University.

Moon, M and E. Smolensky 1977. Improving Measures of Economic Well-being. New York: Academic Press.

Nicholson, J.L. 1976. "Appraisal of Different Methods of Estimating Equivalence Scales and Their Results." Review of Income and Wealth, (2).

Nygard, F. and Sandstrom, A. 1981. Measuring Income Inequality. Stockholm: Almqvist and Wiksell.

Nygard, F. and A. Sandstrom. 1989. "Income inequality measures based on sample surveys." Journal of Econometrics. 42 (1).

O'Higgins, M. et al. 1985. Income Distribution and Redistribution. Luxembourg Income Study Working Paper No:3. Luxembourg: LIS-CEPS Institute.

O'Higgins, M. 1985. "Inequality, Redistribution and Recession: The British Experience, 1976-1982." Journal of Social Policy, 14(3).

OECD. 1978. The Tax/Benefit Position of a Typical Worker in OECD Member Countries. Paris: OECD.

OECD. 1984. Tax Expenditures: A Review of the Issues and Country Practices. Paris: OECD.

OECD. 1985. Social Expenediture 1960 - 1990: Problems of Growth and Control. Paris: OECD.

OECD. 1986. Living Conditions in OECD Countries : A Compendium of Social Indicators. Paris: OECD.

OECD. 1987. Revenue Statistics of OECD Member Countries 1965-1985. Paris: OECD.

OECD. 1988. The Future of Social Protection: The General Debate. Paper distributed to the meeting of the Manpower and Social Affairs Committee, 6-7 July 1988. Paris: OECD.

OECD. 1989. Historical Statistics, 1960-87. Paris: OECD.

Orshansky, M. 1965. "Counting the Poor: Another Look at the Poverty Profile" US Social Security Bulletin, January.

Pahl, J. 1980. "Patterns of Money Management within Marriage." Journal of Social Policy, 9(3) : 313-35.

Pahl, J. 1984. "The Allocation of Money within the Household." In M. Freeman ed. The State, the Law and the Family. London: Tavistock.

Palme, J. 1989. Models of Pensions and Income Inequality: A Comparative Analysis. (Unpublished mimeo). Swedish Institute for Social Research.

Palmer, J. et al. 1988. The Vulnerable. Washington: Urban Institute Press.

Papadakis, E. 1990. Attitudes to State and Private Welfare in Australia. Report to the Social Policy Research Centre. Sydney: University of New South Wales.

Pechman, J. ed. 1987. Comparative Tax Systems: Europe, Canada and Japan. Arlington: Brookings Institution.

Piachaud, D. 1981. "Peter Townsend and the Holy Grail." New Society, September: 419-21.

Piachaud, D. 1982. The Distribution and Redistribution of Incomes. London: Bedford Square Press. .

Piachaud, D. 1988. "Poverty in Britain 1899 to 1983." Journal of Social Policy. 17 (3): 335-349.

Plotnick, R and F. Skidmore. 1975. Progress Against Poverty. New York: Academic Press.

Rainwater, L. 1974. What Money Buys: Inequality and the Social Meaning of Income. New York: Basic Books.

Rein, M. et al. 1987. Stagnation and Renewal in Social Policy. New York: Sharpe.

Ringen, S. 1987. The Possibility of Politics. Oxford: Clarendon.

Ringen, S. 1988. "Direct and Indirect Measures of Poverty." Journal of Social Policy. 17 (3) : 351-365.

Rowntree, B.S. 1902. Poverty: A Study of Town Life. London: Macmillan.

Rowntree, B.S. 1941. Poverty and Progress. London: Longmans.

Rowntree, B.S. and G.R. Lavers. Poverty in the Welfare State. London: Longmans.

Runciman, W.G. 1966. Relative Deprivation and Social Justice. London: Routledge.

Saunders, P. ed. 1980. The Poverty Line: Methodology and Measurement. SWRC Reports and Proceedings No:2. Sydney: University of New South Wales.

Sawyer, M. 1976. Income Distribution in OECD Countries. OECD Economic Outlook - Occasional Studies. Paris: OECD.

Sen, A. 1979. "Issues in the measurement of poverty." Scandinavian Journal of Economics, 81: 285-307.

Sen, A. 1981. Poverty and Famines. Oxford: Oxford University Press.

Sen, A. 1982. Choice, Welfare and Measurement. Oxford: Basil Blackwell.

Sen, A. 1983. "Poor, relatively speaking." Oxford Economic Papers, 35: 153-69.

Shorrocks, A. 1980. "The Class of Additively Decomposable Inequality Measures." Econometrica. 48 (3) : 613-625.

Shorrocks, A. 1982. "Inequality Decomposition by Factor Components." Econometrica. 50 (1) : 193-211.

Sinfield, A. 1978. "Analyses in the Social Division of Welfare." Journal of Social Policy. 7 (2) : 129-156.

Smeeding, T et al. 1985a. An Introduction to the Luxembourg Income Study. Luxembourg Income Study Working Paper No:1. Luxembourg: LIS-CEPS Institute.

Smeeding, T et al. 1985b. Poverty in Major Industrialised Countries. Luxembourg Income Study Working Paper No:2. Luxembourg: LIS-CEPS Institute.

Smeeding, T. et al. 1989. "Patterns of Income and Poverty: The Economic Status of Children and the Elderly in Eight Countries." In T. Smeeding et al The Vulnerable. New York: Urban Institute Press.

Smeeding, T. et al 1990. Poverty, Inequality and Income Distribution in Comparative Perspective. London: Harvester Wheatsheaf.

Summers, R and A. Heston. 1988. "A New Set of International Comparisons of Real Product and Price Levels: Estimates for 130 Countries, 1950-85." Review of Income and Wealth, 34 (1): 1-25.

Theil, H. 1967. Economics and Information Theory. Studies in Mathematical and Managerial Economics, vol. 7. Amsterdam: North-Holland.

Titmuss, R. 1958. Essays on the Welfare State. London: George Allen & Unwin.

Titmuss, R. 1974. Social Policy. London: George Allen & Unwin.

Titmuss, R. 1976. Commitment to Welfare. 2nd Ed. London: George Allen & Unwin.

Townsend, P. 1970. The Concept of Poverty. London: Heineman.

Townsend, P. 1979. Poverty in the United Kingdon. London: Penguin, Harmondsworth.

Townsend, P. 1985. "A Sociological Approach to the Measurement of Poverty: a Rejoinder to Professor Sen." Oxford Economic Papers, 37: 659-68.

Travers, P. 1989. Salami Tactics and the Australian Welfare State. Paper presented to International Seminar on the Sociology of Social Security. Edinburgh.

Varley, R. 1986. Government Household Transfer Database, 1960-1984. Department of Economics and Statistics Working Paper No:36. Paris: OECD.

Ward, M. 1985. Purchasing Power Parities and Real Expenditures in the OECD. Paris: OECD.

Weisbrod, B. 1970. "Collective Action and the Distribution of Income: a Conceptual Approach" in R.H. Haveman and J. Margolis (eds) Public

Expenditures and Policy Analysis. Chicago: Markham Publishing Company.

Whiteford, P. 1985. A Family's Needs:Equivalence Scales, Poverty and Social Security. Department of Social Security, Development Division. Research Paper No:27. Canberra: Australian Government Publishing Service.

Wilensky, H. 1972. The Welfare State and Equality: Structural and Ideological Roots of Public Expenditures. Berkely: University of California Press.

Index